LOST CITIES

PAUL G. BAHN

PHOENIX ILLUSTRATED

First published in Great Britain 1997 by Weidenfeld & Nicolson

This paperback edition first published in 1999 by
Phoenix Illustrated
Orion Publishing Group, Orion House
5, Upper St. Martin's Lane
London WC2H 9EA

A CIP catalogue record for this book is available from the
British Library

ISBN 0-75380-796-3

Picture research: Joanne King
Design by Bradbury and Williams
Designer: Bob Burroughs
Typeset in: Bembo
Printed and bound in Italy

TITLE PAGE: Mohenjo-Daro

List of Contributors

PAUL BAHN, General Editor and contributor, Hull, England

CAROLINE BIRD, School of Archaeology, La Trobe University, Melbourne, Australia (Australasia)

PETER BOGUCKI, School of Engineering and Applied Science, Princeton University, USA (Later Periods, Central and Eastern Europe and ex-USSR)

CONSTANCE CORTEZ, Department of Art History, University of California, Santa Cruz, USA (Mesoamerica)

PHILIP DUKE, Department of Anthropology, Fort Lewis College, Durango, USA (North America)

CHRISTOPHER EDENS, Philadelphia, USA (Near East, Central Asia)

MARK HUDSON, Department of History and Culture, Okayama University, Japan (Far East)

SIMON KANER, Department of Archaeology, University of Cambridge, England (Late periods, Western Europe)

EDDIE OWENS, Department of Classics and Ancient History University College, Swansea, Wales (Classical Archaeology)

STEVEN SNAPE, School of Archaeology, Classics and Oriental Studies, University of Liverpool, England (Egypt and the Levant)

LOUISE STEEL, Department of Archaeology, University of Edinburgh, Scotland (The Aegean)

ANNE THACKERAY, Department of Archaeology, University of the Witwatersrand, South Africa (South Africa)

KAREN WISE, Department of Anthropology, Natural History Museum of Los Angeles County, Los Angeles, USA (South America)

CONTENTS

Preface 8

PREFACE

One of the clichés conjured up in the minds of members of the general public by the word 'archaeologist' is that of an Indiana Jones type of character, hacking a path through impenetrable jungles or trekking through arid deserts, in search of lost cities. Such events have certainly occurred frequently over the past couple of centuries, and indeed lost cities can still be found, even today, in dense jungles and remote deserts.

In this volume we have tried to present a wide variety of towns and cities around the world, of different types and from different periods, in order to emphasize the enormous diversity of the archaeological record.

Our selection primarily comprises major settlements which were abandoned for one reason or another. In some cases we can only speculate as to the cause of a town's neglect and decline, in others, such as Pompeii and Herculaneum, it is both obvious and dramatic. Some may have suffered through climatic or environmental changes (such as drought or flood), through disease and pestilence, through siege and violent destruction, or simply through economic decline.

But the end of a town is only part of its story. Archaeologists are equally interested in why, when and how such settlements arose — there is usually an interplay of many factors — and in particular, how the inhabitants lived their lives.

Emphasis has traditionally been placed on the material remains of a society's élite — the palaces, tombs, temples, pyramids and other monumental structures and artworks which were solidly built, often on a massive scale, and which have therefore survived for our delectation. However, to the archaeologist, it is just as interesting — in fact, often far more fascinating — to investigate the lives and dwellings and workshops of the craftworkers and the lower classes. One can see the uses to which different quarters of a city were devoted, and how the whole system functioned as a whole, as the sum of its parts.

As usual in this series of volumes, we have included many examples which are 'classics', and which simply had to be present — Pompeii, Troy, Machu Picchu, etc.; but equally we have maintained our policy of also including numerous examples which are far less well known, yet are of great interest and of tremendous information value to archaeologists. As is always the case, it was a very difficult task to narrow our selection down to only fifty, when one considers, for instance, the number of suitable candidates from the Classical world, from the Maya or from the Near East.

The old pioneering days, when huge areas of a town or city could be excavated thoroughly and fairly quickly by large groups of cheap labourers, are long gone. Excavation is now a far slower, more painstaking and very expensive enterprise; and at the same time, considerations of conservation are now a top priority. For example, at Pompeii, early excavations from the eighteenth century onward uncovered a large area, and stripped out the statuary, artefacts, wall-paintings and mosaics – now mostly housed in Naples Museum, still splendid but deprived of life and context. On site the result is acres of bare brick, crumbling and weed-infested buildings, shunned by tourists (or closed off to them because of the risk of harm). Moves are now afoot to clean up and consolidate these areas; at the same time the emphasis – both here and at other sites such as Akrotiri – is to proceed slowly, conserving things *in situ*, if possible, as one progresses, thus uncovering ancient buildings which still look just as they did in ancient times. This is surely the better solution, and one which helps bring the past to vivid life.

I well remember being taken, as a schoolboy, on a package tour of Italy, and for me a visit to Pompeii was the impatiently awaited highlight. As the coach approached the site, a little old English lady turned and asked my startled mother what there was to see there: 'Is it a cathedral or something?' On being told, she expressed great disappointment. At the entrance she peered in, turned on her heel and went off for a cup of tea at the nearest café.

We hope that books such as this one may help to enlighten and entertain those people who still, unbelievably, may hold the same sentiments about the past as that lady. But no doubt, to anyone perusing this volume, we are already preaching to the converted.

PAUL G. BAHN

AFRICA

AMARNA

The size and complexity of Amarna are even more remarkable, since it is the most spectacular example of an entire city which was founded, built, occupied, abandoned and destroyed in a single generation. It came about through the desire of King Amenhotep IV (also known as Akhenaten) to abandon Thebes, with its strong connections to the god Amun, and to found a new capital city at the heart of an empire whose religious dogma was now to be dominated by the divine sun-disc, the Aten. Akhenaten founded his new city, to be called Akhetaten, 'Horizon of the Aten', in the fifth year of his reign (c. 1348 BC) and marked its planned limits on the east and west of the Nile by a series of boundary inscriptions cut into the cliffs. On the west side of the Nile, the boundaries of this great metropolis encompassed a broad

Situated in an open plain of a desert bay, close to the Nile in Middle Egypt, 275 km north of Thebes, the ruins of el-Amarna never became 'lost'. The monumental masses of mudbrick at Amarna were obvious to early visitors as representing the remains of a substantial ancient city. However, it is through the extensive excavation of the site by British and German archaeologists from 1891 to the present day that the unique character of this special city has been revealed.

swath of rich agricultural land, while on the west bank was the city itself.

The city needed to be built quickly. Mudbrick could be very rapidly produced and built into the houses, villas and palaces required for ordinary human needs, and the floors and walls of such buildings could be easily plastered and painted with brightly coloured scenes from nature. However, the construction of more important public buildings, particularly temples, required stone. To speed up the process of transport and building, relatively small stone blocks were used, today called *talatat* (Arabic for 'three', since they are approximately three handspans long).

The rays of the Aten are shown as outstretched hands reaching out to Akhenaten and Nefertiti.

A colossal statue of Akhenaten, with its distinct facial features.

Although the mudbrick survived the pillaging of Amarna which followed the death of Akhenaten in his seventeenth regnal year, the stone did not, and the great buildings of Akhetaten were used as a convenient quarry for building projects such as the temple building of Ramesses II just across the river at Hermopolis Magna, from where 1500 *talatat* have been recovered. This dismantling of the most important religious structures at Amarna would also have the effect of attacking those elements of the 'Amarna heresy' most offensive to traditionalists and act as a *damnatio memoriae* for a king who became known, when he needed to be referred to at all, as 'that enemy from Akhetaten'.

Life-size head of Nefertiti, from the workshop of Thuthmose at Amarna.

The City

One of the favourite scenes depicted in the tombs of courtiers which are cut into the cliffs at the northern and southern ends of the bay of Amarna is the royal chariot drive. In this scene, Akhenaten and his principal queen, Nefertiti, are shown driving along the 'Royal Road'. This long, straight avenue forms the backbone of Akhetaten, and the route of the chariot procession took the royal couple past most of the important buildings of the city, clustered around the road. The procession, which may have been a daily event, began at the far north of the site in the so-called 'North City'. This quarter consisted of the North Riverside Palace, which was probably the main residence of the royal family, and a group of large private houses which were probably occupied by the highest ranking courtiers of the king. Travelling south along the road, the chariot would pass the North Palace, a

ABOVE: Stone relief of a procession with ceremonial bull.

LEFT: *Talatat* block, showing masons at work and the cross-section of a house.

self-contained residence probably intended for Meritaten, the king's eldest daughter, then a dense cluster of private houses known as the North Suburb, before reaching the Central City itself, where the road ended. To the west of the road in the Central City was the Great Palace which seems to have consisted of a large central courtyard around which were smaller courts and halls. At the southern end of the palace an enormous hall, containing 544 densely packed brick columns, was built by Akhenaten's short-lived successor, Smenkhkare. Across the road from the Great Palace lay other important public buildings, the most impressive of which was the Great Aten Temple, basically a series of open courts filled with altars for offerings to the Aten. Close by was the King's House, where much of the day-to-day royal business was conducted, and which was connected to the Great Palace by a bridge over the Royal Road. Near the Royal Palace was the 'Record Office', the archive for royal foreign correspondence which produced, firstly from illicit diggings some time before 1887, the so-called 'Amarna Letters', clay tablets with cuneiform texts sent by foreign rulers and vassals of the Egyptian empire to Akhenaten, his father Amenhotep III, and later to Tutankhamen. At the southern end of the city was the Maru-Aten, a cluster of buildings which included an ornamental lake, small island and gardens. This seems to have been a small 'pleasure pavilion' and was also constructed for Meritaten.

Most ordinary people lived in the Central City or in the North Suburb. Well-to-do individuals lived in characteristic villas, with a large central room surrounded by other rooms including bedrooms and bathrooms and open verandahs. Outside the main villa itself (but within its enclosed grounds) would be, typically, granaries, gardens, kitchens, stalls for animals, servants' accommodation and a chapel. However, most people lived in much smaller dwellings, which clustered around the large villas. We know the identities of some of these householders from inscribed objects found within them – for example, the sculptor Thuthmose, who lived in the residential area immediately to the south of the Central City, and from whose studio came a number of pieces of sculpture including the famous head of Nefertiti now in Berlin.

No Egyptian city would be complete without its cemeteries. The royal tomb itself was located in a valley 11 km to the east of the Central City, into the desert, while the high officials of Akhenaten had tombs cut for them in the cliffs at the north and south of the Amarna 'bay'. It may be that the separate Workmen's Village at Amarna, a square block of sixty-nine houses, was the residential area set aside for the artisans who worked on the royal (and private?) tombs at Amarna, just as the Valley of the Kings' workmen lived in the nearby village of Deir el-Medina.

Events at the end of the reign of Akhenaten are confused, but it is clear that, with its prime mover dead, the 'Amarna Experiment' quickly collapsed. King Tutankhamen, although probably born at Amarna and originally called Tutankhaten, has objects bearing his name at Amarna, but his reign represents a return to the *status quo*, the restoration of the traditional state religion and, with it, a move back to Thebes and the abandonment of Akhetaten. ■

TANIS

The collapse of the New Kingdom in 1070 BC broke Egypt up into a number of autonomous regions. This period, Dynasties 21 to 25, is known as the Third Intermediate Period. In the north of Egypt political control was in the hands of a man called Smendes, who had already become effective ruler of northern Egypt in the final years of the last king of the New Kingdom, Ramesses XI. Smendes was, in effect, the founder of a new dynasty, the 21st, which continued to exert control in Lower Egypt, while Upper Egypt was administered by the Theban priesthood of the god Amun. Later (after 945 BC), the predominant influences on political life in Egypt were the powerful families of Libyan origin, probably the descendants of prisoners of war who had been settled in the Delta by Ramesses II and his successors.

The largest archaeological site in the Nile Delta is called Tell San el-Hagar and consists of two large natural sand islands called *geziras* which rise above the flat alluvial plain of the eastern Nile Delta. The great *tell* (mound) is 3 km by 1.5 km and, at its highest, over 30 m tall. In the northern part of the site can be seen a dense scatter of enormous stone statues and building-blocks – this is the temple area, the heart of the ancient city of Tanis, known to the ancient Egyptians as D'nt, the biblical Zoan, and thus the Arabic San el-Hagar, 'San, the stony one'.

Shoshenk I) was based at Tanis, although they originally came to prominence in another eastern Delta city, Bubastis. Tanis seems to have become the most significant centre in north-east Egypt after the abandonment of Pi-Ramesses at the end of the 20th Dynasty. The kings of the 21st and 22nd Dynasties wished to transform

Although retaining their Libyan identity in many ways (including their personal names, such as Osorkon, Shoshenk, Takelot), these local rulers styled themselves as king of Upper and Lower Egypt and required the religious, architectural and artistic paraphernalia to match. The ruling family now referred to as Dynasty 22 (beginning with

The remains of the Amen Temple at Tanis.

Tanis into the 'Thebes of the North' and create a royal city which had those features which defined Thebes in the New Kingdom as the religious capital of Egypt: a great temple to Amun, chief god of the Egyptian empire (as at Karnak), and tombs fit for royal burial (as in the Valley of the Kings).

The method used to build such a city, and particularly to furnish it with colossal stone masonry and 'temple furniture' (statues, obelisks) when access to the granite quarries in the far south of the country may well have been problematic, was to make use of the monuments at the neighbouring and now probably abandoned city of Pi-Ramesses. It is this large-scale borrowing which caused major problems for early archaeologists trying to work out exactly how long Tanis had been occupied, and by whom. The identification of San el-Hagar with Tanis was made as early as 1722, and a plan was drawn of the great mound during the Napoleonic expedition in 1800: obelisks, blocks and a massive enclosure wall were to be seen. Between 1860 and 1864 the French Egyptologist Auguste Mariette excavated in the temple area, recovering many stone fragments inscribed with the name of Ramesses II and groups of well-carved statuary. In 1884 the British archaeologist Flinders Petrie worked on the town site, and in 1929 French Egyptologist Pierre Montet began what was to be the most significant programme of archaeological work on the site.

But by the time Montet started work at Tanis he, like most other Egyptologists, had accepted an erroneous interpretation of the early history of the site. An inscription noted on a royal statue at Tanis mentioned 'Seth, Lord of Avaris'. This, together with finds of Middle Kingdom royal sculpture by Mariette seemed to confirm that Tanis was at least as old as the 12th Dynasty and therefore the most likely candidate for the lost city of Pi-Ramesses. Indeed, even earlier royal names were later found on objects from the site, taking the potential history of Tanis back to the Old Kingdom. Only gradually, after 1928, was it realized that Avaris and Pi-Ramesses lay elsewhere), while Montet's excavations, and those of his successors, have done much to reveal the 'real' early history of Tanis.

The Temple Enclosure

The earliest major builder at Tanis seems to have been Psusennes I, third king of the 21st Dynasty. It was he who built the enclosure wall and temple for the divine family Amun, Mut and Khonsu. Although little of this work now remains, apart from the massive enclosure wall, the existence of the temple(s) to these gods is attested by a fragmentary inscription of dedication. This temple was added to by kings based at Tanis, particularly Siamun and Osorkon III. The work of lime-burners at Tanis has meant that much of the temple buildings has been destroyed for ever; the most substantial remains are the granite portions brought from Pi-Ramesses.

The Royal Tombs

In the south-west corner of the temple precinct Psusennes built his tomb from re-used blocks of limestone and granite. It consisted of simple twin burial chambers for the king and his queen, Mutnodjmet, with a number of side-rooms which were later

Fallen obelisk inscribed with the name of Ramesses II.

occupied by the burials of other Tanitic royals and nobles. In effect, the temple area at Tanis was intended to be a counterpart to both Karnak and the Valley of the Kings – the great state temple also housing the royal tombs. With no desert valleys close to Tanis, some other form of burial needed to be found, and burial within the sacred precincts would keep the king physically close to the god for eternity while ensuring, as far as was possible, the security of the tomb itself. The construction of royal and semi-royal tombs within the precincts of temples of the Late Period is also attested at the Delta sites of Sais and Mendes. The success of the security aspect of this tomb design is amply demonstrated by the fact that the royal burials remained intact until their discovery and excavation by Montet in 1939–40.

The use of the royal tombs after Psusennes is confused; Mutnodjmet's chamber was used for the burial of Psusennes' successor

Below: The outer granite sarcophagus of King Psusennes from the royal necropolis at Tanis.
Opposite: Canopic jar containing the intestines of Prince Hornakht.

Amenemope, while in the 22nd Dynasty Shoshenk II was buried in the same tomb, with other tombs built close by for Osorkon II and Shoshenk III.

Tanis after the Third Intermediate Period

Tanis remained an important city even after it was eclipsed as a royal centre by other northern cities such as Sais, Memphis and, ultimately, Alexandria (p. 40) in the Graeco-Roman period. Additions to the temple precincts continued, most notably under the 30th Dynasty kings Nectanebos I and II, who built new temples for Horus and Khonsu-Neferhotep, and a sacred lake. The second great enclosure wall, 430 m by 370 m, and 15 m thick, was probably built at this time. King Ptolemy II Philadelphus added to the Horus temple, while Ptolemy IV Philopator rebuilt the temple for Mut, which was originally the work of Siamun. Other evidence for Tanis' importance in the Ptolemaic period are the statues of the governors Panemerit and Pikhaas, but Tanis seems to have declined and been largely abandoned before the end of the Roman period. ∎

MEROE

Another name which is applied to southern (Upper) Nubia is Kush. The first kingdom of Kush was centred on the city of Kerma, and flowered briefly during the Second Intermediate Period in Egypt (*c.* 1785–1550 BC), when Egyptian control over Nubia was lost. It was crushed by the re-united Egypt of the 18th Dynasty. The second kingdom of Kush was more successful, surviving for over 1000 years. This period of Nubian independence is sometimes divided into two phases, the Napatan Empire followed by the Meroitic Empire. The reason for this division is the location of the royal burial ground – at Kurru and Nuri near Napata, close to the fourth cataract of the Nile (from *c.* 900 to *c.* 300 BC), and then south of the fifth cataract at Meroe (from

Nubia is the name given to the land of the Nile south of ancient Egypt, mostly located in what is now the Sudan. For two thousand years, from 3000 BC to the collapse of the Egyptian New Kingdom empire in 1070 BC, Nubia was overshadowed by its more powerful northern neighbour. The independent political unity of this region could only occur at times of Egyptian weakness as the policy of Egyptian kings was to control, and later to colonize, an area which was capable of developing into a powerful state, rich in agricultural produce and in gold, much like Egypt itself.

c. 300 BC to *c.* AD 300) – but the whole period seems to be a political continuum with no clear reason known for the change in royal cemeteries.

The name Meroe, which refers to both the city and the kingdom, occurs in the works of Classical authors including Diodorus Siculus, who tells of the ritual killing of the king by the priests. A tradition appears in the Classical authors that Meroe was ruled by a queen called the Candace: indeed, the only biblical reference to Meroe speaks of the baptism of 'a man of Ethiopia, a eunuch of great authority under Candace queen of the Ethiopians' (Acts VIII, 26–39). However, Meroe/Ethiopia remained a semi-legendary land, forgotten until the accidental discovery of the city of Meroe itself by the explorer James Bruce.

Bruce, travelling north along the Nile in 1772, passed the village of Begarawiya, to the south of which were 'heaps of broken pedestals and pieces of obelisks'. He correctly guessed that this was the lost city of Meroe, although this identification was not finally confirmed until 200 years later during the excavations of John Garstang for the University of Liverpool. Between 1910 and 1914 Garstang excavated extensively in and around the 'Royal City' at Meroe; the excavation of the royal cemetery was left to the 1920–23 work of George Reisner, who also excavated the earlier royal pyramids at Kurru and Nuri.

The temples which have survived in Meroe and at other sites in the Meroitic kingdom show that a variety of deities was worshipped. Most important were the gods of Egyptian origin, particularly Amun who had been chief god of the Egyptian empire and now fulfilled that role in the Meroitic kingdom. This was part of an attempt to absorb aspects of Egyptian 'high culture', particularly religion, art, architecture and the presentation of the ruler as all-conquering before the gods. The most important non-Egyptian god was Apedemak, a lion-headed deity which was often shown carrying bow and arrows.

Several of the substantial public buildings excavated by Garstang at Meroe have been identified as temples.

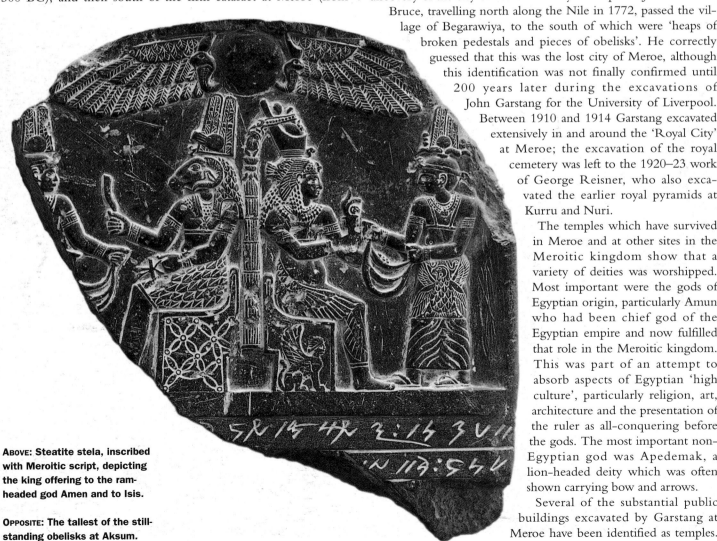

ABOVE: Steatite stela, inscribed with Meroitic script, depicting the king offering to the ram-headed god Amen and to Isis.

OPPOSITE: The tallest of the still-standing obelisks at Aksum.

ABOVE: Pre-Aksumite limestone statuette from Hawile-Assaraw, near Aksum. The plinth carries an inscription in a South Arabian script.

RIGHT: The 'kiosk' of the Meroitic temple complex at Naqa.

The most important of these was the Amun Temple, which consisted of a large outer court, behind which a series of pillared halls, decreasing in size as they led to the sanctuary itself. The Amun enclosure was situated immediately to the east of the walled 'Royal City', which seems to have been the main royal residential quarter of Meroe. Within this city Garstang discovered a large brick-lined pool 7 m square and 3 m deep, with lion-headed water spouts around its edge. He identified this as the 'Royal Baths' which aimed to copy Classical bath-houses, but more recent interpretations of this structure have included a swimming-pool and a water-sanctuary connected to the worship of the Nile itself.

About 1.5 km to the east of the 'Royal City' Garstang found a building he called the 'Sun Temple'. The temple was surrounded by a brick enclosure wall and was raised on a podium with a colonnade running around its edge. In the centre of the podium stood the sanctuary itself, entered through a pylon gateway and

both walled and floored with blue-glazed tiles. Impressive though this structure undoubtedly was, its identification with the 'Table of the Sun' at Meroe, written of by Herodotus, rests on the flimsy evidence of a block bearing a large sun-disk found at the temple.

The small 'Lion Temple' at Meroe was built on a slag heap, which attests to Meroe's role as an industrial centre, particularly in the production of iron, leading one archaeologist to refer to Meroe as 'the Birmingham of ancient Africa'.

The Royal Cemetery

Meroitic royal pyramids are generally much smaller and steeper than their Egyptian counterparts. The first royal pyramid of the Kushite kingdom was built for King Piye (sometimes called Piankhy) at Kurru. This king had conquered Egypt itself, and he and his Nubian successors ruled Egypt as the 25th Dynasty and therefore had the opportunity to see 'real' pyramids at first hand. The desire to emulate their Old Kingdom predecessors translated itself into a rather modest reality – Piye's own pyramid was no more than 8 m broad at its base. The pyramids themselves were solid, with the accompanying burials housed in simple chambers cut into the rock beneath them.

The reasons for the decline of the kingdom and eventual abandonment of the city of Meroe, but it may be that the crucial event was the capture of Meroe by Ezana, ruler of the rising southern kingdom of Aksum.

Aksum

During the middle of the first millennium BC the so-called Pre-Aksumite culture developed in Northern Ethiopia. This seems to have been a mix of local Africans (possibly the descendants of the ancient Kingdom of Punt) and newcomers from south-west Arabia. These immigrants brought with them traditions in monumental stone architecture and sculpture which were to affect the development of the urban civilization of Aksum, which emerged around the beginning of the Christian era, flourished until the sixth century AD, and gradually declined until its disappearance in the Middle Ages.

At its greatest extent, the kingdom of Aksum covered Northern Ethiopia and the Red Sea coast from Sudan to Somalia and at times included the Yemen. The control of the coast was essential to Aksum's prosperity as its major source of wealth was trade, especially between the Roman Empire and India. Besides effecting this trade, it also exported its own African products, including ivory, gold and incense, especially through the sea-port of Adulis. Aksum's mercantile activities were emphasized by minting its own coinage.

At Aksum itself, wealth and royal display were most famously attested by the erection of vast stone obelisks (some 30 m tall) to commemorate deceased monarchs. The form of these obelisks seems to owe little to Egyptian inspiration but are part of the distinct Aksumite cultural tradition.

Under King Ezana (AD 325–360) Aksum embraced Christianity as its state religion. His reign (shortly after the eclipse of Meroe) marks the high water mark of Aksumite power. The establishment of Sassanian Persian control over Yemen and their wars with the Byzantine Empire effectively disrupted the trade on which Aksum's wealth depended and led to its gradual decline. ∎

LEFT: One of the fallen obelisks at Aksum.
OPPOSITE: Statue of a ram, prob-ably representing the god Amen, at the Meroitic Temple complex at Naqa.

SABRATHA

Sabratha, together with Lepcis Magna and Oea, constituted the ancient region of 'Tripolis' on the North African coast. Two factors determined Sabratha's location and development. First, it possessed one of the few natural harbours along this part of the North African coast. Secondly, it is situated at the point where the line of the main coastal route is met by the road which links the harbour to one of the trans-Saharan trade routes via the oasis of Gydamus (Ghadames) to the south.

Sabratha's potential was first recognized by the Phoenician city of Carthage. Certainly by the fifth century BC, if not slightly earlier, Carthage's expanding commercial interests had led to the establishment of a seasonal trading post at the site, from where trade was conducted with the local native population. By the

This original Carthaginian trading post flourished under the Roman empire as a result of its long-distance contacts with the interior of North Africa, whence luxury goods and exotic animals were brought to meet the demands of the Roman cities of the Mediterranean. On several occasions the city suffered from earthquakes and, after a particularly destructive tremor in the middle of the fourth century AD, it was devastated. Although rebuilding took place Sabratha never recovered.

second half of the fourth century BC the appearance of stone buildings suggests the development of a permanent trading station and the growing commercial importance of Sabratha.

However, it was under the peaceful conditions of the Roman imperial period that the city truly prospered. Although isolated from the Gebel, the rich olive-growing region from which Lepcis Magna drew its wealth, Sabratha was well positioned to exploit one of several long-distance trade routes which crossed the Sahara desert. The trade in luxury goods and exotic animals from the interior was the basis of the city's wealth and

View of a residential area close to the centre of Sabratha.

prosperity; and Sabratha's natural harbour, improved by the addition of an artificial mole, allowed easy distribution of these commodities to the markets of the Mediterranean. One such contact is evident from Ostia, Rome's harbour town, where a mosaic floor in the open square of one of the town's trade corporations depicts an elephant, the emblem of Sabratha and an animal eagerly sought after for display in the public shows which became increasingly popular in the capital and other cities of the empire.

Sabratha was typical of the growing prosperity of the towns of Africa; and civic pride and patriotism, resulting from increasing wealth, manifested themselves in a programme of urban expansion and civic development. At Sabratha a new monumental civic centre complex was planned and gradually took shape in the course of the first century AD. Paradoxically the development was assisted by a serious earthquake in *c.* AD 64–70, which destroyed existing buildings that might otherwise have restricted redevelopment. The heart of the development was the construction of a Roman-style forum, associated administrative buildings, and the customary Capitolium. The latter was a temple which was often associated with the forum complex of Romanized cities in the west. Named after the Capitol at Rome, where there was a temple dedicated to Jupiter, it was usually dedicated to the Capitoline triad of Jupiter, Juno and Minerva.

The development of these typically Roman urban forms was complemented by continuing local traditions such as the temple to the Egyptian deity, Serapis. This was positioned at the north-western corner of the forum and was built of local sandstone. Even the grander temple to Liber Pater (Dionysos) was unconventional in the sense that, although it had a Classical plan, the applied stucco facing was gaudily painted. Probably the most impressive development during this period was the enlargement of the temple of Isis. As a goddess of seafarers and calm conditions she became a very popular deity throughout the Mediterranean. At Sabratha, with its commercial interests, Isis was obviously important, and her temple stood on the coast overlooking the sea on the eastern side of the city.

The development of Sabratha in the first century AD was gradual. However, from shortly after the middle of the second century AD Sabratha underwent a veritable explosion of building activity,

A statue of the Roman period from Sabathra.

expansion and renovation, reaching a peak towards the end of the century. Existing buildings throughout the city were extensively remodelled and embellished. Decorative marble was widely employed, and granite was even imported from remote parts of Egypt. New temples were also added during this period, including a lavish one to the emperors Marcus Aurelius and Verus, and an ornate temple to Hercules. These buildings were an indication of the wealth and prosperity of the city and its inhabitants. Moreover, the changes were not confined to public buildings. It was during this same period that many of the streets of Sabratha were paved for the first time, and a comprehensive underground drainage system was installed.

The development and embellishment of cities throughout the empire relied in part on civic funds, but overwhelmingly on the pride and civic patriotism of their leading citizens. Individuals

OPPOSITE: **The reconstructed stage building of the theatre which was built in the second half of the second century AD.**
BELOW: **The remains of a statue, possibly of the goddess Aphrodite.**

were encouraged to contribute their resources to the beautification and enhancement of the city in return for recognition and honours. At Sabratha one such benefactor was Flavius Tullus, who provided the city with a public water supply. Whilst a town might survive without a public supply of water, this feature was really essential to civilized urban life. Water was required for a variety of reasons besides drinking. The leisure facilities of the baths, as well as certain commercial and industrial operations, required large amounts of water. Nevertheless, it was often left to the public-spiritedness and beneficence of wealthy individuals to provide such an amenity. At Sabratha the population relied on water storage cisterns, which are found extensively in houses and buildings throughout the city, until Flavius Tullus provided a public supply, as is recorded in an inscription set up by his son, Caius Flavius Pudens.

As this rapid period of expansion began, Sabratha became the stage for a famous yet curious trial. In *c.* AD 157 the talented advocate, sophist and novelist Apuleius, who wrote the *Golden Ass*, was brought to trial at Sabratha before the provincial governor, who was holding assizes there. Apuleius was an African by birth and had travelled extensively in the eastern provinces, and for a time had even lived in Rome before returning to Africa. It was whilst he was travelling to Egypt that he visited a former student in Oea and married his mother. Her relatives, however, accused Apuleius of winning her by sorcery and the trial was held in Sabratha. The whole affair, including Apuleius' brilliant defence speech, which has survived, gives a remarkable insight into the beliefs and attitudes of the day and, in its allusions to cults to be found at Sabratha, complements what is known from temples and shrines about pagan religion there.

In its public buildings Sabratha increasingly assumed the characteristics of a Romanized town. In contrast the original native character of the city was maintained in its older residential areas which were typically irregular and overcrowded. The frontages often have shops and storerooms inserted into them, and the houses themselves vary in shape, size and configuration, and degree of comfort, according to the availability of land and the wealth of the owner.

The accelerated development of the city in the second half of the second century AD also involved the extension of residential living space. A new domestic quarter was laid out on the eastern side of the city. Unlike in the older quarters the houses and buildings here were set out to a rigid grid pattern, and many of the streets were provided with shallow porticoes to offer pedestrians some protection from the sun and heat. This new district was dominated by a magnificent theatre building, which has partially been restored.

The expansion of the city suggests a rapid rise in prosperity. However, after this there were no major developments. In fact, it appears that the third century was one of stagnation. Then in AD 365 much of the eastern Mediterranean suffered massive damage from a major earthquake and the city of Sabratha suffered extensively in this catastrophe. Although there was some rebuilding in the town centre, much of the outer city was abandoned and, significantly, none of the pagan temples was rebuilt – undoubtedly a significant indication of the growing strength and popularity of Christianity. Occupation continued at Sabratha but its importance as a commercial centre had long since ceased. ■

JENNE-JENO

The appearance of towns in West Africa was until recently commonly thought to have been the result of the external stimulation of the indigenous economy when North African Arabs established trading posts at settlements in order to control trans-Saharan trade. This so-called 'Golden Trade of the Moors', which saw gold, slaves, ivory and other animal products, as well as kola wood, moving north from West Africa across the Sahara desert in exchange for salt, cloth, pottery, glass and foods, became firmly established in the ninth to tenth centuries AD. In some cases trading settlements later expanded into the capitals of powerful West African kingdoms which flourished in the second millennium AD. West African urbanism was thus believed to have a foreign origin, which brought in its wake conversion to Islam, literacy, and the religious architectural forms considered to be the hallmarks of traditional West African towns. Jenne-Jeno, however, provides clear evidence for the indigenous development of West African urbanism long before the arrival of Islamic traders.

Large settlements and indigenous regional trade networks developed in some areas of West Africa from early in the first millennium AD. The clearest available documentation of these developments is from Jenne-Jeno, a site complex on the Inland Niger River Delta in Mali, which was occupied from about 250 BC, grew into a walled town of some 33 hectares by AD 800, and was abandoned by at least 1468, probably around 1400.

'Ancient Jenné'

Jenne-Jeno is located some 3 km south-east of the modern town of Jenné in Mali, in a remarkably fertile area which also provides navigable waterways for the transport of goods. It is a tear-shaped mound of human occupation debris some 2 km round its perimeter and rising up to 8 m above a former channel of the Bani River on the Inland Niger River Delta floodplain, the southernmost basin of the middle Niger River. The 33 hectare surface area of the site is strewn with an astonishing abundance of features and artifacts, including round and rectangular mudbrick foundations, parts of a city wall, concentrations of iron and slag, funerary urns, clay toy figurines, copper ornaments, sandstone grindstones, as well as hundreds of thousands of potsherds.

The earliest known historical record of Jenné dates to AD 1447, when an Italian merchant wrote that he had been told of a West African city-state called Geni. During the sixteenth to seventeenth centuries, chroniclers described Jenné as one of the most important intellectual and trading centres in West Africa, rivalling the famed Timbuktu. Carefully preserved oral traditions maintained that Jenné was founded in the eighth century AD, but pointed to the existence of an earlier town located on the site of Zoboro, also called Jenne-Jeno (meaning 'ancient Jenné' in Songhay), some 3 km south-east of Jenné. Aerial photographs of a huge mound at this location led the husband and wife archaeological team of Roderick J. and Susan Keech McIntosh of Rice University in Texas to embark on an investigation of the site that has continued since 1977.

An Old West African Town

The first occupants of Jenne-Jeno seem to have been iron-using herders and fishermen who settled there permanently in about 250 BC. By AD 99 the settlement covered at least 25 hectares. The people lived

Smith's workshop with three exterior furnaces, dating to about AD 900, from Jenne-Jeno.

Terracotta head found in round smith's workshop at Jenne-Jeno.

although evidence for this may come to light as excavations continue. It is possible that the institution of chief evolved out of the economic need to centralize the administration of kin-based trading networks, rather than being political in origin.

During its heyday in about AD 800, Jenne-Jeno seems to have resembled a rabbit-warren, with narrow alleys weaving between tightly packed compounds of round or rectangular houses joined together by walls. When one house collapsed, another was simply built on top of it. There may have been a central open space. The most noticeable architectural feature of this period was a wall 3.6 m wide at the base, 4 m or more high, and almost 2 km in circumference, built out of solid rows of cylindrical mudbricks. The McIntoshes consider it unlikely that the wall was built for defence; rather, they suggest it could have been intended to protect the town from floods, or possibly to control access to the market, or even as a mark of identity and prestige.

Estimates of the population of Jenne-Jeno at this time range between about 7000 and 13,000. However, Jenne-Jeno was connected to the neighbouring site of Hambarketolo by a causeway and it is thought likely that the two sites functioned as a unit with a combined area of about 42 hectares. Also, some twenty-five smaller sites are located within a 1 km radius of Jenne-Jeno. If the entire complex can be regarded as an entity, population estimates rise to some 27,000 people.

Abandonment

The reasons for the eventual decline and abandonment of Jenne-Jeno are unclear. One possibility is that the town moved to a new site where modern Jenné stands today after the king or an élite converted to Islam, an event reputed to have occurred in the thirteenth century AD, in order to avoid a location considered polluted by pagan practices. However, the cause may have been economic. If, as seems likely from historical records, control of trade fell into the hands of Islamic merchants at about this time, the growing market of the new Islamic neighbouring town of Jenné would have attracted farmers, fishermen and craftsmen and led to the eventual abandonment of Jenne-Jeno and the end of an urban centre that owed its development to indigenous stimuli and flourished for nearly 1000 years. ■

in circular houses made from bent wattle poles and woven reed mats thickly coated on the outside with mud for waterproofing. The presence of iron and slag indicates that the community could smelt and smith metal, while thin-walled fine twine-impressed pottery suggests that specialist craftsmen operated at least on a part-time basis. Great numbers of children's clay toys of wild and domestic animals were made at this time. The economy relied mainly on fish, reedbuck and domesticated cattle. Stone and metals were not available on the floodplain, and were presumably obtained from neighbouring or distant areas in exchange for food surpluses of staples such as dried fish, fish oil and African rice.

During the period between about AD 300 and 800, the site was more intensively occupied and there is more evidence for craft specialists, including masons who worked in *tauf* (solid coursed mud), as well as potters and smiths. The pottery typical of this period suggests affluence and includes luxury items such as carinated bowls with channelled rims painted in white and/or black geometric designs, as well as burnished wares with white geometric designs. Copper and gold ornaments were also present. The economy was based on herding, fishing and the cultivation of millet, sorghum and African rice. Interestingly, available data from houses and burials do not indicate social or economic differences among the inhabitants, nor the existence of an élite group,

Terracotta animal figurines, possibly children's toys, from Jenne-Jeno.

KILWA

By the ninth century AD, African seafaring peoples had spread throughout the East African coast and established small isolated communities sustained by fishing, rice, millet, coconuts and goats. At Kilwa at this time there was a village covering at least 1 hectare of rectangular post-houses with mud and wattle walls. The settlement seems to have been poor, heavily reliant on shellfish collecting for food, and apparently lacked lamps for lighting. Some iron was produced, but the most important local industry was the grinding of shell beads, which were probably used for trade. Imported objects, including Islamic pottery, glass and beads, indicate that the villagers had trading contacts with other, more important, centres on the East African coast, or even lands further afield. A stone inscribed with Arabic letters suggests that Muslims from more northerly East African coastal towns or overseas visited Kilwa or were resident there, but there is no indication that the community as a whole had adopted Islam at this time.

Kilwa Kisiwani is a small coral rock island, some 6 km long and 4 km wide, in a drowned valley off the Tanzanian coast, separated from the African mainland by a deep 1.5 km wide channel. The present-day village of Kilwa Kisiwani in the northern part of the island is located in the central part of the ancient town of Kilwa, which became a wealthy Islamic trading centre boasting fine stone-built mosques and palaces during medieval times.

The Period of the 'Shirazi' dynasty

During the eleventh and twelfth centuries AD, settlements along the East African coast increased in prosperity and large towns appeared. Kilwa expanded to cover 30 hectares and in the late twelfth century became incorporated into a new city-state.

Arabic and Portuguese chronicles record a legend that a dynasty of rulers was established at Kilwa by 'Ali bin al-Hasan (sometimes spelt Husain), the son of a sultan of Shiraz, who sailed with his brothers and his father from the Persian Gulf to settle in seven different places on the East African coast. The story is probably a conflation of memories of various accounts and it seems possible that the settlers in fact originated from further north on the East African coast. Their arrival nevertheless seems to have involved a peaceful business transaction when 'Ali purchased the island from its pagan ruler for a supply of cloth.

Under the rule of three generations of the 'Shirazi' dynasty until the end of the thirteenth century AD, Kilwa developed as a typical Islamic town with a population that fluctuated between about 4000 and 12,000 people. The town was not laid out according to a plan, and irregularly spaced buildings were separated from each other by narrow lanes. Public buildings and the houses of wealthier inhabitants were built from blocks of coral stone cut from reefs at low tide.

Houses must have been cool and dark, and consisted of a sunken courtyard on to which faced a long narrow anteroom, behind which was a main room, with several smaller rooms to the rear. In some more elaborate houses, the anterooms had domes decorated with inset multicoloured bowls. Each house had at least one latrine with adjoining 'bidet'.

At the centre of the town was the Great Mosque, the best-preserved pre-Portuguese building on the East African coast, which attests that Kilwa was now Islamic. The northern and earlier section had a flat roof supported by octagonal masonry columns, but the southern and more recent section was roofed with domes, vaults and arches.

The prosperity of the town was based on trade and its location as an intermediate port between Mogadishu in Somalia and Madagascar, as well as Sofala in Mozambique, where gold and ivory from Great Zimbabwe reached the East African coast. The 'Shirazi' period at Kilwa saw a substantial increase in imported goods from the Islamic world and even rare examples of Chinese porcelain. Although local coins bearing the names of sultans were struck, they are of too little intrinsic value to have been used for large payments, so trade was probably conducted mainly by barter or for payment in gold.

The Dynasty of the Ahdali

A change of dynasty occurred at Kilwa towards the end of the thirteenth century when al-Hasan bin Talut of the Mahdali or Ahdali family, a clan of Sayyids then living in south-west Yemen, became the new ruler. Although traditions state that he seized the city-state by force, but with the help of the people, there is no evidence of an invasion and it seems likely that he was already resident at Kilwa before the coup.

Kilwa continued to flourish under the Ahdalis. The traveller

The ruins of the palace of Husuni Kubwa at Kilwa, Tanzania.

Ibn Battuta, who visited Kilwa in 1331 or 1332, described it as 'one of the finest and most substantially built towns ... most of whose inhabitants are Zinj [East African], jet-black in colour. They have tattoo marks on their faces ...' Kilwa's prosperity was probably a consequence of securing a virtual monopoly on the Zimbabwean gold trade and of establishing ports under her control in the Sofala region. The wealth this trade brought to the town is evidenced by the import of large quantities of Chinese ceramics and glass beads, the increasing production of high-quality cotton cloth, as well as high standards of craftsmanship in carving stone, and, most especially, the building of the palace and emporium of Husuni Kubwa.

The name of this complex is derived from the Arabic *hsun*, meaning a fortified house commonly found in southern Arabia. It was built with its northern end on the most precipitous part of a high cliff from where it has a clear view of the harbour and is well exposed to cooling sea breezes. The triangular northern section comprises the palace proper, while a nearly square southern section was the sultan's commercial centre and consists of a court surrounded by storage rooms. The complex includes staircases, vaults, domes and an octagonal-shaped pool in an unroofed enclosure. Separated from it by a 50 m wide gully is the contemporary rectangular enclosure of Husuni Ndogo, which has exceptionally thick walls, about 1.2 m wide and 2.5 m high, with solid towers along the outside of the walls and isolated structures inside.

Other noteworthy buildings, such as the Small Domed Mosque, the Jangwani Mosque and part of the House of the Mosque probably date from the first half of the fifteenth century.

The Arrival of the Portuguese

The second half of the fifteenth century saw a decline in Kilwa's fortunes as a result of dynastic rivalries, political disputes and fighting, as well as the rise in importance of other towns.

The Great Mosque at Kilwa, Tanzania.

The interior of the Great Mosque at Kilwa, Tanzania.

Vasco da Gama, the Portuguese explorer, had intended to visit Kilwa during his epic voyage around Africa to India in 1498, but was carried past the island by the current. When he did succeed in visiting the island in 1502, he obtained a promise from the sultan to pay tribute to the King of Portugal. When the sultan refused to pay in 1505, a large Portuguese fleet under Francisco d'Almeida occupied the town and pillaged but did not burn it. A fortress called the Gereza was then built, a garrison established, and the succeeding rulers were Omani Arabs who were generally Portuguese nominees. Further disaster struck Kilwa in about 1592, when the marauding Zimba tribe from the mainland overran the town and are reported to have killed and eaten many of the inhabitants.

Kilwa enjoyed a brief revival in the late eighteenth and early nineteenth centuries, as a result of trade in slaves, ivory and copal, when the Makutani palace with a triangular-shaped defensive enclosure was built, but the sultanate ended shortly after 1843 when the last sultan was deported to Muscat.

Kilwa was essentially a mercantile society which functioned as an outpost of the Islamic world. The East African coastal people who were absorbed into this society adopted the Muslim religion and developed a culture which reflected a mixture of Arab and African influences, and which looked to the Indian Ocean rather than the African hinterland. An extraordinary series of excavations was undertaken at Kilwa by Neville Chittick with a crew of about one hundred in eight field seasons between 1958 and 1965, and the town remains the subject of ongoing archaeological investigations. ■

GREAT ZIMBABWE

Great Zimbabwe is situated in the south-east of the southern African country of Zimbabwe, which took its name from the site on achieving independence from Great Britain in 1980. *Dzimbabwe* is the Shona word used for the house, court or grave of a chief. Traditionally, the chief's house comprised a series of stone-walled enclosures built on a hill. Great Zimbabwe is the largest and most impressive of over 150 similar zimbabwes located mainly on the central plateau of Zimbabwe and as far afield as eastern Botswana, the Northern Province of South Africa and western Mozambique, a region known as the Zimbabwe Culture Area.

The site was first occupied by an Early Iron Age farming community, who did not build in stone, from about AD 500 to 900, probably because it promised water, sweet grass for cattle and fer-

Great Zimbabwe is arguably the most famous and dramatic ruined town in sub-Saharan Africa. This haunting stone-walled settlement was the largest and most important capital of a Shona empire that stretched over modern Zimbabwe to northern South Africa, and from eastern Botswana to western Mozambique. Great Zimbabwe covered some 700 hectares and was occupied by about 18,000 people at its zenith in the fourteenth century AD. It has fuelled more legends, exotic tales, mystery and, in recent decades, patriotic feelings, than perhaps any other archaeological site in the world.

tile alluvial soil for cultivation by hoe. Thereafter, Shona people arrived and began building in stone from between 1270 and 1290 until the political importance of the town came to an end between 1420 and 1450. A portion of the site was subsequently occupied in the late fifteenth and early sixteenth centuries.

Unlike most other contemporary southern African societies, social organization in Great Zimbabwe was based on a clear distinction between a ruling class and commoners. The origins of this distinction may have been rooted in religion, or control over cattle and grazing areas, but one of the main stimuli in the evolution of the Zimbabwe Culture was probably gold panned from local streams. In time, the kings of Great Zimbabwe accumulated great wealth and prestige by controlling a trade network which saw the export of gold, ivory and iron to East African coastal trading stations in exchange for glass beads, cotton and silk cloth, and Chinese ceramics.

A Shona Capital

The Great Zimbabwe ruins are organized according to a spatial code which reflects the components of a hierarchically structured Shona society. The site is dominated by a large bare granite hill, Zimbabwe Hill, on top of which are stone-walled enclosures known collectively as the Hill Ruin or Complex. Shona traditions compare the high status of chieftainship with height or mountains, and important leaders used to live in ritual seclusion on high ground as a symbol of their authority. The features, organization and symbols associated with the Hill Complex indicate that it was the compound of a sacred ruler, which included the residence

The Great Enclosure and other structures in the valley at the Great Zimbabwe Ruins.

of the king, or *mambo*, members of his family and officials, as well as places of religious and ritual importance. The most famous objects found in the Hill Complex are seven unique grey-green soapstone raptor-like birds (an eighth one, found in the valley below, is represented on the flag of modern Zimbabwe), which are considered of religious significance. Each is about 300 mm long and sits atop a pillar a metre or more high. In Shona cosmology, some birds are thought to carry messages from ancestors and to be able to mediate between 'The Great One' and living people.

The lower slopes of the hill contain several terraces for the homes of noblemen and the base is partly surrounded by the Inner Perimeter Wall. In the valley below, an Outer Perimeter Wall encloses not only the hill, but also a central area including the quarters for the royal wives and the famous Great Enclosure (also known as the Elliptical Building). Shona kings had many wives (some as many as 1000), because wives represented political allegiances and symbolized wealth, power and success. The wives did not live in the palace on the hill, but in their own area with their own servants, under the control of the first wife or *vahozi*.

Many consider the Great Enclosure to epitomize the monumental grandeur of the town and to be its most important architectural achievement. It is estimated that the outer wall of this enclosure contains 900,000 stone blocks. A portion which stands 11 m high is decorated by a double chevron design that extends over 85 m and is considered to be symbolic of young manhood. This wall was probably built in stages, without scaffolding, by building one section to its full height and then using the fill as a ramp to extend it horizontally. The stones were all quarried locally by making use of natural cracks that occur on the granite domes of Zimbabwe and cause the rock to peel in even layers. The location, organization, artifacts, symbols and structures within the Great Enclosure are thought to indicate that it was used as a pre-marital initiation school for young men and women. For example, the much-photographed giant conical tower within the enclosure is considered to represent a huge granary, a male symbol.

The common people lived in high-density housing in the valley area of the town, while lesser chiefs from other areas maintained small palaces on the outskirts of the town for use when they came to Great Zimbabwe for important meetings.

Abandonment

Great Zimbabwe was not destroyed, but abandoned, probably for social and environmental reasons. The large number of people living at the site would have strained resources like bark (which was used for nets as well as bags and blankets), firewood and fertile soil, and this would have created social tension. By the time Portuguese explorers arrived in south-east Africa in the sixteenth century, the Shona capital had moved to other centres. Historical records and Shona oral traditions nevertheless indicate that the Zimbabwe Culture persisted in some areas and zimbabwes continued to be built until the nineteenth century.

Discovery and Early Interpretations

Great Zimbabwe was made known to the Western world by Carl Mauch, an adventurous young German geologist. Inspired by old stories from Portuguese explorers, traders and missionaries that King Solomon's Ophir lay in the East African hinterland, Mauch

The Conical Tower and walling within the Great Enclosure at the Great Zimbabwe Ruins.

set off in 1871 to find the 'most mysterious part of Africa'. His 1872 account of overgrown impressive stone walls and his romantic interpretation that they were built by the Queen of Sheba aroused tremendous popular interest and gave credence to the myth that the ruins were the work of foreigners.

After the 1890 colonization of the area by the British South Africa Company of Cecil Rhodes, who was convinced the ruins were a long-lost Phoenician city, exotic interpretations often invoking Arabians, Egyptians or Indians were the order of the day in a *milieu* that considered Africans too lazy and barbarous to have built such magnificence.

These interpretations were rejected by two investigations by trained archaeologists sponsored by the British Association for the Advancement of Science. The first, by David Randall MacIver in 1906, dated the ruins to medieval times by linking the stone walls with fourteenth to sixteenth century AD objects imported from the Near East and China. This was confirmed by the second investigation under Gertrude Caton-Thompson in 1929, who also unequivocally established the 'essentially African' interpretation of the site.

Despite overwhelming evidence for a medieval age and African origin obtained from numerous scientific investigations over the following decades, Great Zimbabwe continues to be burdened with exotic interpretations in popular accounts that deny Africans were capable of great indigenous architectural achievements. Africans, on the other hand, have come to regard the ruins as a symbol of past glories and freedom from colonial rule. It is probably true to say that the archaeology of no other site is as explicitly political or excites such passion as that of Great Zimbabwe. ■

uMGUNGUNDLOVU

owards the end of the eighteenth century AD in the south-east area of southern Africa, competition between chiefs for control of trade with ships visiting the East African coast played an important role in triggering social, political and, especially, military changes in the region. By the mid 1820s the Zulu king Shaka had established a single unified Zulu kingdom which stretched over much of modern KwaZulu-Natal Province of South Africa, and which was the most feared and formidable military power in the region at the time.

Shaka was assassinated on 24 September 1828 as the result of a conspiracy in which his half-brothers Dingane and Mahlangane were involved. When Dingane had Mahlangane killed and succeeded to the Zulu kingship some weeks later, he continued Shaka's custom of building military towns in the heart of the kingdom. The largest of these was uMgungundlovu, to which Dingane moved with large numbers of women and warriors on its completion in 1829.

The site chosen for his capital was a gently sloping hill in wooded savanna, iSangoyane, on which one of Dingane's

uMgungundlovu, thought to mean 'the secret meeting place of the elephant', was built by the Zulu king Dingane ka Senzangakhona on a hill in the Makosini Valley in central KwaZulu–Natal Province, South Africa, as his capital and military headquarters. It was occupied from about December 1829 until it was destroyed by fire during December 1838. The site is important in southern African history as a remarkable example of the military towns characteristic of nineteenth-century Zulu kingdoms, and enjoys notoriety as the place at which the Voortrekker leader Piet Retief and his party were killed on Dingane's orders on 6 February 1838.

ancestors, known in later records as Nkosinkulu, had been buried and possibly had a homestead in the late seventeenth or early eighteenth century. Dingane spent most of the next nine years at uMgungundlovu, from where he co-ordinated the internal affairs of the Zulu kingdom, maintained a large military garrison, and conducted trade with Europeans from Delagoa Bay (now called Maputo in Mozambique) and Port Natal (now Durban in South Africa).

Description of the Site

A number of European visitors, traders and missionaries who visited uMgungundlovu have left descriptions of the site, and their information is supplemented by a series of archaeological excavations undertaken since 1974.

These sources indicate that uMgungundlovu was oval in shape and surrounded by a high reed fence. At the head of the town opposite the main entrance was a royal area, or *isigodlo*, where

Captain A. F. Gardiner's sketch of the layout of uMgungundlovu within a ring of reed fencing.

Dingane and his retinue lived, with two arcs of densely packed standardized thatched warrior houses going downslope to the main entrance and enclosing an open space. The town probably contained about 1100 houses and had a population of about 5500. The missionary Allen Gardiner described it as looking like 'a distant racecourse' and 'an immense assemblage of haystacks'. Dingane himself was described as 'tall, corpulent and fleshy'.

The houses in the *isigodlo* were larger and less densely packed than those of the warriors, and were partitioned into small groups by high fences. This area was divided into a 'white' *isigodlo*, where Dingane's personal retinue lived, and a 'black' *isigodlo*, where hundreds of *undlunkulu* or 'royal girls' lived. An open space between these two areas may have been a cattle enclosure, or more probably a dancing square.

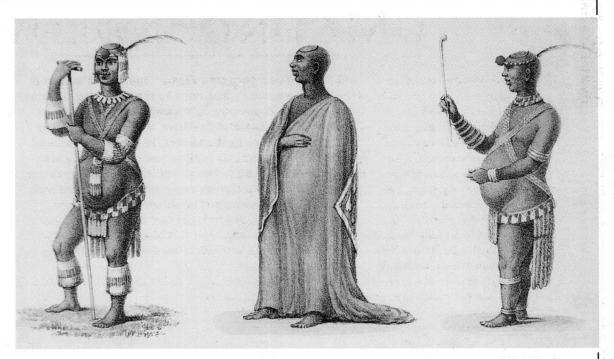

Sketches of Dingane (including his dancing outfits) by Captain Gardiner.

Dingane's personal quarters are believed to have been on the eastern side of the *isigodlo*. According to some contemporary accounts, his house was a beautiful circular building about 20 m in diameter, held up by twenty-one or twenty-two posts covered in beads, although other accounts mention only nine or ten posts. It is possible that Dingane used various houses for different purposes and slept and ate in one small house containing only a single post.

Some of the houses in the *isigodlo* may have been occupied by protective warriors and at least one house was specially designed for storing weapons. This structure contained at least three sets of small post holes which are thought to have supported wooden racks on which shields and spears were stored off the ground and protected from insect damage.

Behind the *isigodlo* was the *Bheje* enclosure, which may have housed members of the royal family, as well as serving specialist purposes like smithing and grain storage. A pit in this enclosure was found to contain a schist mould for making brass beads and bangles. Brass was obtained from traders at Delagoa Bay in exchange for ivory and cattle.

Meals at uMgungundlovu

It seems that uMgungundlovu was not self-sufficient in food and that large quantities of beer and grain were brought to the town by relatives of the warriors who lived there. Contemporary accounts comment that there was no cultivation of crops in the vicinity.

Animal bones from uMgungundlovu indicate that almost all the meat consumed in the town came from cattle, evidence of the high social status of the community. Sheep, goats and wild animals seem to have been of little importance. Most of the cattle consumed were old. Gardiner reported that the meat was tough

and that Dingane himself each day selected the cattle to be slaughtered to feed his warriors. Bones of some younger cattle excavated from the royal enclosures however suggest that the ruling élite occasionally enjoyed a more tender meal.

The meat was cooked in pots large enough to contain the half metapodials (foot bones) and it seems the head rather than the leg meat was regarded as more favoured. Horns were apparently burnt for religious or ritual reasons.

Destruction

Dingane signed a treaty to cede territory to the Voortrekker leader Piet Retief on 6 February 1838. The Voortrekkers were a group of some 15,000 Afrikaans-speaking farmers who left the eastern frontier of the Cape Colony between 1834 and 1840 and moved north-east to escape British rule, search for new grazing lands as well as commercial opportunities, and establish their own states in the South African interior. While Retief and his party were attending a farewell entertainment at uMgungundlovu, Dingane ordered them killed. The Zulu army was subsequently defeated by the Voortrekkers at the Battle of Blood River on 16 December 1838, after which Dingane burned part of his capital and abandoned it. Shortly afterwards, the Voortrekkers burned what was left of the site. The intense heat of the burning wood and thatch superstructure of the houses baked their clay floors and thus ensured their preservation to the present day.

Dingane built a new capital, also called uMgungundlovu, further to the north-east and he was killed in mysterious circumstances near the modern Swaziland border, probably in 1840. The Zulu kingdom retained its autonomy within reduced borders, but, after the discovery of diamonds and gold in the South African interior from the 1860s onwards, South African society began the process of transformation from farming communities to a centralized industrial way of life. ■

ALEXANDRIA

Among the cities of Egypt, Alexandria was established very late, almost 3000 years after the foundation of Egypt's first capital city, Memphis (across the river, west of modern Cairo), by the semi-legendary conqueror-king Menes. Alexandria was, of course, founded by and (like sixteen other cities of the Macedonian empire) bears the name of, an even more famous conqueror-king, Alexander the Great. It was chosen as the new capital of Egypt largely on the strength of its natural advantages as a seaport, lying on a 2 km wide neck of land between the Mediterranean Sea to the north and Lake Mareotis to the south. An artificial causeway, the Heptastadion, was built to run north to the off-shore Pharos Island, thus creating the Eastern and Western Harbours, the Eastern being the

In AD 642 Alexandria, like Egypt itself, was abandoned by the Eastern Roman empire to the irresistible Arab invaders who had swept up from the Arabian Peninsula and would, eight centuries later, take Constantinople itself. The Arab general Amr ibn al-As reported back to the Caliph Omar that the city he had captured without a fight contained '4000 palaces, 4000 baths, 400 theatres' among the public buildings of what was one of the truly great cities of the ancient world.

principal 'Great Harbour'. The pre-existing Egyptian city of Rhakotis does not seem to have taken full advantage of the natural assets of its situation, but the Greek newcomers were well able to see the potential of what was to become *the* major seaport of the Hellenistic and Roman Eastern Mediterranean.

The rest of the city was planned on a Greek grid pattern, possibly by a Macedonian architect called Dinocrates, possibly by Alexander himself, depending on which story one chooses to believe. The main axes of this grid were two main streets which crossed each other at right angles. The east–west avenue was

The remains of ancient Alexandria, like this theatre, sit within the modern city.

Above: 'Pompey's Pillar' and sphinx, close to the ruins of the Temple of Serapis.
Right: The catacombs at Alexandria.

'Canopus Street', which ran the full width of the city from the Moon Gate in the west to the Sun Gate in the east. It was crossed by 'Soma Street', which started in the south near Lake Mareotis and headed north towards the Mediterranean. Where these streets crossed was, in more ways than one, the heart of the city; here stood the Soma, the tomb of Alexander himself (now reputed to lie under the Mosque of Nebi Daniel). The king's body was brought here, via a sojourn at Memphis, from Babylon, having been hijacked by one of Alexander's generals, Ptolemy, who used it as a political tool and established himself and his family as dynastic rulers of Egypt. The Soma was also the last resting place of these Ptolemaic rulers, the Ptolemies and Cleopatras, some of whose remains were still present close to Alexander's own when the Roman Octavian, soon to become the Emperor Augustus, himself came to Alexandria as a conqueror after his defeat of Cleopatra VII.

Alexandria was very different from other, more ancient cities of Egypt and, although it was the capital of the Ptolemaic kingdom of Egypt, it was referred to as 'Alexandria-adjoining-Egypt', stressing its separateness. In many ways Alexandria embodied Alexander's vision of his empire as a cosmopolitan mix of peoples and ideas; a polyglot city where Greeks, Egyptians and a large Jewish community made up the most substantial elements of an international community which specialized not just in commerce but also in the production of new forms of culture and religion through the fusion of ancient and modern elements.

The major districts of the city included the Palace Enclosure, an administrative complex located on a spur of land jutting out into the Mediterranean at the eastern end of the Great Harbour. To the south lay the Museion, a district dedicated to learning whose buildings included the Great Library, which first attempted to emulate, then eclipsed, the library at Athens. Like Athens in its heyday, the schools of learning at Alexandria were able to attract some of the best minds of the age, including Euclid and the geographer Eratosthenes.

At the eastern tip of Pharos Island was the great lighthouse, one of the seven wonders of the ancient world, built by Sostratus of Cnidus for Ptolemy II. The exact form of the building has been much discussed, but it seems most likely to have been a tower, over 100 m tall, the lowest portion of which was square, surmounted by an octagonal shaft, topped by a cylindrical column. The lighthouse seems to have survived in some sort of form until the Middle Ages when a series of earthquakes may have proved the final blows for the great building. The fort built by the Sultan Qaitbey in 1477, and still standing in good condition today, is often regarded as being built on the ruins of the Pharos lighthouse. Recent archaeological work at Alexandria has concentrated on the antiquities lying underwater close to the Qaitbey fort, where thousands of architectural elements of Pharaonic and Greek-style buildings lie alongside colossal statues. The Pharaonic pieces, including monuments of Ramesses II, seem to have been brought to Alexandria from other sites (particularly Heliopolis, near modern Cairo) to embellish the new city, just as earlier Tanis was embellished (see p. 18).

Alexandria was not only a centre for learning but also a major centre for religion. It was here that the Old Testament was translated into Greek, perhaps principally for the benefit of a largely assimilated and Greek-speaking Jewish community. Alexandria was the melting pot of religions of the Eastern Mediterranean, where new synthetic gods were created, like the Greek/Egyptian Serapis. It was also, after the arrival (supposedly in the person of St Mark) and spread of Christianity, the place where some of the most vigorous debates of the early Church were thrashed out (sometimes in the most literal sense!). The main temple of Serapis, the Serapeum, lay in the south-western part of the city in the old district of Rhakotis. Close to the ruins of this temple now lie the best examples of what are, apart from the submerged blocks of the Pharos, the most substantial remains of ancient Alexandria: its cemeteries. In particular, the catacombs of Kom el-Shuqafa, with their painted underground tombs cut from the living rock in a mixture of Egyptian and Hellenistic styles, are one of the most romantic of archaeological sites. ■

AKROTIRI ON THERA

The area of Akrotiri has been estimated at around 20 hectares and the town probably had a population of several thousand. Only a small percentage of the town has been explored, and the quality of the architecture and finds suggests that excavations have concentrated on one of the wealthier quarters. Large houses of irregular plan lined winding streets, which were too narrow for wheeled transport but were wide enough for pack animals to pass each other. The high standard of civilization enjoyed by the inhabitants of Akrotiri is demonstrated by the sophistication of the town's sanitation. Sewers, narrow stone-lined trenches leading to pits, ran beneath the paved streets and were connected to the inside lavatories.

The preservation of architecture at Akrotiri is remarkable and gives a clear picture of a second millennium BC town in the Aegean. There was a common concept behind the internal arrangement of the houses, suggesting that they were used for a similar range of activities, but there was no standard house plan, as individual requirements and personal preference allowed for a certain flexibility. The houses were built of rubble and mudbrick reinforced with timber, and there was extensive use of ashlar masonry (squared blocks of cut stone) in the large public or ceremonial buildings. As a rule, the buildings had an upper storey and some were preserved to a height of three storeys. The internal

One of the most exciting discoveries in the Greek world is that of the Bronze Age town of Akrotiri on the island of Thera (Santorini), which was destroyed in a volcanic eruption in the seventeenth century BC. Between 1967 and 1979 the site was excavated by the Greek archaeologist Spyridon Marinatos, who found the remains of a sophisticated and prosperous urban civilization perfectly preserved beneath the volcanic ash, similar to the Roman town of Pompeii.

Here food, such as cereals, dried fruit and oil, was stored in large jars or *pithoi*, some of which were sunk into the floor or in benches. Most houses were equipped with mill installations for grinding grain, and pestles and mortars, and most households were largely self-sufficient. The residential and reception areas were located on the upper storeys. Here the rooms are large and airy, with big windows to let in light. Most houses were provided with toilets, basically stone benches with wooden seats which were connected to the outside sewerage system by clay pipes. Many houses also had bathrooms but, as water was in scarce supply on the island, these were presumably restricted to the wealthier inhabitants. The walls of the bathrooms were plastered halfway up, to protect them from splashing water, and were painted yellow. In the West House there was a clay bath tub, and nearby a bronze vase, probably used to pour water. This recalls the wall-paintings around the lustral basin (a sunken, stone-lined pool, probably for ritual cleansing or bathing) on the ground floor of the West House, depicting young men preparing for a bath and water being carried in fine metal vases.

walls were plastered and some were decorated with elegant wall paintings (the famous frescoes of Thera), using the same techniques as the wall-paintings in the Minoan palaces on Crete.

The ground floor was used for storage and as a work area, and was ventilated by small windows looking out on to the street.

Many everyday objects were found inside the houses, and these can be used to reconstruct daily life in ancient Thera. Most common is pottery, which had a wide range of uses: to store food and transport traded commodities, and as cooking and eating utensils. Alongside the local pottery there are Minoan vases, imported from the Cretan palaces. The wall-paintings also illustrate the use of metal vases and wicker baskets. The volcanic destruction of Akrotiri gives a unique insight into the furniture used in a Bronze Age town. It was made of wood, which does not

The massive eruption which destroyed the town of Akrotiri tore out the heart of the island.

The substantial houses with mudbrick walls on stone foundations have been preserved to a height of two or more storeys.

usually survive on archaeological sites, but a negative of the furniture was preserved within the ash. Plaster casts taken from these hollows illustrate a wide range of finely carved items, including beds, tables, chairs and stools. On the other hand very few valuables have been recovered from Akrotiri, as most of these were taken away by the inhabitants when they fled the island before the final destructive eruption. However, the richly adorned women and girls from the wall-paintings depicting saffron-gathering give some idea of the type of jewellery that the wealthier inhabitants might have worn.

Several of the buildings give the impression of elaborate public structures with some sort of ceremonial or administrative function. Some of these 'public' buildings, such as the largely unexcavated Xeste 4 (*xeste* being the Greek for squared masonry), were quite massive. It is unlikely that in general the inhabitants of Akrotiri had access to these buildings, although an open space in front of the West House might have functioned as a public area. The 'public' buildings were lined with ashlar masonry and several Minoan (Cretan) architectural features are incorporated in their

Many of the houses were decorated with fine naturalistic wall paintings, such as these of a rocky landscape and a fisherman with his catch.

design, such as the lustral basin, and the pier and door partition (a low stone partition-wall with several openings). The amount of water that would have been used and the elaborate architecture of the lustral basins imply that these were probably intended for ceremonial rather than private use. Some of the more intricate wall-paintings from Thera are found in these public buildings. The scenes around the lustral basin in Xeste 3 depict young men with shaven heads (a classic indication of adolescence in contemporary Egyptian art) preparing to bathe, using fine metal vases. These suggest that the ceremony in the lustral basin of Xeste 3 might have been connected with some form of initiation rite,

ABOVE: The island of Santorini.
RIGHT: Agricultural produce, such as oil or grain, was stored in huge clay jars, or *pithoi*.

perhaps a ceremony associated with the transition from adolescence to adulthood?

The wall-paintings, whether they were public, ceremonial or private, indicate a certain sophistication of society and the existence of a social class with the wealth to commission such works of art and the leisure time to appreciate them. Some of the imagery relates to that found in the Minoan palaces on Crete, such as the young girls in Minoan dress gathering saffron flowers; but on the whole the Akrotiri wall-paintings are more naturalistic and sophisticated. Similar wall-paintings are also found on palaces in the southern Levant and Egypt.

The prosperity of the town of Akrotiri was based on sea-trade. Akrotiri bay was a natural safe harbour, perfectly placed for trade with the prosperous palace centres on Crete; and lead weights using the Minoan weight system and Linear A writing (the system used in the Cretan palaces) have been found at Akrotiri. Possibly the Therans traded textiles, and numerous clay loomweights and crushed murex shells, used to manufacture red dye, have been found on the site. The port itself has not been excavated, but we have some idea of what it might have looked like from the magnificent Ship Procession wall-paintings from the West House. ■

GOURNIA

The Minoans were fine craftsmen, particularly renowned throughout the Aegean, East Mediterranean and Egypt for their fine stone and metal vases. The characteristic feature of the Minoan civilization is the palace – a large rambling structure built around a central court and frequently

Excavations on Crete in the early years of this century, principally by Sir Arthur Evans at Knossos, uncovered the remains of a prosperous Bronze Age civilization of the early second millennium BC which Evans named Minoan after the legendary king Minos of ancient Greek mythology. One of the most famous Minoan towns is Gournia in east Crete, overlooking the Bay of Mirabello, which was excavated at the turn of the century by an American archaeologist, Harriet Boyd Hawes.

decorated with fine wall-paintings. In addition to these palaces the Cretan landscape was populated by large country mansions or villas (miniature versions of the palaces) and prosperous towns and trading emporia.

Gournia is one of the most completely excavated Minoan towns: of a total area of probably some 5 hectares, 2.5 hectares have been uncovered, revealing more than sixty houses and a large public building at the centre. The town occupied a strategic position, commanding routes between the eastern extreme of the island and the west of Crete, and the narrow north–south strip below the Bay of Mirabello. Much of its prosperity was probably based on its importance as a trading centre, with a bustling harbour nearby at Sphoungaras. The town was built around a low hill, and its central part was enclosed by a large ring road, the main thoroughfare, with numerous smaller roads and alleyways running at right-angles to it. This complex network of paved roads divided the town into discrete blocks, or insulae. Another example of the high level of public organization was the elaborate drainage system of stone-built water channels, fed by clay pipes from the houses. As is the case in many contemporary towns in the Aegean and Near East, the inhabitants of Gournia appear to have enjoyed a comfortable lifestyle with a high level of sanita-

tion. A supply of new clay pipes in one of the storerooms in the public building suggest that at Gournia this was under central control.

Gournia was dominated by the large public building at the centre of the town, on top of the acropolis. This was possibly a palace similar to the more famous Minoan examples, and probably functioned as the economic pulse of Gournia and the seat of local administration, reflecting some of the roles of the larger palace centres at Knossos, Phaistos and Mallia. The building was monumental in construction and was designed to impress both the local inhabitants and visitors to Gournia. The façades, for example, were dressed with large cut blocks of sandstone (ashlar masonry), a sign of wealth and rank in Minoan society. Otherwise the construction resembled that of the town houses. The walls were rubble-built or mudbrick on the upper storeys and were covered with plaster, but unlike in the palace centres they were not decorated with fine wall paintings. There was a lavish use of timber, in particular for columns, window frames, doorways and stairways, and the floors were paved with stone slabs of different colours, for a decorative effect. The bathroom had a stone floor, which was covered with several coatings of a fine plaster. A line of storerooms was located behind the elaborate west façade, reminiscent of the architectural layout of the larger Minoan palaces. In addition to the storerooms there were residential suites and fine reception rooms where the ruler or aristocracy of Gournia received visiting dignitaries, and a series of small shrines. Other architectural features of the palaces are likewise replicated in the public building at Gournia, such as the lustral basin – a paved sunken area possibly used for ceremonial bathing.

Although the Minoan civilization was literate, Bronze Age Crete is essentially prehistoric. Writing formed an integral part of the palace administration of Crete, and numerous clay tablets, used to record economic transactions in a syllabic writing system (Linear A), have been found. But they are in an unknown language which has yet to be deciphered and which is neither Indo-European nor Semitic, and has no known relative. The main body of texts are from the palaces, but none has been found at the so-called palace at Gournia.

A large paved square adjacent to the palace was probably used by the inhabitants of the town as a public meeting place, for economic and legal transactions and other activities where they came in contact with its administrative centre. Alongside there was a small shrine.

Numerous buildings have been excavated at Gournia, most of which appear to be domestic houses rather than shops, hostels or workshops. One carpenter's workshop has been identified, and

Excavations at Gournia at the beginning of the century.

The site of Gournia overlooking the Bay of Mirabello.

two metal-working installations; and in the southern part of the town there was a potter's workshop. The majority of households appear to have been largely self-sufficient and equipped with their own storage areas and workshops for processing agricultural produce. The largest houses, which probably belonged to prosperous merchants, fronted on to the main road. A series of faience plaques from Knossos (the Town Mosaic) gives us some impression of the appearance of the houses which typically had a paved court near the entrance which opened on to other areas of the building. In some cases these were colonnaded, providing a shaded area for people to gather in the summer, and brightly decorated with a 'mosaic' of red, green and white stone slabs. The ground floor was set aside specifically for domestic activities such as the storage of agricultural produce (grain, olives, olive oil) in large clay storage jars or *pithoi*, the preparation and cooking of food on portable hearths, and presumably other activities which do not survive archaeologically – like spinning and weaving wool, and social gatherings. The private living quarters of the houses, and possibly the reception areas, were located in the upper storeys. While the central authority controlled the disposal of waste water, individual houses were responsible for their own water supply and were suitably equipped with wells and cisterns.

An interesting feature of life at Gournia was its proximity to the dead. The large cemetery on the north spur of the ridge, appar-

ently used by the wealthier inhabitants of the town, dominated the approach to Gournia. The burial chambers were built as single-storey houses, but in every way reflected the architecture and layout of homes of the living in the town, including narrow storerooms designed to store food for the deceased in their afterlife. The cemetery with its house tombs was part of the urban design of Gournia, an extension of the living space implying a close relationship between the town's inhabitants and their ancestors. ∎

Only the stone foundations of the houses are preserved at Gournia.

ENKOMI

Enkomi was a major cosmopolitan trading centre and had wide-ranging contacts throughout the East Mediterranean, with Egypt, the city-kingdoms along the Levantine coast and the Aegean. Her prosperity and foreign contacts are particularly evident in the elaborate range of grave gifts deposited in the tombs of the wealthier citizens. Principal among these are the finely decorated pottery drinking sets imported from the Aegean. The large *kraters* used for mixing wine, and often decorated with chariot scenes, are particularly popular. Exquisite vases made of faience (a form of glass paste) were imported from Egypt and the Levant, along with fine ivories – for example, duck-shaped cosmetic boxes and elaborately carved mirror cases and gaming boxes. The wealth and range of gold jewellery is particularly remarkable, and includes a fine Egyptian-style pectoral (necklace), seal-rings (with engraved scenes, which could be used to stamp seals), and a variety of necklaces and earrings.

In the earliest town at Enkomi, houses of varying sizes were scattered around the landscape, separated by open spaces, courts and gardens, with no evidence of any coherent planning. In the thirteenth century BC, however, there was a dramatic change in the appearance and organization of the town, coinciding with her period of greatest prosperity and perhaps reflecting a more organized form of political control. Enkomi was laid out on a regular

To the north-west of modern Famagusta lie the remains of one of the most important Late Bronze Age towns on Cyprus, the site of Enkomi. It was occupied from around the sixteenth century BC, but the most prosperous period of the town's history was during the thirteenth and twelfth centuries BC. For a long time Enkomi was the only Late Bronze Age town known on Cyprus, but today excavations at other sites, principally at Kition, have increased our knowledge of the urban communities which flourished on the island during the latter part of the second millennium BC.

grid plan and was cut in two by an arterial north–south road. The main road was lined by a number of large buildings, faced with large cut-stone blocks. In the centre of the town was a small paved open space where people could gather. This reorganization of Enkomi survived a massive conflagration at the beginning of the twelfth century BC, one of a wave of destructions that afflicted the major centres of the East Mediterranean, many of which disappeared (for example, the Aegean palaces, Ugarit (p. 98), the Hittite empire). Although Enkomi was destroyed, the town was rebuilt and retained the same basic grid plan.

As part of the programme of urban development, Enkomi was fortified during the thirteenth century. A massive wall (1 m or more thick), built of enormous, unworked boulders, encircled the town, enclosing an area of around 11 hectares. Following its destruction around 1200 BC, the fortifications were reinforced to a thickness of 4 m. The wall was penetrated by massive gates at various points around its perimeter. Beneath the west gate there are channels, part of an underground drainage system which evacuated used water from the town. The main water supply was furnished by a system of wells within the town limits. When these wells ceased to be used, they were turned into rubbish dumps. Occasionally, though, the dumping in disused wells appears to have little to do with the disposal of rubbish: for example, in one well there was a cache of bronzes.

Houses at Enkomi conform to a traditional Cypriot plan. In the centre there is an open court, and rooms are grouped around three sides. Unlike the inhabitants of other contemporary towns in the East Mediterranean, the residents of Enkomi do not appear to have enjoyed the highest standard of comfort and civilization. Rather than an advanced sewerage system, such as that seen at Akrotiri on Thera (see p. 44), the inhabitants of Enkomi only had pits for latrines, though they did have clay bath tubs. The dead of

Many of the tombs at Enkomi were richly equipped with a variety of gold jewellery, such as this gold mouth-piece.

ABOVE: Silver bowl with inland decoration of bulls' heads.
RIGHT: This cast bronze statue of a deity, the Horned God, was found in the ruins of an imposing sanctuary of the twelfth century BC.

Enkomi were buried within the living space of the town, in tombs located under courts or beneath the streets.

While Enkomi was reorganized during the thirteenth century BC, it was only in the twelfth century that there was a major programme of public buildings within the town walls – characterized by the appearance of a number of monumental buildings with elaborate façades of cut stone (ashlar) masonry. The most famous are Bâtiment 18, the Sanctuary of the Horned God and the Sanctuary of the Ingot God.

The metals trade was central to the trading system which developed in the East Mediterranean during the second millennium BC, and Cyprus achieved particular preeminence as a major centre of copper production. Enkomi's prosperity was largely dependent on the metals trade, and many copper-bronze workshops were located within the town walls. One of the major workshops of the thirteenth and twelfth centuries was by the north gate, as the prevailing southerly winds would blow the noxious fumes away from the main residential areas. The copper foundry was housed in a large architectural unit divided into three main sectors. The central sector was residential, and had two large rectangular halls, used as dining-rooms. The east part of the building was used for domestic activities such as cooking, and the foundry was located in the west wing. A large slag heap (the by-product of copper smelting) was piled up in the court to the north of the foundry, and inside the foundry there were moulds for weapons, tools and pins.

Even after the destructions which shook the prosperous East Mediterranean world around 1200 BC and removed many of the markets for Cypriot copper, Enkomi continued to be a major bronze-working centre. If anything, the height of the town's prosperity, when many of the more remarkable bronze objects were manufactured, dates to the twelfth century. Among these artifacts are the magnificent four-sided bronze stands with elaborate figured decoration, the bronze tripods, and the various cast statuettes of deities, in particular the Ingot God and the Horned God. A market for these fabulous pieces was found in the west where many have been uncovered in Sardinia, southern Italy, Crete and on the island of Euboea.

Unlike her neighbours in the Near East and Egypt, Cyprus is essentially prehistoric throughout the second millennium, although the ancient Cypriots were not illiterate. A system of writing peculiar to the island was developed, and used on a variety of media. The script (Cypro-Minoan) has a certain resemblance to the writing systems used in the Aegean palaces of Crete and the Greek mainland, but the language remains unknown. Therefore the political system prevalent on the island is likewise unknown. Certainly the planning involved in the reorganization of Enkomi in the thirteenth century BC would have required central control, and the wealth deposited in the tombs is suggestive of an aristocracy. But just who was at the apex of Cypriot society is unknown. There is a possibility that (a part of) Cyprus might equate with the powerful copper-producing kingdom of Alashiya known from the Amarna letters (an Egyptian archive of letters written to the pharaoh from the rulers of neighbouring kingdoms, p. 17). Enkomi has always remained the most popular choice for the 'capital' of the king of Alashiya, but if this is the case, the king's palace has never been found. ■

DELOS

The barren, waterless island of Delos in the centre of the Aegean is small (measuring only 5 km north to south by 1.3 km east to west), yet it played an important part in the history of the Greek world. Delos owed its importance to two factors. First, it was famed as the birthplace of Apollo and Artemis. Already renowned in the *Odyssey*, by the seventh century BC it was developing as a cult centre to Apollo and its annual festival was attracting visitors from other Aegean islands and even the mainland. From the sixth century BC onwards its importance as a cult centre to Apollo increased, especially for the Ionian Greeks, when the Athenian tyrant, Pisistratus, in an effort to extend Athens' control over the Cyclades, purified the sanctuary by removing interred remains from its environs. The importance of Delos was further enhanced in 478–7 BC: after the defeat of the Persians, the island was

The rocky, barren Cycladic island of Delos can justifiably be regarded as the Pompeii of the Aegean. Today remote and accessible only with difficulty from the neighbouring holiday island of Mykonos, its long-abandoned temples, public buildings, houses and streets still capture the atmosphere of this once flourishing centre for the cult of Apollo, and prosperous and cosmopolitan trading and commercial city.

chosen to be the centre of the Athenian-dominated Ionian Confederacy of Delos, and the site of the league's treasury.

The sanctuary to Apollo, adjoining the harbour, remained the heart of the town. Its monuments reflect the continued importance of the sanctuary and the interest of the Greeks in it throughout the island's history. The focal point of the sanctuary was the three temples to Apollo. The oldest and most venerable was the '*poros*' temple, which was constructed in the sixth century. Athenian domination of the sanctuary is indicated by the 'Athenian' temple which dated to

RIGHT: The terrace of the lions, late seventh century BC.

BELOW: Streets and houses at Delos.

Colonnaded courtyard with mosaic floor of the house of Diadumenos.

approximately 420 BC. The third and largest of the temples was the so-called peripheral temple, begun in 477 BC but not completed until the third century BC. The growing importance of the sanctuary attracted other monuments, buildings and dedications. However, it was from the third century BC onwards that the sanctuary was significantly embellished as a result of the interests of competing Hellenistic kings. Philip V of Macedon dedicated a portico to the south of the temples, the architrave of which was inscribed with the words 'From Philip, king of the Macedonians and son of king Demetrius, to Apollo'. Another Macedonian king, Antigonus Gonatas, also dedicated a portico. One of the most enigmatic buildings of the sanctuary is the so-called 'sanctuary of the bulls'. Its purpose is totally obscure. It was an elongated building decorated with sea creatures, and could conceivably have housed a ship and been dedicated to a naval victory. Excavations also brought to light the administrative records of the sanctuary; the details of the accounts and the inventories of offerings made to the temples give remarkable insight into the civic organization and religious institutions of the town and the sanctuary.

Secondly, in the Hellenistic period, and especially after 166 BC, when the Romans handed control of the city back to Athens and declared it a free port, Delos became an important trading and commercial centre. As a rival to the island of Rhodes, recently sacked by the Romans, Delos flourished and the town expanded as foreign traders and businessmen were drawn to it from other parts of the ancient world. It became one of the centres for the slave trade in the eastern Mediterranean and, at its height, up to 10,000 slaves per day were reputedly changing hands in the slave markets of the island.

The commercial importance of Delos is witnessed by its harbour installations, no fewer than five *agoras*, and numerous other commercial buildings, developed by indigenous and foreign businessmen and entrepreneurs. Particularly impressive is the '*agora* of the Italians'. Not only is it the grandest building on the island, but it is probably also unique in the Greek world. It acted as a commercial and social centre and meeting place for the large Italian community which established itself on the island. Construction was begun about 110 BC, but it was still not complete when the soldiers of Mithridates, king of Pontus, ravaged the island in 88 BC. The '*agora* of the Italians' and other buildings, constructed for the use of the religious associations of Italian traders and other nationalities, are indicative of the thriving cosmopolitan community which lived on the island. There were Athenians and other Greeks, Egyptians, Phoenicians, traders from Palestine and a small Jewish community. They brought with them their own deities and, on the slopes of Mt Cynthus, the highest point on the island, a terrace for the sanctuaries of foreign deities was set aside.

These different groups tended to remain mutually exclusive and formed associations on the basis of nationality and profession, often under the patronage of a particular deity. Inscriptions inform us of associations dedicated to Herakles from Tyre. There were associations of Italian merchants under the patronage of Apollo, Hermes and Poseidon; a group of slaves under the patronage of the household deities, the Lares. A group of merchants from

Beirut under the patronage of Syrian Poseidon formed themselves into an 'association of the Poseidoniastes of Berytos at Delos, merchants, shippers and warehousemen'. Its associated building, 'the establishment of the Poseidoniastes of Beirut', acted as a sanctuary, meeting place and trade centre, as well as offering accommodation to passing merchants.

During this period of commercial prosperity in the later part of the second century BC the city expanded greatly. A new quarter of fine houses and other buildings was regularly laid out at the northern end of the island. In contrast, the area to the south of the sanctuary extending to the theatre offers a unique example of the residential district of a Greek town, with narrow and irregular streets insinuating themselves between equally irregular houses. The houses vary in size, shape, configuration and comfort according to the wealth of the owner and the space available, but conform to a typical plan with a central courtyard, colonnaded if space and resources allowed, which acted both as an open-air room and offered light and air to the surrounding rooms. Upper storeys are common, and many houses had small latrines linked to the street drains. Several of the houses were sumptuously adorned with statuary, wall-paintings and mosaics, indicating the wealth of their occupants. Lock-up shops, independent of the houses into which they were set, lined two main streets of the district in particular and are an indication of a thriving local economy.

The economic success of the island was short-lived. In 88 BC Delos was captured and sacked during the first Mithridatic war. A second catastrophe occurred in 69 BC. Pirates under the command of Athenodorus, an ally of Mithridates, again attacked the island and sacked it despite the efforts of the Roman general Triarius to defend the city with a hastily erected wall. These disasters, together with the growing commercial competition of Italian towns such as Puteoli and the eventual refoundation of Corinth, strategically placed on the Isthmus of Corinth, ensured that Delos never recovered its commercial position. The population shrank, and all that remained was a small community primarily to service the sanctuary. ■

RIGHT: The horned altar to the Hellenized form of the Egyptian deity Serapis.

BELOW: This semi-artificial cave on the slopes of Mt Cynthus was probably dedicated to Heracles.

BISKUPIN

Excavations at Biskupin that began in 1933 revealed the waterlogged remains of a fortified Iron Age settlement built of timber and many thousands of artifacts, which provide a glimpse of everyday life over 2500 years ago.

In north-central Poland there is a whole series of waterlogged settlements which provides a fascinating glimpse of life during the first millennium BC. The best-known of these is Biskupin, located about 60 km north-east of the city of Poznan, where excavations which began in the 1930s and continue on a limited scale today have revealed the remains of a settlement dating to about 700 to 500 BC. Because the settlement was waterlogged, the plan of the wooden houses and streets was preserved in remarkable detail, along with artifacts made from wood and fibre, which are rarely found on dry sites, numerous bones and seeds, grindstones and metal ornaments and tools.

The area around Biskupin is characterized by numerous small lakes left by the last Ice Age. On peninsulas and islands formed by these lakes, and on the short streams that wind through this region, numerous prehistoric settlements from many different periods have been found. Over the years the water levels have fluctuated, and when they were lower, about 3000 years ago, settlement began on the Biskupin peninsula (which probably was originally an island). Around 500 BC the water levels rose again, and the remains of the settlement were buried under water and peat, to be discovered again almost 2500 years later.

In 1933 a local schoolteacher named Walenty Szwajcer noticed timbers protruding from Lake Biskupin. Flood control in a nearby river had lowered the water level of the lake, and the peaty sur-face of the peninsula had become exposed. Szwajcer made the mental connection between the timbers that he saw and what he knew of the famous Lake Dwellings which had been discovered in Switzerland in 1854, and he realized that this could be a significant archaeological find. He reported his discovery to Professor Józef Kostrzewski, the director of the Great Poland Museum in Poznan and professor at the University of Poznan, who realized the potential of the site. On 20 June 1934 Kostrzewski began excavations at Biskupin.

Over the following six years, Kostrzewski and his assistants uncovered an astonishing patchwork of waterlogged timbers. The size of the project grew from a small team of students to a crew of nearly 200 workmen. As the excavations expanded, the timbers took on regular arrangements and gradually the outlines of walls and streets emerged. Scattered among the timbers were hundreds of thousands of artifacts made from pottery, stone, metal and wood that dated the site to the early half of the first millennium BC, around 700 years before Christ. Clearly, the peninsula at Biskupin had masked the traces of a prehistoric town which could be excavated nearly in its entirety, and by 1939 about half the settlement had been uncovered. Thirteen rows of houses, each about 10 by 7 m with walls preserved to a height of about 1.5 m, formed the core of the settlement. Between them were streets paved with logs, while surrounding the entire settlement was a rampart made from timber cribbing, protected at the lake shore by a wooden breakwater of sharpened logs.

Kostrzewski's excavations were very large and technically advanced for their time. For example, in 1935 a balloon borrowed from the Polish army was used to take photographs of the excavated area from heights of up to 150 m. Botanists, zoologists and geomorphologists were engaged to analyse the rich organic finds and sediments. Dendrochronology, or tree-ring dating, which had been pioneered in the early twentieth century in the south-western United States, was attempted in 1938 as a means of providing calendar dates for the settlement. This work indicated

A camera attached to a balloon photographed the streets, houses and rampart of Biskupin as the peat was gradually removed.

that the oak timbers were cut in 625 and 680 BC and the pine timbers about 500 BC, suggesting two phases of construction. Divers explored the lake nearby and discovered two dugout canoes and the traces of a causeway.

In Poland the excavations were widely publicized and, although the site was not easy to reach, thousands of visitors made the journey to view the settlement emerging from the bog. The Biskupin project was celebrated in the press, inspired several novels and even provided the subject for one of the first films made about archaeological excavations.

Several days before the outbreak of the Second World War, the gate of the settlement which had long been sought by the archaeologists was discovered, but work came to an end a few days later. In 1942 German archaeologists carried out some limited investigation of the site. After the war, excavations were resumed by Kostrzewski's student, Zdzislaw Rajewski of the State Archaeological Museum in Warsaw, which assumed control of the project. The excavations at Biskupin were given high priority by the postwar Polish government, which attached much importance to establishing the continuity of cultural traditions in this area, and it became a permanent archaeological station. In 1949 a museum was established at Biskupin to house the finds from the excavations, and reconstruction of a segment of the rampart and some of the streets and houses began in 1968.

By the early 1970s, about 75 per cent of the Biskupin settlement had been excavated and the details had become very clear. The Iron Age settlement covered about 20 sq km, surrounded by a rampart about 4 m thick built from timber cribs filled with sand and stones and plastered with clay, which was protected from wave erosion by a breakwater of oak logs. A single gate controlled access to the settlement. Just within the walls ran a circular perimeter street paved with logs, off which branched eleven parallel streets across the centre of the settlement, separated by rows of timber houses, over one hundred in all. The houses had party walls and consisted of a uniform module of an anteroom beside the door and a central area with a stone hearth. Rather complicated joinery was used, with the horizontal timbers mortised into uprights. A huge amount of wood was used in the construction and maintenance of the settlement, as well as for cooking and for working metals, which must have had an immense impact on the local forest cover.

The inhabitants of Biskupin were farmers and herders, and it seems likely that livestock was also accommodated within the houses. The animal bones found in the settlement indicated that pigs were important food animals, but cattle were kept for milk and as draft animals as well as for meat. Millet, wheat, barley and beans were the main crops, and were grown on the fields of the firmer ground south of the peninsula.

When inhabitants of Biskupin died, their cremated bones were buried in an urn in a cemetery across the lake. Kostrzewski and Rajewski estimated the settlement's population at between 1000 and 1200, although others suggest that the number of inhabitants was in the range of 200 to 500. The causes of the abandonment of Biskupin are unclear. The traditional explanation has been that the settlement was doomed by the progressively wetter climate in the middle of the first millennium BC. The settlement was flooded, which forced its inhabitants to relocate. On the other hand, it is also possible that social causes such as overpopulation,

The reconstructed main gate of the Biskupin settlement, showing the rows of houses which would have lined the streets over 2500 years ago.

over-exploitation of the local environment, and conflict with neighbouring groups may have played a role.

It is important to note that Biskupin is not unique in north-central Poland. About twenty such sites are known: for example, sites at Sobiejuchy, Izdebno, Kruszwica and Smuszewo have been investigated, although not nearly as extensively as Biskupin. All seem to have a similar layout and use of timber construction. These strongholds appear to have existed simultaneously, suggesting small polities which controlled particular parts of this lake belt, although this system appears to have collapsed within a few centuries, due perhaps to the same factors which caused the decline of Biskupin.

Biskupin has been developed as a tourist attraction, with over 200,000 visitors annually. A number of houses, the gate tower, and part of the rampart have been reconstructed. The interiors of the houses have been furnished to illustrate the activities of their inhabitants, and the museum depicts the history of settlement in the Biskupin area. ■

ENTREMONT

Entremont, in the heart of Provence, was the capital of the Saluvii, a military confederation of Celtic and Ligurian tribes who dominated the southern stretches of the valley of the Rhône. To the south lay the Greek colony of Massilia, modern Marseilles, a trading entrepôt that spread Greek influence into western and central Europe up the Rhône and other river valleys. To the north lay the routes to the Alpine passes leading to central Europe. To the west was Spain. Conquest was eventually to come from the east, from Italy and Rome.

Early discoveries of extraordinary statues at Entremont in the nineteenth century caused French scholars to marvel at the achievements of their Celtic ancestors. The writings of the Classical historians and the results of recent excavations, including a Sanctuary of Skulls replete with dramatic imagery of severed heads and cross-legged deities or heroes overseeing the road to the afterlife, give an unrivalled picture of religious belief and flourishing commerce in an early European urban centre at the edge of the Roman world on the eve of the conquest of southern Gaul.

The buildings, ramparts and streets of Entremont underwent seemingly endless reconstruction and repair, partly as a result of the building materials. The earliest settlement at the site, the Upper City, dates to between 190 and 170 BC. Perched on the top of the limestone plateau, this settlement was similar to many other hilltop sites built by the Celtic inhabitants of France. Stone-built fortifications enclosed and protected large numbers of identical small houses, their flat roofs made out of wattle and daub, laid out along parallel streets. Each dwelling contained one or more pottery *dolia*, holding grain or water, and a hearth. Some

hearths also functioned as altars.

After some forty years, around 150-140 BC, Entremont was re-organized and enlarged. The Lower City was laid out, grand public buildings appeared, along with two-storey houses, now divided into a number of rooms. An artisan quarter developed, with metalworking smithies, leather workshops, pottery kilns and weaving looms. Most of the population, however, was involved in agricultural production. Many querns for milling flour were discovered. The remains of *areae* for oil-presses attest to the importance of that still valuable commodity, olive oil. The masonry ramparts encircling the town were 2.5 m wide and up to 4 m high, with openings at the base to act as drains. Curvilinear, rubble-filled towers were built every 19 m along the wall, intended to provide an effective defence against battering rams. Over 34 sq km in area, Entremont dwarfed other Ligurian settlements. In its development we can see the birth of one of the earliest non-Classical European urban centres.

Entremont grew wealthy on the profits of trade with the Greek commercial centre at Massilia and the Celtic world, but in the

The Saluvian capital of Entremont from the air (LEFT). On one pillar from the Sanctuary (ABOVE), at the heart of the Upper City, were engraved twelve mouthless severed heads – vanquished foes or the heroic dead?

protection of commercial interests lay the seeds of Entremont's destruction. Among the most highly prized imports were amphorae of Italian wine, while other desired commodities included salted fish and pickling brine from southern Spain. The entrepreneurial class developed a taste for personal adornment, and the ornaments produced by local metal-workshops were complemented by coloured glass beads and bracelets and coral from Massilia. Everyday pottery, produced locally, contrasted with the fine wares imported from Massilia. Slaves, minerals and agricultural products flowed the other way in exchange. Coexistence with the Greek outpost was not entirely harmonious, however, and when Massilia appealed to Rome for assistance against Ligurian pirates to protect the trade routes between Spain and Italy, Rome embarked on a series of campaigns to subjugate southern Gaul. Roman historians including Appian and Livy recorded the events for posterity.

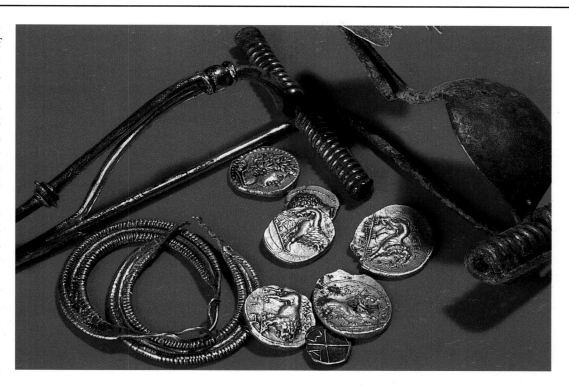

Coins stashed away before the Roman sack of the city.

Entremont resisted the first campaign, of 125 BC, but was not able to withstand the assault by the forces under the consul C. Sextius Calvinus in 123 BC. A devastating catapult bombardment left the city littered with stone balls. The piles of clay slingstones, iron daggers, arrows and javelins tell of a spirited but ultimately fruitless defence against the Roman attackers who entered the town on the road from the north-east, where many iron spearheads, *pilae*, were later discovered. Entremont was ransacked. Pottery *dolia* were smashed in the streets. Coin hoards, hidden away in the small houses before the battle, were pillaged – only a few survived for archaeologists to discover: stashes of Massilian obols and Greek drachmas. The Saluvian king and his princes fled to safety in the land of the Allobriges to the north. With the exception of some 900 Roman sympathizers and collaborators, the inhabitants of Entremont were deported. Entremont was abandoned, returning to rural obscurity.

For all their development of an urban lifestyle influenced by the Greek colonists at Massilia, the inhabitants of Entremont retained their deeply held indigenous religious beliefs. Between two stone towers, which jutted out from the northern outer face of the ramparts of the Upper City, was a porticoed building, its roof supported by a series of stone columns. Carved on these pillars were symbols of death. One bore a serpent, signifying the afterlife throughout much of the Mediterranean world. Along the entire length of another pillar, 2.6 m, were engraved some twelve severed heads, the bottom one upside down. Each was mouthless, the loss of speech symbolizing death. Two skull-shaped sockets, originally holding severed heads, were cut into a fragment of lintel that also bore an engraved mouthless head. Classical authors

such as Strabo describe the Celtic custom of cutting off and displaying the heads of the enemy.

The Sanctuary opened on to a road known as the Sacred Way. Many remarkable statues carved from the local limestone lined this road, including seated and standing figures depicting deities and heroes. Male warrior figures wore leather pectorals and short breeches, leaving the stomach bare. Long swords hung from their waists; necks and wrists were adorned with torcs and bracelets. Different hairstyles are carefully depicted, including fine curls. The heads of female statues, although fewer in number, were modelled with greater finesse, their long tresses coiled back over the forehead. These statues, although displaying individuality of features, were as involved in the pageant of death as the carvings on the Sanctuary pillars. One sitting hero rested his left hand on a severed head, his right holding an iron thunderbolt. This laying of the hand on a severed head could represent either the victor claiming ultimate control over the victim, or the gentle caress of the ancestral deity.

The Sanctuary was a focus of activity in the final stages of the life of Entremont. The remains of twenty or so human skulls were found in the Sanctuary and on the Sacred Way. Puncture marks through some of the skulls show how they were nailed to stakes shortly after decapitation, to be displayed on wooden platforms, the flesh stripped from their necks. Many skull fragments were found in the upper layers of the Sacred Way, along with a ball fired from a catapult, probably during the final siege of 123 BC. Similar catapult balls had fractured two skulls. Did these skulls belong to vanquished enemies or to revered ancestors? Whatever the answer, the Sanctuary of the Skulls is a vivid testimony to the funerary and animistic nature of Saluvian religion, providing a home for the heroic dead at the heart of this early European town. ■

POMPEII AND HERCULANEUM

In two letters addressed to the great Roman historian of the imperial period, Cornelius Tacitus, the younger Pliny tells of the death of his uncle in the eruption and his own flight with his mother from Misenum in order to escape the effects of the volcano. His account vividly recalls the destructive power of the volcano with its 'broad sheets of fire and leaping flames', and the panic which it created. He describes the ash like snowdrifts, and the fear and shouts of the people. 'We had scarcely sat down to rest when darkness fell, not the darkness of a moonless or cloudy night, but as if a lamp had been put out in a closed room.

When Mount Vesuvius erupted on 24 August AD 79 it destroyed, in the words of the younger Pliny, 'the loveliest regions of the earth, a fate shared by whole cities and their people'. Certainly the catastrophe which befell the district around Vesuvius on that fateful day destroyed several towns and villages in addition to many villas. The most famous of these are Pompeii and Herculaneum, where excavations have uncovered two unique examples of prosperous towns of southern Italy.

You could hear the shrieks of the women, the wailing of the infants, and the shouting of men; some were calling their parents, others their children or their wives, trying to recognize them by their voice.' These events occurred at Misenum, 16 km from Vesuvius. Closer to Vesuvius, Pompeii and Hercula-neum were two of several towns and villages which were completely swamped by the volcanic ash and lava.

On that fateful day, Pliny's uncle, the elder Pliny, who was commander of the fleet based at Misenum and was watching the spectacular eruption, had received a letter from a friend's wife,

RIGHT: A street tavern in Hercula-neum.

OPPOSITE: The garden wall of the house of Lucius Ceius Secundus at Pompeii was painted with scenes from Africa.

BELOW RIGHT: A statue of Apollo in the guise of an archer in the temple of Apollo at Pompeii.

imploring him to help her. She lived at the foot of Vesuvius and was trapped, her only means of escape by boat. He immediately ordered the fleet to put to sea, whilst he made for Stabiae, 8 km south of Pompeii. By the time he arrived at Stabiae in the mid-afternoon, Pompeii, being closer to the centre of the eruption, was already covered by a thick layer of pumice and ash, driven by the wind which was blowing from the north-north-west. Eventually the deposit attained a depth of over 5 m. This has offered archaeologists a unique opportunity to explore an almost intact prosperous Italian city of the late first century AD.

Today the visitor to Pompeii can walk along the paved streets with their raised pedestrian pavements, visit the temples, the bath houses and the amphitheatre, where in AD 59 there was a serious riot between the spectators from Pompeii and those from the neighbouring town of Nuceria, and wander through the residential districts. It is here with the shops, tavernas and brothels, with graffiti inscribed on the walls of buildings, that the true atmosphere of an ancient Italian town can be felt. There is a mixture of rich and poor houses. Some are spacious with well cultivated gardens; others are small, with overhanging balconies, encroaching on to the street. Many of the better quality houses were finely decorated with wall-paintings and mosaics.

If the streets, shops and houses are evidence of the vitality of Pompeii, it is the detailed finds, preserved at the moment when the ash and pumice descended, which capture the tragedy and suddenness of the catastrophe. Food and drink were hastily abandoned. In one baker's shop loaves were left baking in the oven. Many of the 20,000 inhabitants fled the city, taking with them their valuables and whatever else they could carry. However, as many as 2000 people died in and around the city. Some were killed by pieces of lava and stones, which had been hurled high into the air by the force of the initial explosion and then had come crashing down. Others had died as buildings collapsed. Many, delaying their escape until it was too late, perished from

ABOVE: Inscribed pottery vessels from a shop at Herculaneum.

LEFT: A mosaic of a chained dog inscribed with the warning 'Beware of the dog'. The remains of a chained dog were found at Pompeii.

RIGHT: The garden of the house of the Vettii at Pompeii. The surrounding porticoes offered shade from the heat.

the suffocating effects of falling ash and the poisonous fumes and gases which belched from the crater. In one house (Menander) a group of ten slaves died on the stairs, one of them still with a lamp, whilst the doorman together with his daughter choked as they tried to protect themselves with cushions from the falling ash and debris. In another house (Pansa) the mistress and three of her servants died, the valuables, which she had tried to save, strewn around her. Pliny's uncle also died: 'he stood leaning on two

slaves and then suddenly collapsed, I imagine because the dense fumes choked his breathing by blocking his windpipe . . . When daylight returned on the 26th . . . his body was found intact and uninjured, still clothed and looking more like sleep than death.' At the gladiatorial barracks over sixty gladiators were found, including two who remained locked and chained in the establishment's prison. In the panic to escape even dogs were forgotten and left to die, still chained up.

Herculaneum, which takes its name from its legendary founder, Hercules, lies immediately to the west of the volcano and suffered a different fate. The town escaped the effects of falling ash because of the direction of the wind. However, it was overwhelmed by mud-lava. The large quantities of steam escaping from the volcano mixed with spray from the sea, churned up by the

BELOW: Detail from the tomb of a freedwoman. The ship entering harbour is possibly a symbol of death.
RIGHT: Pornographic paintings and graffiti on the wall of this building indicate that it was a brothel.

violence of the eruption and the attendant earthquakes, and fell as scorching rain. On the ground it washed down the surface lava and earth from the slopes of the mountain to produce irresistible rivers of boiling mud which swamped the city. Once cool the mud formed a hard impermeable layer up to 15 m thick.

Pompeii was a bustling industrial centre, market town and harbour for the surrounding region. Herculaneum, on the other hand, was a popular resort for wealthy Romans. Many of the public buildings remain under the tufa, but the lifestyle of the inhabitants is reflected in the well-appointed villas, with marble and bronze statues, and fine furniture and fittings. Its importance as a place of leisure and relaxation is witnessed by the papyrus library, where the rich, educated inhabitants could pass their time in scholarly pursuits.

After the eruption subsided, no attempt was made by the central government to restore or reconstruct. Some inhabitants returned to Pompeii to dig in the cooling ash in an attempt to recover personal valuables and remove even statues and the marble facing from public buildings. At Herculaneum, as the mud cooled and solidified, such looting was impossible. The survivors were relocated and the sites were lost until chance digging in the seventeenth and eighteenth centuries once again brought Herculaneum and Pompeii to the attention of the world. ■

RIGHT: The Via dell'Abbondanza was one of the main streets of Pompeii. The raised stepping stones were for pedestrians.
BELOW: The sign above this building close to the forum indicates that it was a wine merchants' shop.

NOVGOROD

Excavations at the medieval Russian town of Novgorod have revealed many layers of construction which began in the ninth century AD, including timber buildings and streets. Nearly 700 unusual birchbark manuscripts record the everyday life of the inhabitants of the town.

Novgorod, located on the Volkhov River about 160 km south of St Petersburg, is one of the oldest towns in Russia. The medieval settlement on the site dates from the middle of the ninth century AD. Although some scholars have attributed Novgorod's founding to the arrival of Viking merchants, this idea is hotly disputed by others who argue that the town arose from indigenous Slavic inhabitants. Over the next several centuries, Novgorod emerged as a large, prosperous city situated on a trade route between the Baltic and Byzantium. As a result of large-scale archaeological excavations and documentary evidence, much is known about life in this early Russian town. Excavations at Novgorod began in 1929 under the direction of Artemii Artsikhovsky and have continued since then under a variety of directors. Since 1951 the Novgorod excavations, at one point some of the largest archaeological excavations in Russia, have been more or less continuous, and have taken place in many parts of the town.

The clay soil which lies beneath Novgorod impedes drainage, so the 6 m or so of accumulation of archaeological deposits in the city centre have been waterlogged. This resulted in an extraordi-

nary quality of preservation not only of wood (especially of house walls and timber streets) but also of leather and wooden utensils, musical instruments, and even toys. Analysis of tree-rings in the larger timbers has led to the development of a chronology which permits the dating of structures with a precision of the order of fifteen to twenty-five years.

The plan of ancient Novgorod is formed by a network of streets which wound through the old town. Due to the damp conditions, the streets were surfaced with timbers, using a method which involved first laying three or four thin birch or pine poles along the length of the street. Upon this footing was laid a deck of split logs of about 40–50 cm in diameter side-by-side across the width of the street. Along Saints Cosmas and Damian Street, a total of twenty-eight paving levels have been identified and dated by their tree-rings. The earliest street at this location was laid down in AD 953 and the latest in 1462.

Novgorod's streets were lined with timber buildings, and the remarkable preservation of their lower walls permits their reconstruction in some detail. Domestic buildings were log cabins, built using combinations of several basic modules. Some stood possibly two or even three storeys tall. They were clustered into compounds of a house and its outbuildings around a yard. Such a compound would have been enclosed by a stake fence which separated the complex from the street and from adjacent buildings.

The artisans who worked in these compounds specialized in the manufacture of leather goods, jewellery, shoes, metal and glass objects, and pottery. In fact, it is possible to determine that there were districts of the city in which specific crafts predominated. Novgorod was linked to a trading network that encompassed much of northern Europe and extended even to the Indian Ocean. A remarkable array of goods passed through Novgorod, including wine, incense, spices, nuts, exotic

Excavations at Novgorod are conducted amidst the buildings which have been built since medieval times.

ABOVE: The everyday lives of the inhabitants of Novgorod are revealed through the birch-bark manuscripts known as *beresty.*
RIGHT: A small stone icon reflects the role of religion in Novgorod life.

woods, and cloth. The town was a hub of mercantile activity by Scandinavian merchants, who called it 'Hólmgard', and Slavic artisans and traders. The wealth and power that came from such commerce enabled Novgorod to emerge as the leading town in the northern part of the nascent Russian state in the tenth century AD.

The heart of medieval Novgorod was surrounded by a rampart to form a citadel, or 'kremlin', as early as the tenth century. Originally, the rampart was constructed of timber and earth, but over the next several centuries it was replaced by stone walls with defensive towers. Today, the most prominent feature of the Novgorod kremlin is the onion-domed Cathedral of St Sophia, which began as a wooden church at the end of the tenth century and was replaced in the eleventh century by the present stone church. The kremlin was the seat of the prince who nominally ruled Novgorod, but much of the governing power resided in the popular assembly, or *veche,* which made laws and decided on administrative matters.

Perhaps the most remarkable finds at Novgorod have been over 700 birchbark manuscripts, known as *beresty,* preserved in the waterlogged deposits. *Beresty* were written between the middle of the eleventh century and the early fifteenth century. The first of these was discovered in 1951 in a level dating between AD 1369

and 1409, but more were later found in earlier levels. The *beresty* were pieces of birchbark that were boiled to remove the coarse outer layers. The fine inner layers were then inscribed without ink using styluses made from bone or metal. The contents of the *beresty* describe numerous aspects of life in Novgorod, from mundane household records to legal, governmental and commercial discussions. They reveal a level of literacy hitherto unexpected in medieval Russia and, moreover, indicate that a large segment of the population could read and write to some extent.

Since only about 2 per cent of the area of ancient Novgorod has been excavated, archaeologists have estimated that over 20,000 *beresty* remain buried in the medieval layers under the modern town. *Beresty* have recently come to light in other ancient towns in north-western Russia, such as Pskov, and these documents will be a continual source of new information about medieval Russia. When combined with the hundreds of thousands of artifacts and the preserved houses and streets, they offer a fascinating glimpse into the life of this region almost 1000 years ago. ■

ASIA

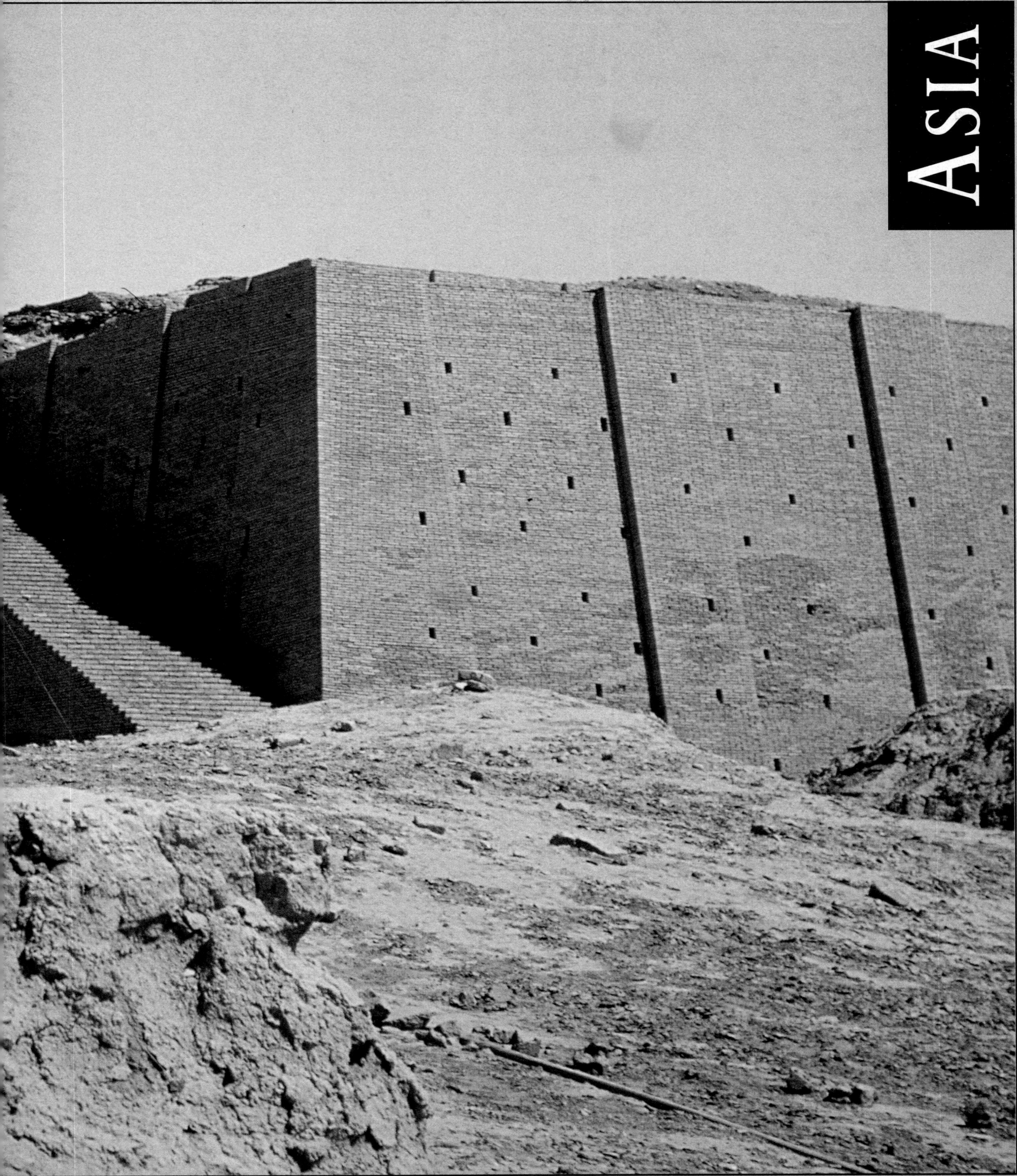

WARKA/URUK

Before 4000 BC, Sumer (southern Mesopotamia) hosted a farming culture that had been slowly developing small towns over the previous two millennia; after 3500 BC, a bureaucratic state governed a population concentrated in cities. These developments occurred during the time that archaeologists call the Uruk period, named after the city at Uruk, the biblical Erech and modern Warka. The remains at Uruk represent the world's oldest city, the capital of an early state, where officials invented writing to keep track of government affairs.

Although the first archaeological investigation of Uruk happened in 1849, systematic work did not begin until 1912, when the German Oriental Society began excavations. Despite the interruptions of two world wars and the vagaries of regional politics, the Germans have continued work at Uruk, under a succession of directors, into the present decade. Concentrating on monumental buildings with a public function, the Germans have uncovered the palace of King Sinkasid (the ruler of a kingdom

The south of Iraq today is uninviting and isolated, marked by extensive marshes and scattered sand dunes, and home to a sparse, often nomadic population. Yet the world's first urban society developed here in Sumer during the first half of the fourth millennium BC.

during the nineteenth century BC), and temples from the city's late periods of the occupation (Hellenistic and Parthian times, roughly 300 BC to AD 200). However, the main monuments, including those of the Uruk period, lie in two cultic precincts in the centre of the city.

As so many other ancient Mesopotamian cities, Uruk was first occupied during the 'Ubaid period, perhaps 4500 BC. Initially perhaps two separate villages, Uruk expanded rapidly during the fourth millennium, and by 3300 BC had grown to cover no less than 200 hectares, with possibly 40,000 residents. Uruk and other new Mesopotamian cities reflect a new kind of social organization, one that required new hierarchical relationships between people, new expressions of increasing differences in social status, and new technologies and organizations for making commodities. Many goods required access to the exotic raw materials – metals,

The ziggurat was the Uruk's most prominent monument.

Mesopotamian architects developed arches by the third millennium BC, continuing to use this device until the end of the Mesopotamian civilization.

Uruk's builders used coloured cones, pressed into clay walls, to create patterned mosaics.

stones, woods – that came from distant sources in the mountains of Turkey or Iran. In pursuit of these goods, Uruk traders, and even colonists, established a string of settlements and outposts in northern Mesopotamia and the neighbouring mountains.

Uruk's growth continued unabated, and by *c.* 2800 BC the city had reached some 550 hectares in size, with a concomitant rise in population; a wall now encircled the settlement. Unfortunately, later building destroyed most traces of this giant city, at least in the areas the Germans have explored. At this time (the Early Dynastic period, roughly 2900–2300 BC), Sumer was divided into numerous city-states often at war with each other over regional supremacy. This period witnessed one of the most urban civilizations of the ancient world – one modern estimate places an astonishing 80 per cent of Sumerians in cities at *c.* 2500 BC. Such a high level proved insupportable over the long term for an ancient agrarian society, and southern Mesopotamia became increasingly rural, and even depopulated, over the next couple of millennia. Uruk's individual history roughly mirrors these regional trends. Beginning the third millennium as the metropolis of Sumer, Uruk ended it as a much smaller city of local importance, subordinated to more powerful neighbours like Ur (see p. 80). The slide continued, despite brief periods of autonomy, and the site was even abandoned late in the eighteenth century BC. Although it was reoccupied several centuries later, and even attained a local importance for the Eanna and other ritual monuments, by then the centres of regional power had shifted permanently to the north (for instance Babylon): Uruk never again matched the brilliance of its beginning.

Although the Uruk period has been known for more than six decades, today Warka still presents the best evidence for it in southern Mesopotamia. Excavation of Warka's early periods has concentrated on two central sacred areas, the Abu and Eanna precincts. These excavations have uncovered temple buildings, together with many fine pieces of art, and remains of the world's first bureaucracy. These two areas proved so rewarding that the German excavators have not uncovered other kinds of places,

whether residential quarters with their houses and lanes, industrial quarters for the mundane crafts like potting, or other evidence of daily life. Impressions about the Uruk culture, and especially the Late Uruk phase (*c.* 3500–3100 BC), have therefore come only from the special contexts of the temples, associated buildings and their rubbish.

The exposed architecture of the Abu precinct reveals continuous building on the same spot. This Mesopotamian tradition of preserving sacred spaces, maintained and upgraded through time, is best illustrated at the site of Eridu, near Ur, where archaeologists revealed a superimposed succession of sixteen increasingly elaborate temples built in the same spot for some 2000 years. The earliest detected shrine in the Abu precinct goes back to perhaps 1000 years before the best-preserved Uruk period

The artisans of Uruk created many beautiful objects of stone, to be used in cultic observances.

monument. This building, called the White Temple because of its bright gypsum plaster, stood atop a mudbrick platform that covered 70 by 60 m, and rose to a height of 13 m. A staircase gave access to the temple, which covered only a small portion (22 by 17 m) of the platform. The temple's floor plan was tripartite, with a regular row of rooms flanking each side of a long central hall that ran down the length of the structure; this basic tripartite plan goes back to 'Ubaid domestic buildings. The idea of elevating the temple upon a large high podium was a common practice in Mesopotamia at this time, and gave rise during the third millennium to that characteristically Mesopotamian structure, the ziggurat (three or four platforms stacked on top of each other, again with the temple on top).

Eanna (literally the 'house of heaven') was the cult centre of Inanna, the Sumerian goddess whose persona encompassed both war and fertility. About half a kilometre from the Abu precinct, a wall enclosed a large space, about 200 by 400 m, within which lay many big buildings, usually with the same tripartite plan and set upon terraces. These structures could be very large, one covering 80 by 50 m. Stairways gave access to the terraces on which stood the temples. In one instance, a pair of stairways rose to a colonnaded portico, with two rows of columns and half-pillars ornamenting the adjacent walls. Other buildings were square, with banks of rooms arranged around a large central courtyard. In at least one case, the structure was built of limestone blocks, brought from a quarry at least 80 km away, instead of the usual mudbrick. Some walls are decorated with clay (or, more rarely, stone) cones with painted flat ends, that were pressed into a wall's mud plaster to create colourful geometric designs. In addition, a large sunken square courtyard served some special, now obscure function.

However spectacular this architecture was, several circumstances greatly enhance its significance. Nothing identifiable as a palace has been found amid the early architecture at Uruk, and elsewhere in Sumer palaces seem to appear only in Early Dynastic times. This chronology corroborates the Sumerian story that Gilgamesh, a mythologized ruler of Uruk who probably lived around 2800 BC, set himself up as the first king outside the previously existing government by community elders. During Uruk times, much of civil authority was probably vested in the temple communities. The temples were not merely cult centres, with or without political clout – they were one of the bedrock institutions of Mesopotamian society, with attached agricultural lands and personnel to farm them, craftsmen as well as ritual specialists, and accumulated wealth that underwrote loans and other banking activities. The nascent power of this institution is already evident in early Uruk, for this is the context of the world's first bureaucratic machinery.

The bureaucratic functionaries of the Late Uruk period developed two new devices to aid their work. One invention was the cylinder seal, which replaced the older stamp seal. A cylinder seal had a design that could be rolled out across a large surface of clay, such as a jar stopper or door lock, thus guaranteeing the contents of the jar or room, and inhibiting unauthorized persons from tampering with them. The cylinder was also used to seal the spherical clay envelopes called *bullae*. A *bulla* would hold several clay geometric shapes, called tokens, whose shape was also impressed into the surface of the *bulla*. The tokens denoted numbers of things (such as sheep or textiles), and the *bulla* system helped keep track of the institutional economy of the temple. The Uruk accountants soon simplified this cumbersome system, when they inscribed the same information on a solid rectangular clay tablet, which they continued to impress with a cylinder seal. They then added abstract signs to identify commodities more precisely, thus laying the foundations of the cuneiform writing system that Mesopotamian scribes were to use for the next 3000 years. The pronouncements and boasts of kings, the recording of myth and cult observances, the procedures for magicians, diviners, physicians and other occult specialists, and private letters between ordinary people eventually sprang, later during the third millennium BC, from these beginnings. And these innovative Uruk practices also laid the distant foundations of the modern world. ∎

The temple of Inanna, renovated in the mid-second millennium BC.

UR

Ur: its name evokes many responses today – Ur of the Chaldees, Abraham's birthplace, the dynastic seat of a powerful if short-lived empire 4000 years ago, the even more ancient brilliance of the Royal Cemetery. In large measure, Leonard Woolley's popular accounts of his excavations at Ur have kept the place fresh in the public mind, helping to make it perhaps the most recognized ancient Sumerian city, despite being a relatively small one. Woolley dug at Ur from 1922 until 1934, during which time he gained a comprehensive understanding of the city's history from its prehistoric beginnings nearly 7000 years ago to its final abandonment around 400 BC.

Ur, the modern name of which is Tell Muqayyar, lies near the bank of a former branch of the Euphrates River in the deep south of Sumer (southern Mesopotamia), near the former head of the Persian Gulf. This location, convenient for transportation and long-distance trade, early attracted settlement whose beginning recedes into the mists of prehistory. Woolley encountered, at the bottom of deep soundings, the remains of flimsy huts, painted pottery and burials that go back to roughly 5000 BC. A thick deposit of river silt, covering these traces of prehistoric occupation, seemed to Woolley to echo the story of the Flood that is recorded in both biblical and Mesopotamian myths. The Mesopotamian civilization set down its deep urban roots during the fourth millennium BC, when Uruk (see p. 176) was the premier Sumerian city. Woolley found only traces of monumental architecture (remains of a platform on which presumably there had been a public building decorated with painted wall cones) belonging to this time.

The following thousand years was a period of massive change. For much of the third millennium BC, southern Mesopotamia was divided among competing city-states that formed shifting partnerships in a perpetual dance for supremacy. During this Early Dynastic period (c. 2900–2330 BC), Ur was sometimes the seat of powerful dynasties (the cuneiform document today called the Sumerian King List records two dynasties). Magnificent palaces,

Sir Leonard Woolley digging at Ur, uncovering the statuette of a worshipper in a chapel in the residential quarter, early second millennium BC.

temples and other buildings surely adorned the Early Dynastic city, but such structures remain mostly obscured by later construction. To this period, however, belongs the glorious Royal Cemetery. The cemetery, active over five centuries, contained more than 2000 graves, of which Woolley distinguished only sixteen as royal. These few tombs are subterranean chambers rather than simple pits, often graced with vaulted roofs. Some objects, inscribed with people's names, seem to identify the burials of Meskalamdug, Akalamdug, the queen Pu-abi and other members of a ruling house of Ur around 2500 BC. Interestingly, the Sumerian King List does not mention these names. The Royal Cemetery yielded many celebrated pieces of Sumerian art, like the 'Standard of Ur', a panel showing scenes of warfare and peace composed with nacre and lapis lazuli inlay; inlay-decorated lyres, gaming boards, and figures of a ram caught in a thicket; and the electrum helmet of Meskalamdug. Some tombs also contained the remains of oxen yoked to wagons, and the skeletons of many male and female attendants, all apparently sacrificed to serve the royal personage in the afterlife.

The Early Dynastic dance of city-states ended when Sargon (c. 2330–2280 BC), the Akkadian upstart, defeated all the Sumerian cities and then extended the weight of his hand well beyond the previous ambition of Sumerian dynasts. Woolley could find little at Ur that he could attribute to the new masters of Sumer. Akkadian suzerainty endured for another century, before giving way to external invasion and political chaos (the Sumerian King List makes the sardonic remark 'Who was king? Who was not king?' about this period). From this wreckage arose a new dynasty at Ur, the third dynasty that the King List names for the city. Although spanning a mere century (c. 2100–2000 BC), the Ur III dynasty marked the peak of Ur's power and wealth. Its kings again seized all of Mesopotamia as far north as Ashur, and imposed an orderly, even rigid, bureaucratic administration over its large dominion. Naturally, the city greatly benefited from its new role as the imperial seat, and Ur III construction projects radically changed the city, even giving it a new skyline.

For a very long time, Mesopotamian builders had been elevating temples by placing them on platforms. This practice gave rise to ziggurats, large stepped towers composed of successively smaller platforms stacked on top of each other. Although earlier examples may exist (buried as the core of later larger structures), Ur-Nammu (2112–2095 BC), the first Ur III king, erected the oldest surviving ziggurat. Ur-Nammu's ziggurat rose in three stages, each terrace with slanted sides to give the effect of a stepped pyramid. The bottom stage covered 60 by 45 m and stood about 15 m high, its corners oriented to the cardinal points in the traditional Mesopotamian fashion. The upper two stages are less well preserved. A grand staircase mounted the structure, leading directly from the facing plaza to the cult chamber that perched on the ziggurat's summit. Two ancillary stairways rose from the adjacent corners to meet the central staircase at the top of the first stage. The entire structure was a solid mass of mudbrick, faced with a 2.4 m thick skin of baked brick set in asphalt.

The ziggurat formed one element in the precinct of the temple dedicated to Nanna, moon god and patron deity of Ur. Nanna's main temple lay against the ziggurat's north-west side, while several other major buildings and plazas filled the remains of the walled sacred precinct (*temenos*). One important building was the Giparu, the residence for the chief priestess of the Nanna cult, a position often filled by royal daughters. This structure lay within a nearly square (80 by 76 m) enclosure formed by a wall 5 m thick. The interior space fell neatly into two halves, separated by a long corridor, one half focused on rituals of the Nanna cult and the other on the residential needs of the priestess and her entourage. Another building, the Ehursag, presents some architectural features characteristic of Mesopotamian palaces. Just outside the *temenos* opposite the Ehursag, in the area of the Royal Cemetery, lies a block of three connected buildings, beneath which were underground chambers. Although they were empty of contents, Woolley identified these structures as mausolea of the Ur III kings. The *temenos* lay in the midst of a 50 hectare city enclosed by a town wall and rampart, just beyond which flowed a now extinct branch of the Euphrates River.

The bureaucracy of the Ur III kingdom could not keep the barbarians from the gates, and an invading Elamite army sacked and looted Ur. The literary memory of the event emphasized the carnage, exemplified in these verses (Thorkild Jacobsen's translation) from 'The Lamentation for Ur':

> Its people('s corpses), not potsherds,
> littered the approaches.
> The walls were gaping;
> the high gates, the roads,
> were piled with dead.
> In the wide streets,
> where feasting crowds (once) gathered,
> jumbled they lay.

But the physical destruction, although heavy, was not complete, and Ur soon flourished again.

The next two centuries (roughly 2000-1800 BC) represented a return to the squabbling politics of petty kingdoms. In the end, a single strongman emerged to sweep away all other contestants,

The great ziggurat at Ur, during excavation; Woolley's workmen have paused on the ramps for a portrait.

this time Hammurabi (1792-1750 BC), the king of Babylon. During this period, however, Ur no longer maintained its independence, at first falling within the domain of stronger neighbours like Isin and Larsa, and then succumbing to Hammurabi's army. The 'foreign' kings, conscious of Ur's imperial heritage, invested in restoring and maintaining the city's monuments, including the ziggurat, giparu and other structures within the ritual centre. The city walls were rebuilt, now enclosing some 60 hectares, but during this time extra-mural suburbs, not systematically investigated, seem to have surrounded the walled centre, creating a much larger city (perhaps of the order of 300 hectares). In addition to documenting the reconstructed religious architecture, Woolley uncovered two residential areas. One of these districts lay near the *temenos* and seems to have housed mostly temple officials. The other district, near the south-east stretch of town wall, presented a rabbit-warren of narrow twisting streets and irregularly shaped houses of different sizes. Most houses were arranged as rooms around a central courtyard, some possibly standing two storeys tall. Many of the larger houses possessed facilities that Woolley thought to be domestic chapel rooms, an indication of the growing belief in personal gods that presaged biblical sentiments (for example, a later cuneiform prayer entreats 'many are my iniquities, slip them off (me) like a garment'). This quarter housed a diverse population, including a copper merchant whose clients accused him of sharp practices, a school headmaster, and a greasy-spoon restaurateur.

Hammurabi's rule marked a turning point in Mesopotamian geography, as the centres of power shifted for ever to the north. Occupation at Ur went on for nearly another two millennia, always under the patronage of an outside power. These rulers continued to take an interest in maintaining the traditional religious buildings of the place, and rebuilt some of them on an ever larger scale. But stripped of its political and economic position, Ur now evoked only cultic and historical memories. ■

TROY

Schliemann identified the second city as Homer's Troy, but it was in fact an Early Bronze Age town of the late third millennium BC. Troy II was a small fortified citadel measuring around 100 m in diameter. Seven separate strata have been identified, which demonstrate increasing architectural expertise, alongside the growth of the settlement and its increasing prosperity. The first fortification wall, built of unworked stones to a height of 3 m and surmounted by a massive mudbrick wall, was protected at 10 m intervals by square towers. The citadel was entered by two main gates in the south and the west, over each of which rose a massive tower. The fortifications of Troy IIc and IId are particularly imposing. A greater area was enclosed, and two new stately gates with a tripartite plan were built (the south-east and south-west gates). The south-west gateway was approached by a paved ramp, used by wheeled vehicles.

Inside the citadel there were two paved courtyards, one enclosed by a colonnade. This was probably a public, communal area, perhaps for an assembly or market. Opposite the entrance to the colonnaded court there was an imposing rectangular building, the great megaron. The megaron's plan, a spacious pillared porch leading into a great hall with a huge central hearth, recalls the Greek mainland palaces of the fourteenth and thirteenth centuries BC. Like the fortifications, the megaron was built of mudbrick on a stone foundation, and the walls were half-timbered. The sheer size of the building and its imposing location, dominating the centre of the citadel, suggests that the megaron was the home of the local chief.

The wealth of Troy II is illustrated not only by its impressive architecture, but also by the famous treasure hoards found by

Few archaeological exploits capture the imagination more than Heinrich Schliemann's discovery of the legendary city of Troy. His determination to establish the veracity of the Trojan War led him to an obscure mound (Hissarlik) on the western coast of Turkey which he excavated during four major campaigns between 1870 and 1890. Further excavations, by Dörpfeld, Blegen and currently by Korfmann, have confirmed the identity of the site as Troy. Nine separate cities have been unearthed, spanning the period from the third millennium BC to Roman times. The most important are Troys II, VI and VIIa which have each been identified in turn with the city of Homeric epic.

Schliemann within the settlement, in the final phase of the second town. These include exquisite gold jewellery, such as the famous diadem worn by Sophia Schliemann, metal vessels and a set of four stone battle axes. Fortunately for the archaeologists, these treasures were abandoned by the inhabitants of Troy II when they hurriedly fled the town before it was destroyed by fire, and they tell us much about the life of the wealthier residents of the city. The men appear to have been formidable warriors; the women wore elaborate gold jewellery. The majority of Trojans ate off simple clay pots, but the chief, his family and associates used fine metal vessels.

The prosperity of Troy II was based on its importance as an agricultural and trading centre. There is considerable evidence for a maritime trade network around the northern Aegean at this time, in the form of pottery, and the various metals used in the town (copper, tin, silver and gold) were all imported. Quantities of sheep bones have been recovered from the site which, together with numerous spindle whorls, suggest that sheep-rearing and the manufacture of woollen textiles were important elements of the local economy.

Troy VI, the most famous and imposing of the cities, was occupied between around 1800 and 1300 BC. Blegen suggested that her inhabitants were newcomers, who were responsible for the introduction of various novel features and improved technical skills, as seen in the pottery and architecture. The famous fortifications of Troy VI were rebuilt on three separate occasions, and the latest walls are the best preserved and most imposing. They were built of cut limestone blocks supporting a substantial superstructure of mudbrick and were over 4 m thick. The citadel was entered by at least five major gates, each protected by a tower. One of these towers enclosed a huge stone-lined cistern, which ensured the town's water supply in times of siege. The walls are an amazing feat of military engineering and suggest that Troy was a major economic centre, but the area enclosed is very small in comparison with many contemporary towns elsewhere in Greece and the Near East. Recently, however, a geomagnetic

Watercolour of Schliemann's 1870–82 excavations of Troy.

ABOVE: The main southern gate into Troy VI.

RIGHT: Plan of ancient Troy.

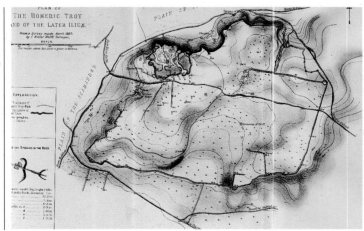

survey south of the mound of Troy has located a second, outer defence wall, thereby dramatically increasing Troy VI to a size more appropriate for a prosperous second millennium BC town. The citadel itself, where the ruler of Troy lived, was the focus of public life and required particular protection.

The internal layout of the citadel area shows some evidence of town planning, although the buildings were arranged in concentric rings climbing the terraces of the citadel, rather than forming a grid system. The residence of the ruler of Troy VI has not been located, but there are a series of large free-standing buildings within the citadel. These buildings, some of which stood two

BELOW: The ruins at the site of Troy.

RIGHT: The fortification walls and tower protecting Troy VI.

storeys high, had walls of mudbrick and timber on stone foundations, and were probably the residences of important citizens of Troy.

The burial ground of the ruler of Troy and his followers has not been found, but to the south of the citadel, on the edge of the Trojan plateau, there was a simple cremation cemetery, probably belonging to the ordinary citizens. The cremated remains were placed in clay jars and buried in shallow pits, with only a few provisions for the afterlife.

In daily life the majority of the inhabitants used clay vessels, but their obvious affinities with metal vases imply that these pots imitated the luxury dinner sets of the ruler of Troy. In general, though, despite the obvious prosperity of Troy VI very few luxuries have been salvaged from its remains, although there are occasional ivories, some glass paste beads, and five alabaster sword pommels. The inhabitants of Troy appear to have been forewarned of impending disaster and abandoned the town, taking their valuables with them, before the massive walls of Troy VI were toppled by an earthquake.

After the earthquake people returned to Troy, but the town took on a very different character to its imposing predecessor and was destroyed within a generation. The inhabitants of Troy VIIa rebuilt the fortifications using assorted materials, including fallen blocks from the previous walls and smaller, unworked stones. Within these walls they lived in a maze of small overcrowded rooms, very different from the fine free-standing buildings of Troy VI. Large clay storage jars sunk into the floor contained food supplies (grain and oil), perhaps provision in case of siege. The general impression is that Troy VIIa was rebuilt hastily and that there was an overriding concern for quick protection from imminent danger. The form this danger took is suggested by the sudden destruction of the town by fire. Several skeletons were found in the destruction level, the victims of an attack who had no chance to flee. Is this then the city described by Homer in the *Iliad*? ∎

MOHENJO-DARO

Archaeologists first detected the Indus civilization in 1920, and since then have excavated numerous sites, among them the city at Mohenjo-Daro, in the Sind. Mohenjo-Daro, like other cities and towns of the Indus civilization, projects the image of a curiously regimented and standardized society that still defies modern understanding. The cities of the Indus civilization disappeared abruptly around 2000 BC, leaving only vague echoes of a failed urban experiment as their legacy.

India often conjures up images of immense cities like Bombay and Calcutta, teeming with people. These modern cities are inheritors of an urban tradition that began nearly 3000 years ago in the Ganges drainage, not long before the lifetime of the Buddha. However, the emerging Iron Age towns could not claim to be the first cities of the Indian subcontinent. Around 2500 BC an urban society emerged in the Indus River valley (today mostly in Pakistan), spreading out to Gujarat and Haryana in India.

The Indus civilization (often called Harappan, after another important city) sprang up as a rapid synthesis of several antecedent (Early Harappan) cultures. The transformation was rapid, as the culture took something like a century to move from multiple regional village and town societies to a single urban society that spread from Gujarat and the Indian Ocean to the Punjab and the Himalayan foothills, with outposts as far east as the Delhi area, in the Ganges drainage. The society actively penetrated neighbouring areas, setting up colonies as far away as northern Afghanistan. Between 2500 and 2000 BC, at least four large cities held a large proportion of the total population, although many people continued to pursue a more familiar village life. Rather than growing organically, with the irregular twisting streets and oddly shaped houses typical of ancient Near Eastern towns, the Indus cities seem to have been built as planned developments with a regular street grid, modular houses, unified sanitation facilities and other hallmarks of urban planning.

Mohenjo-Daro, located on the right bank of the Indus River about 400 km upstream from the ocean, is the best-known of the large Indus cities. Its builders used burnt, or baked, brick for much of its construction, a circumstance that left the buried city in a remarkably good state of preservation – visitors today can walk down 4000-year-old streets, complete with pavements and drains, with the walls of adjoining buildings rising overhead. Mohenjo-Daro was doubly fortunate to have escaped the more recent ravages of peasants and engineers who mined other cities like Harappa for these very same baked bricks. Like many cities and towns of the Indus civilization, Mohenjo-Daro was laid out in two distinct parts: a citadel and a lower town separated by empty space (elsewhere sometimes by a wall).

The citadel rose some 5 m above the surrounding plain by virtue of its giant brick platform that covered about 8 hectares. The citadel may have been further distinguished by an enclosing wall, a feature evident at other Indus cities but obscured here by later river alluvium. On top of this impressive terrace sat public buildings, probably administrative and cultic. Made of burnt brick, these facilities included a large, ventilated structure that is commonly identified as a granary, a large asphalt-lined 'bath' perhaps used during ritual purification, a suite of rooms that the excavators called the priests' quarters, and a large colonnaded hall.

The lower town, where people lived and worked, extended over 80 hectares or more, and held perhaps 20,000 people (some estimate twice this figure). The main streets were up to 10 m wide, and formed a regular, apparently planned grid of blocks, roughly 370 by 250 m in area, oriented towards the cardinal points of the compass; smaller streets and alleys gave access to the buildings within these blocks of residential apartments, barracks and workshops. The individual residential units, set around courtyards, contained anywhere from one to dozens of rooms, with staircases leading to the roof or upper storeys. Covered drains, connected to the toilets of private houses, ran under the streets in a surprisingly sophisticated sewerage system. An estimated 700 brick-lined wells, each serving a group of households, supplied the city-dwellers with water.

In addition to its residential function, the Lower Town hosted many different workshops where the goods of daily life were made. Potters, who decorated many of their products with painted representations of plants, fish and animals, were concentrated in the northern end of town, with more isolated kilns scattered throughout the city. Some shops made characteristic Indus goods such as stoneware bangles, while others fashioned bracelets and inlay elements from shells brought from the Indian Ocean. Flint knappers made the long regular blades that served as knives and common agricultural tools, as well as the cubes and spheroids

Excavation of residential areas at Mohenjo-Daro revealed deeply buried brick houses, and brick-lined well shafts sunk from higher levels.

in a standardized graduated series of weights for use in commerce. Metalworkers produced copper and bronze objects, both tools and objets d'art. Stoneworkers turned out beads made from various chalcedonies and also lapis lazuli and serpentine. The Indus civilization developed a decorative technique, still used today, of etching designs in carnelian beads with an alkali paste, and the characteristic Indus etched carnelian beads were traded as far away as Mesopotamia and the Iranian plateau. Craftsmen also turned out steatite products, most notably seals. The Indus civilization adopted a square form of stamp seal, decorated with a limited range of animal motifs and inscriptions in the still undeciphered Indus script. This writing system is preserved only in short texts on objects like the seals, amulets and pottery vessels, which has made decipherment so far elusive; most scholars nowadays believe that the Indus tongue was Dravidian, a language family that includes Tamil, spoken today in southern India and Sri Lanka.

The regularity of the street lay-out and of the residential architecture, and the sophisticated drains, and other municipal works give the impression of town planning and indeed of a regimented society. The artifacts within these settlements, both large and small, also seemed to be uniform. The painted pottery, the chipped stone and metal tools, the steatite seals, and the other inscribed objects appeared to be identical from place to place over the 1200 km between the Indian Ocean and the Himalayan foothills. The modern reaction to this seeming uniformity has often been negative, exemplified by one disparaging observation that Indus cities like Mohenjo-Daro 'imply all too effectively the elaborate organization of an urban mercantile class whose products lack not only the barbaric spontaneity of the older and more primitive cultures, but even the cheery *nouveau riche* vulgarity of Early Dynastic Sumer . . . and display instead a dead level of

LEFT: As deposits of earlier occupations thickened, renovations left ever higher walls of houses along the ancient streets of Mohenjo-Daro. **ABOVE:** Although the political organization of the Indus civilization remains an enigma, many scholars have identified this bearded figure, carved in steatite, as a priest-king.

bourgeois mediocrity in almost every branch of the visual arts and crafts'. Part of the modern difficulty lies in being unable to identify the social sources of authority and organization in the Indus culture: no palace or anything that could be described as royal has been discovered, little public or ostentatious art, and even temples remain obscure. Many scholars see religion as the organizing theme of Harappan society, which priest-kings ruled by their association with rituals and the gods. These ideas remain largely speculation. More interestingly, perhaps, some elements of Indus art seem to evoke a spirit typical of later India, including the seated figure in a lotus position. These elements appear to imply that, despite the abrupt and total collapse of city life, and the disappearance of many typical Indus practices like the writing system around 2000 BC, this experiment with urbanism was in some distant way connected to the flourishing of Iron Age towns in the Ganges area more than a millennium later. Even if this connection with historical India proves tenuous, Mohenjo-Daro and the Indus civilization provide an example of ancient cities that differs fundamentally from the more familiar Near Eastern pattern. ■

MEGIDDO: THE CITY
OF ARMAGEDDON

Megiddo's very long sequence of occupation illustrates the fortunes of town life in the southern Levant, and also traces a shift through time from small town to city-state capital, to special function as a military and/or administrative centre. Megiddo's urban fabric changed radically with each of these manifestations, showing how closely its broader social or political context can mould the very appearance of a city.

Compared to Mesopotamian cities, the ancient towns of the southern Levant – modern Israel and Jordan – tended to be modestly proportioned, most covering less than 25 hectares even during the Iron Age. Town life in the region also seems fragile, periodically almost disappearing, and even during the most intensely urban phases a large proportion of the population lived in villages. Even so, towns served important functions in the ancient societies of the southern Levant.

The Megiddo mound today covers a mere 6 hectares, and the town never expanded beyond some 12 hectares, making it a medium-sized town by local standards. Megiddo's importance stems from its long and varied history, the succession of towns recording many basic changes in the region's political, ethnic and religious history, as well as the ebb and flow of international currents, and broad changes in the character of settlement. Megiddo, the Armageddon of the biblical Revelations (where the kings will assemble for the final battle), is set on the west side of the Jezreel valley, which acts as a passage from the Jordan River valley to the Mediterranean coast. Although the Mt Carmel range flanks the site to the south, a pass across these hills enters the Jezreel near Megiddo, placing it at a regionally important crossroads.

The site attracted some of the first archaeological excavations in Palestine, beginning before the First World War. An ambitious American team from the Oriental Institute (Chicago) carried out the most important digging, when it attempted the strategy of 'the permanent acquisition of the whole *tell*, and of excavation over its entire area . . . of each successive stratum of ruins as a complete whole'. The Megiddo project, which ran between 1925 and 1939, surely counts as the most lavishly funded excavation in the history of Near Eastern archaeology (the dig house even equipped with tennis courts). But despite the deep pockets of its sponsor, John D. Rockefeller Jr, the project could not cope with the Great Depression, and the team was able to uncover completely only the upper levels. Even so, a succession of Bronze Age towns over several large areas of the mound were exposed. More recent, smaller scale excavations have tried to resolve stratigraphic questions that the Chicago team left behind.

The earliest traces of human life on this spot go back to the early Neolithic, before the invention of pottery (a period called the Pre-Pottery Neolithic B, dated to 7400–6200 BC). The first substantial remains date to the Chalcolithic (4500–3500 BC) and Early Bronze I (3500–3100 BC) periods, when the village contained a scatter of small single-room houses. Even at this early date, a large structure fronting on a large walled courtyard can be identified as a temple. The settlement took a more urban form with the following periods, the Early Bronze II and III (3100–2300 BC). A wall was constructed, at first only around the previously established temple area, and subsequently doubled to an 8 m thickness around the whole town. The sacred area shifted somewhat to the west, and was incrementally enlarged. In its early phases, this precinct contained a circular stone podium, 8 m in diameter and over 1 m high; the often charred bones of sacrificial animals littered the space around the podium. The spacious, broad cult room had its altar opposite the doorway that was entered through a portico with two columns. A later phase of construction added a pair of adjoining cult rooms, each similar in plan to the initial sanctuary. Private houses along narrow streets surrounded the temple area.

The town experienced a decline during Early Bronze IV (2300–2000 BC) times, when flimsy domestic structures were

The ruler of Megiddo at the end of the Late Bronze Age left a hoard of carved ivories. Many of these, like this small head, adorned furniture.

scattered across the site. The sanctuary continued in use, although the pair of cult rooms was abandoned and the main temple was reduced in size. This period was one of widespread abandonment of settled life in many parts of the southern Levant, and saw a general shift towards animal herding.

A growing connection to Syria eventually helped stimulate a revival of town life around 2000 BC. A new town wall was built, now in the borrowed Syrian style with massive ramparts and sloping bank, a characteristic feature of towns of the Middle Bronze Age (2000–1550 BC). The wall enclosed a lower town as well as the older upper town, bringing Megiddo to its peak size (10–12 hectares) early in the MBA. The gate, on the north side of town, took the form of a bent axis, in which a walled ramp ran along the outside of the town wall and then took a sharp turn as it approached the portals. Later in the same period the gate was remodelled as a straight entrance with two chambers (or three piers) between a pair of massive towers. This key point in the town soon attracted large, even palatial buildings. The traditional cult centre continued to attract devotion, and the area was now walled off, keeping this sacred space separate from the domestic residences that sprang up around it. A large palace, arranged in several wings of courtyards, halls and storerooms, was soon founded on the west side of the sacred precinct. During this period, the southern Levant was divided into a series of city-states; Megiddo and its palaces were the political and administrative centre of one of these states.

The southern Levant lost its independence during the Late Bronze Age (1550–1200 BC), when the Egyptian New Kingdom pharaohs used local rulers as vassals. Although subordinate to foreign suzerains, the élites at Megiddo prospered. A new palatial complex emerged around the north gate, shifting the town's civic centre to this area. The new elaborate palace, formed around multiple courtyards and decorated with wall-paintings, yielded some of the most spectacular finds of the LBA. A hoard of ivory plaques, gold vessels, beads of gold and lapis lazuli, and other precious objects was hidden below the floor of one room. And early in the twelfth century, three sunken rooms, or cellars, held a treasure of ivory furniture inlays, the carved decoration rendered in the various styles of this international period. A district of modestly sized private houses south of the palace were also uncovered.

The LBA settlement ended with a destruction around 1150 BC. The next occupation was a mere village, whose poorly built houses covered a small portion of the mound (perhaps only 1 hectare). Many researchers identify this village as an early Israelite settlement. It soon gave way to a richer, unwalled Philistine town, with a rich metalworking industry that continued the Bronze Age tradition. Despite these relatively swift changes in the material culture, and presumed ethnicity, of the town's inhabitants, the traditional Bronze Age temple precinct continued to function well into the Iron Age.

The next two towns were walled administrative and military establishments that completely remodelled Megiddo's appearance. The first belonged to the newly arisen United Kingdom of David and Solomon. The town contained three separate palaces set at various points against the town wall, and an additional large, probably administrative building, along with extensive domestic architecture. A small two-entry gate with a ramp approach gave access through the casemate town wall. The finest buildings of the

Although seeming to reflect biblical references to Solomon's chariot cities, Megiddo's stables were actually built a century later.

town made common use of ashlar masonry and proto-Ionic capitals (so named because of their resemblance to the later Ionic order of the Classical world), recalling the architectural sophistication of Solomon's building in Jerusalem. These remains illuminate the nature of Solomon's military and administrative centres, mentioned in various biblical passages.

Fire destroyed Solomon's Megiddo, towards the end of the tenth century. The subsequent rebuilt town had an extremely strong military character, with large areas converted to army facilities. Most notable of these are the four-entry gatehouse, the two stables compounds and the water system. The Oriental Institute excavators wanted to identify this town as Solomon's work, thus illustrating the biblical testimony that 'Solomon gathered together chariots and horsemen; he had fourteen hundred chariots and twelve thousand horsemen, whom he stationed in the chariot

LEFT: Strong gateways with three sets of piers and two interior chambers came into fashion in the Levant around 2000 BC. This example dates to the early Iron Age over a thousand years later.
ABOVE: These ivory lenticular discs, carved in animal figures or geometric designs on one side only, may have been gaming pieces.

cities and with the king in Jerusalem' (1 Kings 9:19, 10:26). However, later reconsideration of the associated pottery showed that the levels must date to the ninth century BC, and the stables were perhaps the work of Ahab, the king of Samaria. Even without their Solomonic association, the stables are impressive. The complex to the north falls on three sides of a plaza, a palace abutting to the south. The southern complex faces a 50 by 50 m parade ground in the centre of which stood a large watering trough. These installations could hold some 300 to 330 horses. Other important facilities included a large walled compound enclosing a palatial building, a secondary gate between this compound and the southern stables, and an elaborate four-entry gate on the north wall. A sophisticated water system, cut through bedrock, allowed access to a spring via a horizontal gallery that ran from the blocked-up spring to a vertical shaft in the centre of the town. This garrison town was destroyed late in the ninth century BC, perhaps as the result of an Aramaean raid.

The next town, belonging to the eighth century, represents a completely different function, with ensuing remodelling of the town lay-out. Now, for the first time, the town streets were laid out in a regular grid. The city blocks so formed were 55–60 m long and 22 m wide. The private houses along these streets were set around a courtyard, representing a change in the architectural canon; in contrast to the heavily military character of the previous town, ordinary dwellings covered about 80 per cent of the town. The administrative centre, as earlier in time, lay just inside the north city gate, with blocks of rooms falling on either side of it. This town was an administrative centre for the Assyrian occupation of Samaria, which Tiglath-pileser III (744–727 BC) had conquered. Although Megiddo continued to host settlement over the next three centuries, these later towns held diminishing importance. The place was finally abandoned around 400 BC. ∎

BABYLON

The German archaeologist Robert Koldewey excavated at Babylon for nearly two decades (1899–1917), uncovering many of the principal monuments of the city of Nebuchadnezzar. Thanks to Koldewey's labours, Babylon can today be regarded in a less rhetorical vein, as the first 'national' capital of southern Mesopotamia, the seat of Marduk, Babylonia's patron deity, and the home not just of Nebuchadnezzar (604–562 BC), but also of Hammurabi (1792–1750 BC), the law-giver.

During the first few centuries of the first millennium, Babylonia was at the nadir of its fortunes, suffering from severe political fragmentation, plague, famine, declining population, Bedouin raids and other calamities. Taking advantage of this weakness, the

Sited on a branch of the Euphrates River, 90 km south-west of Baghdad, Babylon attracted some of the earliest careful descriptions of ancient Mesopotamian sites. These accounts inevitably relied heavily on biblical references (including the allegorical Tower of Babel) and Greek writers like Herodotus. Thanks to these texts, Babylon was never forgotten, having passed into tradition as a place of oppression and exile.

resurgent Assyrians occupied Babylonia for over a century. Babylon was both the centre of the Assyrian occupation and a leader of resistance to it – it benefited from Assyrian building programmes, but was sacked in 689 BC after a failed revolt.

Fortune soon reversed the situation. The combined forces of the Babylonians, Medes and Scythians rose up and swept away the tattered remains of the Assyrian empire, sacking Nineveh in 612. The Babylonian king, Nabopolassar (625–605 BC), had been battling the Assyrian occupiers within his own homeland since taking the throne; he was now in a position to extend Babylon's sway into the post-Assyr-

Glazed moulded brick lions striding along Babylon's Processional Way.

Pieter Breughel's fanciful painting of the Tower of Babel bears only slight resemblance to Babylon's ziggurat.

ian power vacuum. His successor, Nebuchadnezzar (604–562 BC), accomplished this task, and in the process defeated the kingdom of Judah and carried many Jews into the Babylonian exile. But the seemingly powerful Babylonian empire proved a brittle creation, falling with stunning swiftness to the rising power of the eastern mountains, the Achaemenid Persians, in 539 BC. The Achaemenid kings continued to treat the city as an imperial centre, and often spent their winters there. The Greeks in their turn occupied Babylon, and Alexander the Great died there in 323 BC, after his return from India.

The high water table prevented the German archaeologists from uncovering Babylon's older phases, except for only a small area (known as the Merkes) where a deep hole reached levels that date back to the first few centuries of the second millennium (the Old Babylonian period, c. 2000–1600 BC). As a result, the early phases of the city's history remain poorly known. The cuneiform texts do allude to certain features of the town at various times. The place, albeit relatively unimportant, already existed at the beginning of the Akkadian period (c. 2330–2150 BC), when it contained at least two temples. Half a millennium later, Babylon was the royal seat of the most powerful dynasty of its time, that of Hammurabi, who managed to unite Babylonia and Assyria into a single, short-lived kingdom. The wealth of empire flowed into Babylon and doubtless underwrote the construction that graced the city. Texts of the period allude to Esagila, the temple of the chief god Marduk, and many other temples, as well as a cloister district and the city walls. A late thirteenth century BC description summarizes the main features of the city, naming eight gates through the city wall, ten quarters or districts within, and at least fifty-three temples plus other shrines and buildings.

Babylon was already large at the time of this description, but imperial attentions, first of Assyrian and then of Babylonian rulers, greatly enlarged and embellished the city. At its apogee, during Nebuchadnezzar's reign, the city spread over 8.5 sq km, making it the largest ancient Mesopotamian city, larger even than

Assyrian capitals like Nineveh (p. 106), and Nimrud (p. 102). The outer city wall, stretching some 18 km, presented a triple circuit of durable baked brick and rubble, 30 m wide, with towers marking regular intervals; a perimeter moat further strengthened this massive defensive arrangement. The Greek writer Herodotus described the wall as being so wide that a four-horse chariot could reverse direction on its top. A large walled compound, today called Tell Babil, sat in the outer wall's north-east corner, marking the location of Nebuchadnezzar's summer palace. But most of the city's main buildings lay within the inner city.

The inner city formed a long rectangle, more than 4 sq km in size, that straddled the Euphrates River. A pair of thick mudbrick

Moulded glazed brick creatures adorned the Ishtar Gate at Babylon.

walls, separated by a street, and an outer embankment and canal connected to the Euphrates marked off this inner precinct of the city. Within these walls the main streets formed an irregular grid oriented, in typical Babylonian fashion, more north-west/south-east and north-east/south-west than to the cardinal points. The German excavations led by Koldewey focused on the portion of the inner city on the east bank of the Euphrates: here lay the political and ritual centre of Nebuchadnezzar's empire.

The Processional Way provided the main axis for this ceremonial complex. The avenue, some 20 m wide and stretching 250 m south from the famous Ishtar Gate, ran between walls decorated with glazed bricks depicting lions and rosettes in low relief. The Ishtar Gate, named after the Babylonian goddess of love and of war, was a high-arched passage between heavy square towers set in the inner city wall. The German excavations found that the gate had passed through three distinct phases of construction, in which its decoration became more elaborate. In the final phase, the

RIGHT: Nebuchadnezzar's throne room, ornamented in the same manner, with lions and trees.
BELOW: An artist's impression of the Hanging Gardens of Babylon.

The artists of Babylon worked in other media, like stone used for recording land titles (kudurru). These 'boundary stones' bore both cuneiform text and carved symbols and figures.

gate's glazed brickwork represented white and yellow dragons and bulls moulded in low relief, marching across a blue background. The gate, 25 m high, sat on a platform 15 m above its surroundings, giving an impressive display of splendour and power to anyone seeking to enter the heart of the Babylonian capital.

Nebuchadnezzar's main palace lay just inside the Ishtar Gate, sprawling between the Processional Way and the river. The palace, also constructed on a 15 m high platform, focused on five large courtyards, around which blocks of halls and chambers sheltered the royal household and its activities. The throne room, over 50 m long, and fronting the central courtyard in the heart of the palace, was decorated with multicoloured glazed moulded bricks showing a procession of lions and stylized trees-of-life. A group of underground rooms with vaulted ceilings and equipped with wells and asphalt water-proofing form the palace's northwest corner, adjacent to the Ishtar Gate. Koldewey believed that these remains once supported the famous Hanging Gardens of Babylon, one of the seven wonders of the ancient world. This identification remains uncertain, and recent considerations of the evidence suggest that the hanging gardens were actually located in Nineveh (p. 106).

A kilometre further along, the Processional Way passed, on the left, a pair of enclosed plazas that contained Etemenanki and Esagila, the ritual centre of Babylonia. A street separating these two monuments ran from the Processional Way to the river, where a bridge (120 m long and supported by seven or more piers) permitted passage to the western half of the inner city. The Etemenanki, literally 'the house that is the foundation of heaven and earth', was a ziggurat, the stepped tower that inspired the biblical story about the Tower of Babel. Only the foundation wall was discovered in excavation (the structure had been dismantled), leaving the ziggurat's overall configuration in doubt. The bottom stage of the ziggurat formed a square, 91 m on each side, with the main staircase (9 m wide) mounting the structure from the south. Esagila, immediately to the south, was the temple of Marduk, the national god of Babylonia. The complex contained not merely the cult room for the statue of Marduk, but also made space for various other deities. Greek authors reported that the statue and other equipment of the Marduk cult used over twenty tons of gold, and that the rituals required over two tons of imported frankincense each year.

Babylon continued to serve as an important centre after the invading Persians swept away Nebuchadnezzar's empire in 539 BC. The Persians maintained Babylonian traditional temples, and supported the worship of the traditional gods. And when the Greeks in their turn took Mesopotamia two centuries later, they also tolerated the local cults and even contributed new buildings, including a theatre, to the city fabric. But the centres of power, whether political or cultural, had shifted away from the old Babylonian heartland. Occupation at Babylon continued, on a gradually reduced scale, through the Parthian occupation of Mesopotamia, but with ever attenuating connection to its own glorious past, before it became an abandoned mass of melted mudbrick. ∎

UGARIT

The most important period of occupation at Ugarit was during the Middle and Late Bronze Age, between around 1800 and 1200 BC. Two main sources of evidence are available to reconstruct everyday life in Ugarit: the archaeological remains and the many archives recovered from the site. These texts were written in Ugaritic (a Semitic language) using an early alphabetic script on clay tablets. The prosperity of the city is evident from the richness of many of the objects recovered from the settlement and its tombs. These include fine carved ivories, a range of elaborate bronzes (tripods, cast figurines of statuettes), and many imports from Egypt, Cyprus and the Aegean. The wealth of Ugarit was based on its importance as a trading port, favourably located on the intersection of land and sea routes between Anatolia, Mesopotamia, Syro-Palestine and the Mediterranean.

Ugarit was the capital of a small coastal kingdom. The royal dynasty of Ugarit was founded in the nineteenth or eighteenth century BC, and the names of some of the rulers are recorded on a badly preserved tablet, the King List of Ugarit. The king was

Twenty-five miles south of the mouth of the Orontes, on the coast of Syria, is an important *tell* (mound) site, Ras Shamra, and its associated harbour at Minet el-Beidha. These have been identified as the ancient kingdom of Ugarit, known from the Amarna letters (p. 17) (diplomatic correspondence of the mid fourteenth century BC between the Egyptian pharaoh and the rulers of the Near East). Continuously occupied from the neolithic period (sixth millennium BC) to the twelfth century BC, Ugarit then lay forgotten until it was rediscovered in 1928 by a farmer working in his fields.

responsible for the internal administration of the city, its legal, economic and military organization, and also external contacts – diplomatic and trading relations with other kings throughout the Near East, such as the Egyptian pharaoh and the king of Alashiya (probably Cyprus). The king also had a religious function: he was the intermediary between the people of Ugarit and their gods, and was himself a divine personage. The royal family lived in a large palace which commanded the northwest part of the *tell*. It was built in various stages between the fifteenth and thirteenth centuries BC, expanding in size in step with increasing administrative complexity and the corresponding growth of the king's court. The main entrance to the palace was approached by a flight of shallow steps, and was flanked by a pair of wooden columns. Inside there were six large courtyards, a number of smaller courts and an interior garden, each surrounded by suites of rooms. The palace was an imposing edifice, constructed of fine, cut-stone blocks. Traces of plaster were found on some of the internal walls, but there is no evidence that these were decorated with wall-paintings, unlike in contemporary palaces, such as at Alalakh, on the Orontes, and Knossos, on Crete.

There was a functional division of space within the palace. The royal family's private apartments were located on the upper storey, while the public areas, working space, guard rooms and storerooms were on the ground floor. The palace was the administrative hub of the kingdom and its economic centre, as is reflected by the five separate archives that have been found within its ruins, comprising commercial, administrative, legal and military documents. It also functioned as the ceremonial, diplomatic centre of the kingdom, where the king received visiting dignitaries and embassies from neighbouring rulers. Texts in Akkadian (the diplomatic language

View of the site of Ugarit, with tombs in the foreground.

The site of Ugarit was very wealthy, as is reflected by the fine jewellery found at the site, such as this gold and bead necklace.

of the ancient Near East), Cypro-Minoan, Hittite and Egyptian reflect the wide range of diplomatic and economic ties beyond the kingdom of Ugarit.

The archives give a clear picture of the religious life of the inhabitants of Ugarit. The head of the Ugaritic pantheon was the god El, but numerous other gods were also worshipped, prominent amongst them Baal (the god of rain who brought fertility to the arid land of Ugarit). The city was dominated by two stone-built temples on the acropolis in the north-east part of the *tell*. The larger of the two was dedicated to Baal and the other to Dagan (also associated with fertility). The temples conform to a common plan found throughout the Levant at this time. There was an outer enclosure with an altar for sacrifice, and an impressive temple building, built of cut-stone masonry. The main temple building had an inner room which would have housed the cult statue of the god and an outer room for cult activity. But the focus of communal religious activity would have been in the open area in front of the temple building and within the enclosure wall, where the sacrifices were carried out. Sacrifices to the gods were varied and included animals (sheep and lambs, oxen, kids) and agricultural produce (oil and honey).

Between the two temples there was a large building of dressed stone masonry, comprising a series of paved rooms around a central courtyard. A bronze hoard or foundation deposit found beneath the threshold included a tripod decorated with miniature pomegranates and five bronze tools inscribed 'chief of the priests'. This identified the building as the house of the high priest of Ugarit. Three archives were found in the house, including numerous mythological texts and also writing exercises that were used to train scribes. These archives indicate that writing was more than a mere administrative tool, and that literacy was widespread amongst the higher echelons of Ugaritic society and had a religious as well as a bureaucratic function.

The residential areas of Ugarit are located to the east of the palace (the homes of the wealthier citizens) and on the southern slopes of the acropolis below the temples (the homes of the craftsmen of the town). The houses are grouped along straight streets, and conform to the same basic plan: courtyard houses with subterranean family tomb vaults. As a rule they had bathrooms and sanitation. The scale and sophistication of the architecture of the houses near the palace, belonging to the wealthier citizens, is remarkable. They had a stone façade and an upper storey, where the family lived, while the ground floor was a general reception and work area (similar in concept to the palace). Some houses were very large. The house of Rap'anu, for example, had over thirty rooms on the ground floor. Private libraries for private and official correspondence indicate a general level of literacy among the wider citizenship of Ugarit, and no doubt facilitated the trading activities of the wealthy merchants.

Ugarit was a flourishing centre of trade and industry, and in the fifteenth century a new quarter was built near the harbour. This was residential, industrial and commercial. Metal foundries have been found in this area as well as at the main *tell* site. Warehouses near the harbour housed imports and exports. One contained rows of transport amphorae, either for oil or wine, very possibly local produce. Texts refer to the production of both olive oil and wine at Ugarit, and an olive-press has been found with presses and vats *in situ*. Other traded commodities included grain, textiles and luxuries (cosmetics, ivories, metalwork). ■

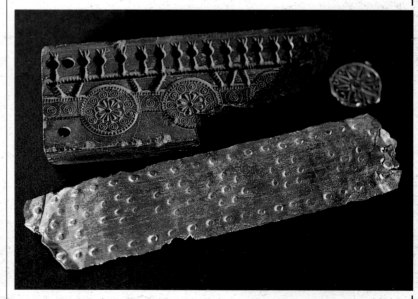

Stone moulds used to make this fine gold jewellery were found at Ugarit.

BOGAZKÖY

Near Eastern politics during the Late Bronze Age resembled in many ways those of more recent times, as powerful kingdoms played 'the great game' in a struggle for control over the eastern Mediterranean seaboard. Among the contestants figured several still familiar names, like Egypt and Assyria, and also some less well-known players like the Mitanni and the Hittites. For over two centuries the Hittites more than held their own against all comers, and gained dominion over large portions of Anatolia and western Syria. The Hittite kings built their capital city Hattusha, the modern Bogazköy, in central Anatolia, on the lavish scale fit for a Bronze Age superpower.

Hattusha lies about 150 km east of Ankara, nestled in the hills through which flow tributaries in the Kizil Irmak (or Halys River) drainage. The ruined city sprawls across a rising slope, gaining some 300 m in height over a distance of 2 km. Although sloping gently from south to north, the eastern and western sides are more precipitous, a natural protection further strengthened by strong walls whose outer circuit encloses about 200 hectares. The city incorporated several craggy hills that interrupt this slope, including Büyükkale on the east-central edge of the city where the Hittites established a royal citadel.

The Hittites, who spoke an Indo-European language, were relative newcomers to Anatolia, having arrived during the middle of the third millennium BC. Hittite tradition credits Labarna with establishing the Hittite occupation of Bogazköy, and beginning the period known as the Old Kingdom (*c.* 1650–1500 BC). His dynasty soon trod the world stage, when Hattushili I expanded Hittite power into northern Syria, and Mursili I raided and sacked Babylon in 1595, thereby bringing to an end Hammurabi's dynasty (see p. 93). But this experiment with regional domination ended in regicide and civil strife; the Hittites withdrew to the highland fastness of central Anatolia for a period.

The coronation of Suppiluliuma I, an energetic ruler, changed matters. Again expanding into north Syria, over the next two centuries the Hittites confronted the other great Near Eastern powers of the time. This New Kingdom period (*c.* 1420–1200 BC) is best known from the voluminous written sources that the Hittites themselves left behind. The archives at Hattusha were composed in many different languages. Scribes used cuneiform to record several Indo-European languages, including Hittite, and other tongues also found their way into the records; Akkadian was used for international affairs and in the transmission of Mesopotamian literature. The archives present a multifaceted view of the élite circles of Hittite society. Formal state records – royal decrees, treaties, law codes, annals and letters – and administrative records (for instance inventories, censuses, land grants) are abundant, as are literary works, epics, myths, many religious texts (festivals and rituals of the cultic calendar, prayers) and school texts. The archives even include procedural texts of magical incantations for getting rid of ghosts, winning love, and so forth, and more practical manuals on horse-training.

Although the evident massive stone architecture of the site was the work of the New Kingdom builders, the German excavations since 1906 indicate that Bogazköy was first occupied near the end of the Early Bronze Age, shortly before 2000 BC. The initial settlement was small, and centred on Büyükkale and the adjacent portions of the Lower Town. During the eighteenth century BC the town was part of the Assyrian karum-system, in which merchant families from the city-state of Assur in northern Mesopotamia established business offices in various towns of eastern and central Anatolia, seeking profits by trafficking silver, copper, tin, textiles and other goods. These foreign merchants, identified by their private

Copious storage facilities in the Great Temple at Hattusha kept this Hittite institution running.

archives of cuneiform tablets, lived in the Lower Town, and probably entered into formal treaty arrangements with the local ruler, who doubtless resided in Büyükkale. The Old Kingdom city grew larger, and a casemate wall, some 8 m wide and erected on a wide embankment, now enclosed the Lower City.

The wealth and prestige of the New Kingdom empire encouraged the Hittite Great Kings to undertake massive building projects that doubled the size of Hattusha, when the Upper City was constructed up-slope from the older Lower City. On Büyükkale, the new palace complex now sprawled over the entire citadel, within the new casemate wall and three strengthened gates. The palace incorporated several very spacious open courtyards, set at different levels. Several wings of the palace buildings contained only parallel rows of long narrow chambers on their ground floors, seemingly the royal storehouses. Stairs led to a second floor, where columns may have allowed a more open plan, including the proposed location of the royal audience hall. Archives were kept in several different places, one in a colonnaded library and another in a second-floor depository from where they fell to the ground when the building burned.

The kings built other palaces, especially in the new Upper City. Nisantepe, a rocky outcrop south-west of Büyükkale, contained a palace formed as four wings around a central area. The building seems to represent a halentuwa-house, a place halfway between a palace and a temple where a king becomes ritually worthy of making cultic observances. The king reached this place along a viaduct that led directly from a gate in the Büyükkale wall to Nisantepe across the hollow that separated these two promontories. The viaduct, at least 85 m long and 10 m high, is the oldest example of this type of construction known in the Near East. The Upper City as a whole seems to have been mostly devoted to temple architecture and to cult observances and festivals.

German archaeologists have uncovered over two dozen temples within the Upper City. While most of these structures are modestly sized (covering *c.* 500–1500 sq m), several are considerably larger and more elaborate. For example, Temple 5 has a floor plan (extending over some 3000 sq m) that resembles in many aspects palace architecture elsewhere in the city. The temple enclosure wall also encompassed an open air altar and three single chamber structures ornamented with reliefs of the royal personage. The temple seems dedicated to a royal mortuary cult, focused on three thirteenth-century kings, with an attached residence.

Temple 5 lay near the King's Gate, named after a male figure brandishing a weapon, carved in relief on to the flat surface of an inner door jamb. This entrance was one of three ceremonial gates that pierced the southern end of the Upper City wall. The Sphinx Gate lay at the highest, southernmost point of the Upper City, where an artificial buttress enhanced the hill slope. Two huge upright stones, each ornamented with the head and forequarters of a sphinx carved in relief, formed the gate's outer portal. A long tunnel ran under the entire gate complex, its hidden entrance allowing unobserved passage through the defences. The third gate, named the Lion Gate for the similarly rendered head and forequarters of this beast on the outer jambs, pierced the south-west stretch of the Upper City wall. Cultic texts indicate that these gates, the city wall and the temples formed a vast ceremonial complex, in which ritual celebrants went through the King's Gate, along a processional way that skirted the outside of

The Lion Gate into the Upper Town at Hattusha.

the city gate to the Sphinx Gate, and then on to the Lion Gate and back into the city.

The Great Temple (Temple 1) in the Lower City reinforces this impression of pervasive religion. This temple presents a pair of cult rooms, side by side, for worship of the two principal deities, the storm god Hatti and the sun goddess Arinna. These cult rooms stand at the back of the temple, reached only after passing through the portal complex, then the long central courtyard, and through a colonnaded vestibule to small anterooms. Additional rooms and corridors frame the central courtyard. This temple building stands at the centre of a larger complex, where blocks of long storerooms appear on all four sides of the temple plaza. Another compound of offices and storerooms stood across a street to the south-west. The temple complex housed a large community of temple personnel that included not just priests of the cult but also musicians, weavers, potters, smiths, carpenters, stonecutters and other craftsmen. The storerooms came equipped with large jars for holding the grain, oils, wine and other produce that kept this community going.

Hattusha was more than a royal-ritual city, and the German archaeologists have uncovered residential quarters at various points around it. Even the predominantly cultic Upper City contained residential areas, and even some industrial quarters (represented by smelting ovens and pottery kilns). The most extensively exposed residential district lies between the Great Temple and the Lower Town wall, where twisting streets form irregular blocks of ramshackle houses. But the lives of these more ordinary residents of Hattusha remain less well known than those of the kingly court and the temple households.

The cataclysmic upheavals that came with the twelfth century completely changed the political and social landscape of western Asia, sweeping away the Bronze Age world. The Hittite empire collapsed, and Hattusha was sacked and abandoned by marauding barbarians from the Black Sea coast. ■

NIMRUD

Nimrud, the ancient Kalhu and biblical Calah, holds an honourable place in the history of archaeology, being the site where Austen Henry Layard first brought back to life the spectacle of ancient Assyria, edifying and titillating his Victorian audience with gruesome corroboration of biblical history. Layard excavated much of Assurnasirpal's palace, and opened other palaces and temples. Since then,

Assyria is most remembered in the Bible for the empire of the late eighth and seventh centuries BC, when Tiglath-pileser III and his successors controlled a vast region between the Iranian mountains on the east and the Mediterranean Sea and Egypt on the west. But Assyria also created a short-lived empire a century earlier, when ambitious rulers like Assurnasirpal II (883–859 BC) and his son Shalmaneser III (858–824) campaigned almost yearly through neighbouring regions. These ninth-century kings, and Assurnasirpal especially, seemed to revel in their cruel treatment of vanquished foes. The same texts linger over the spoils that the victorious Assyrian kings carried home from the wars.

quered peoples whom he uprooted from their native lands. But archaeologists have been disproportionately attracted to excavating the grand buildings and rich artwork of temples and palaces – almost nothing is known of the more ordinary houses and streets of the city.

The royal architecture was centred in two mounded areas, today called the citadel and the arsenal, each with its own surrounding wall. Other Assyrian

archaeologists have repeatedly returned to the site, most notably Sir Max Mallowan after the Second World War, when he discovered important archives of cuneiform tablets and many beautiful carved ivories in the royal precinct. Most recently, Iraqi archaeologists uncovered spectacularly wealthy royal graves beneath the floor of Assurnasirpal's palace.

This century and a half of archaeological investigations provides a clear picture of only some aspects of the city. Surface finds of prehistoric pottery show the first settlement was long before the imperial Assyrian city. But most of the known architecture is the responsibility of ninth-century Assyrian kings, who built this city as the new capital of their aggressively expanding empire. The city walls enclose 3.6 sq km, almost all of which was given over to the residences, workshops, streets, open spaces and gardens of the lower town. Many of the people who lived here must have been foreigners, for Assurnasirpal populated his new city with con-

capitals duplicate this city plan – two separate walled compounds, one devoted to royal and cultic administration and the other to military affairs, both set in the perimeter wall of the much larger lower city. The arsenal (Fort Shalmaneser) sat in the south-east corner of the town. Its wall encircled 30 hectares, where stood a palatial building (itself covering about 6 hectares) within a parade ground. The archives found in this building refer to troops, horses and stockpiles of arms, and give details about the organization of the Assyrian cavalry. Other records deal with tax collection and legal affairs (like loans of silver made by temples), indicating that the 'arsenal' staff carried out many functions in addition to their military duties. Indeed, the queen maintained a household, managed by its own staff in a partially segregated area of the building.

The citadel, placed in the town's south-west corner, was the royal seat, graced by multiple palaces, temples, a ziggurat (the staged tower typical of Mesopotamian cities) and other monumental buildings. This royal precinct was substantial, its 20 hectares the size of a respectable town. Here Assurnasirpal built a palace, as he put it, 'as [his] royal residence (and) for [his] lordly leisure for eternity'. He also built the temple of Nabu, the patron god of scribes, where vassal treaties that subordinated defeated lands were stored. Later kings built other palaces in the citadel, even after Sargon had moved the Assyrian capital to Khorsabad. In effect, the citadel was jam-packed with the architecture, both secular and ritual, of the imperial government.

Assurnasirpal's palace, which archaeologists also call the Northwest Palace, was the architectural centrepiece of the city. It lay at the western edge of the citadel, adjacent to that structure's massive mudbrick walls (37 m thick and at least 15 m high). Even now not completely excavated, the building stretched 200 m in length and at least 120 m in width. The ground plan reflects the organization evident in palaces from other Assyrian cities like Nineveh (p. 106), with a clear separation between administrative offices and storerooms in the north wing, and private apartments and possibly the harem in the south wing. The central rooms, between the two wings, were given over to more public displays of power and regal authority, including the throne room. Massive

This elaborately carved and ornamented ivory plaque was found at the bottom of a well within Assurnasirpal's palace at Nimrud.

The 'Black Obelisk' of Shalmaneser III, at Nimrud, records the submission to Assyrian authority of Jehu, king of Israel, and delivery of tribute.

guardian figures of human headed bulls flanked important doorways, to ward off evil.

At conspicuous places throughout the palace, Assurnasirpal placed cuneiform inscriptions that lauded his military victories and described his building at Nimrud. These descriptions mention the fragrant woods such as cedar, cypress and juniper that lined the palace's brick walls, and refer to the giant guardian figures at doorways and the wall reliefs that recount Assurnasirpal's

victories. The king also exulted in his pleasure gardens, planted with strange trees taken from the various parts of his dominion, where 'fragrance pervades the walkways [and] streams of water (as numerous) as the stars of heaven flow'. One inscription recounts the lavish ten-day inaugural festivities, attended by nearly 70,000 people, to mark the completion of Assurnasirpal's new palace.

The south wing of Assurnasirpal's palace concealed spectacularly rich burials of royal women and others of the court, who were placed in vaulted chambers below the tiled floors of certain rooms. One such tomb held the body of Mulissu-mukannishat Ninua, a queen of Assurnasirpal. Hundreds of golden ornaments,

including a crown, had been placed in three bronze coffins to accompany her. The coffin in a second tomb held the remains of two (or three) royal women who lived over a century later. Thousands of objects covered the women, prominent among which were exquisitely wrought golden jewellery and ornaments, often embellished with inlay – a fringe of flowers, a mesh headband with pendant medallions, anklets, bracelets and rings; tiny gold flowers had been sewn on to the burial garments. Gold was also used for various bottles, goblets, pots, and toiletries. Other materials appear among this mass of gold, like an ivory box, a bronze mirror and glass vessels. A third tomb contained a middle-aged man, with whom was a wealth of gold jewellery, a silver bowl and other items of ivory and semi-precious stones.

These rich burials give a vivid illustration of Assyrian wealth, gained through conquest, loot and tribute. The grave goods also betray the effects of empire on Assyrian arts and crafts. For example, one gold bowl is decorated with boats in a papyrus marsh, an Egyptian theme rendered in Phoenician style. Carved ivory objects, including boxes, bowls, small figures and furniture ornaments, have been recovered in large numbers from many buildings in both the citadel and arsenal. The ivories reflect styles and themes from several different regional traditions, including Phoenician (with a strong Egyptian influence), North Syrian and Assyrian. The Assyrian kings often listed ivory-decorated furniture among booty seized from conquered places, while foreign craftsmen laboured alongside Assyrian sculptors in the workshops of Nimrud. However violent their origin, both the carved ivories and the golden jewellery reveal an appreciation for delicate art, and help balance the impression of Assyrian brutality.

Nimrud remained the Assyrian capital until king Sargon (721–705 BC) built a new city at Khorsabad to the north. Although no longer the imperial centre, Nimrud remained an important administrative centre. Destroyed by Assyria's enemies during the calamitous end of the empire (612 BC), Nimrud housed later occupation, the most notable of which came after Alexander the Great, the Greek empire-builder without equal. But Nimrud never again held the world stage as it had when Assurnasirpal and Shalmaneser asserted Assyrian dominion over so many unfortunate neighbours during the ninth century. ■

NINEVEH

During its eight decades at the centre of Assyrian power, Nineveh grew to an immense size, feeding on the benefits of tribute and looting that gave it such an evil reputation for later generations. Archaeologists have worked at Nineveh since the 1840s, when Paul Emile Botta and Austen Henry Layard invented Mesopotamian archaeology. Their labours, and the work of those that followed, exposed the spectacular palaces and temples of Assyrian kings, revealing their wealth and sophistication, and also their ingenuity and even sensitivity.

Nineveh sprawls along the east bank of the Tigris River, opposite the modern town of Mosul in northern Iraq. A small stream, the Khosr, meanders through the city before flowing into the Tigris. Most of the ruined city is low and flat, being demarcated most obviously by the massive city walls that stretch some 5 km and enclose about 7.5 sq km, making Nineveh one of the largest ancient Near Eastern cities until Classical times. The walls formed a double cordon, the inner mudbrick curtain standing perhaps 25 m high; the outer wall was lower but stronger, being made of

Nineveh, queen city of the Near East, served as the capital of the Assyrian empire at the height of its power. The Assyrian kings made a habit of moving their courts to new places – Nimrud (p. 102) had been the capital until Sargon II (721–705 BC) shifted it to his new foundation at Khorsabad, partly to get away from the entrenched special interests that inevitably had developed at the previous capital. Sargon's successor, Sennacherib (704–681 BC), seeking similar fresh air, then moved the royal seat to Nineveh, where it remained until the end of the Assyrian empire.

limestone. A series of moats and ditches lay beyond the walls, encircling the city. Fifteen gates at various points around its circumference pierced the walls, giving access to the lower town. On the western side of the city, the walls ran between two mounded areas, spaced about 1 km apart. Today called Kuyunjik and Nebi Yunus, these mounds mark the location of two older, once separate towns on the Tigris River.

Unlike other new Assyrian capitals (Khorsabad and Nimrud) which were created upon small, unimportant places, Nineveh's history extends back into the darkness of prehistory. Deep excavation near the Ishtar Temple exposed superimposed occupation levels that go back to 6000 BC. The excavations show that the town had already grown to cover most of the Kuyunjik area by about 3500 BC. By the mid third millennium BC, cities had arisen in Assyria and North Syria, and Nineveh was surely among their number. Although overshadowed by the city at Ashur to the south, Nineveh was renowned for its Temple of Ishtar: the earliest textual allusion to this regionally important cult refers to the temple's construction by Manishtushu (c. 2270–2255 BC), a ruler of the first imperial dynasty of Mesopotamia, the Akkadians. A life-size copper head of an Akkadian king, perhaps of the dynasty's founder, Sargon (c. 2330–2280 BC), one of the treasures of Mesopotamian art, was found at Nineveh. In the thirteenth century BC, kings of the first Assyrian empire erected palaces on the Kuyunjik mound, even while Ashur remained the principal city of the region. These adornments in turn attracted a growing population, which began settling in the flat areas around Kuyunjik early in the first millennium BC. But Sennacherib's new capital remade the city. He built the walls and laid out the lower town. More spectacularly, Sennacherib and

LEFT: The Kuyunjik mound at Nineveh.
RIGHT: Assyrian palaces were carved with stone reliefs, showing royal deeds. Assurbanipal is shown in this lion-hunting scene.

his successors Esarhaddon and Assurbanipal built palaces, temples and other monumental buildings on Kuyunjik, and the 'arsenal' on Nebi Yunus. This tripartite division of royal precinct, arsenal and large lower town was a standard configuration for royal Assyrian cities, repeated in places like Nimrud and Khorsabad.

The 'arsenal' at Nineveh remains basically unexcavated. Although probably analogous to the better known Nimrud arsenal (see p. 102), only Sennacherib's inscriptions attest to the construction of the arsenal 'for setting in order the camp, mustering the steeds, the mules, the chariots, the harnesses, the battle equipment and the spoils of the enemy, every type of thing which Ashur, the king of the gods, has granted me as my regal lot, for exercising the horses (and) for manoeuvring the chariots'.

The royal buildings of Kuyunjik offered some of the most important discoveries of Assyrian archaeology. Assurbanipal (668–627 BC), the last great Assyrian king, built a palace on the

The Kuyunjik mound excavations provide basic details for this artist's rendering of how Nineveh may have looked in the seventh century BC.

north edge of the mound. He was a cultured man, one of only three rulers in Mesopotamian history to claim the ability to read and write. As part of his activities, he collected an enormous library, seeking out antique 'books' from Babylonia. When Assurbanipal's North Palace was excavated during the nineteenth century, the newly discovered library provided a treasury of Mesopotamian literature and learning. The North Palace also contained some of the finest decorative art in the Assyrian repertoire, including famous scenes such as the royal lion hunt.

Sennacherib's palace, which he described as an 'eternal foundation', was built along the basic plan evident in other Assyrian palaces and even in large private houses. The palace, which seems to have been an astonishing half a kilometre long, was arranged in two sections, each centred on a large courtyard. The outer section, immediately available after passing through the ceremonial portal, contained the palace's public face with its administrative offices, service rooms, storerooms, stables, and similarly functional spaces of a large institutional building. The inner section held the private suites and chambers of the royal family and its intimate attendants. Positioned in the intermediate portion of the palace, serving both to join and to buffer the public and private spheres, sat the throne room and other large quarters emblematic of royal authority and prestige. Enormous stone statues of human-headed winged bulls guarded the main doorways of the palace. Alabaster panels, carved in scenes and descriptions of the king's deeds in warfare, hunting, ritual observances and feasting, ornamented the walls of the ceremonial rooms and passages. Layard estimated that he uncovered nearly 3 km of these carvings in the Sennacherib palace alone. A kind of visual propaganda more immediately comprehensible than the accompanying cuneiform inscriptions, the wall reliefs showed the king as the source of Assyrian power and prestige, and also as the life-giver and the guarantor of order in the cosmos.

Sennacherib also boasted of the gardens he created within the city. Royal gardens, usually planted with strange trees from the various parts of the empire, were a common feature of royal Assyrian towns, and usually required special waterworks to keep

Excavations have allowed Iraqi archaeologists to reconstruct the outer defensive line, with its towers and crenellated parapets.

Assyrian stoneworkers often captured individual moments in expressive detail in wall reliefs, like the dying lions in Assurbanipal's royal hunt.

them flourishing. Sennacherib brought water via a system of canals, aqueducts and tunnels from 55 km away, and then raised the water to the garden on top of the Kuyunjik mound with an invention (for which Sennacherib claimed credit) that seems to have anticipated, by several centuries, Archimedes' screw. The effect of the terraced garden with its wonderful watering system, plus the perennial confusion of Nineveh with Babylon among both biblical and Classical authors, makes plausible the recent suggestion that the famous Hanging Gardens of Babylon, one of the seven wonders of the ancient world, were really in Nineveh.

Outside these royal precincts, some aspects of more ordinary life in the lower town have also come to light, thanks to recent surveys and excavations. In its early phases, the lower town seems to have focused on an area just north of Kuyunjik, where several centuries of building and other activities created a low rise. The well-to-do of Sennacherib's city built houses on this gentle rise, placing them above the more common masses elsewhere in the lower city. Here the houses focused on large central courtyards, surrounded by blocks of rooms often at least two storeys tall. The streets were often wide, doubtless giving an airy feel to the quarter. Further north, by contrast, the buildings were crowded together, and plentiful industrial debris attests to the concentrated activities of potters and metalworkers.

Nineveh fell in 612 BC to the allied Medes and Babylonians who had risen to overthrow the Assyrian yoke. The violence of this cataclysm is vividly illustrated by the dozen skeletons in a tumble just inside a city gate, the bodies of Ninevites slain in a hail of arrows while fleeing the final assault. The destruction of imperial Nineveh was a fitting end to this 'blood-stained city, steeped in deceit, full of pillage, never empty of prey', in the triumphant words of the biblical prophet Nahum. ∎

PERSEPOLIS

During the middle decades of the sixth century BC, Cyrus the Persian (559–530 BC) defeated the other great powers of the time and created an empire that extended from Bactria in Central Asia to the Mediterranean Sea. His successor, Cambyses (529–522 BC), added Egypt to the empire, but soon after died while dealing with an attempted *coup d'etat*. Darius I (521–486 BC) came to power despite dubious claims to the throne. His uneasiness at the situation is reflected in the defensiveness of language in his apologetic autobiography ('according to righteousness have I walked; neither to weak nor to strong have I done wrong'). As part of his campaign to legitimate his newly won position, he established a new royal seat to replace the traditional Achaemenid centre at Parsagadae, where his great predecessor Cyrus was buried. The new capital, Persepolis (the Greek name, 'city of the Persians', for a place the Persians themselves called Parsa), lay beneath a range

The Achaemenid Persians, familiar to the western historical consciousness through Classical eyes after the attempted conquest of Greece during the fifth century BC, created an empire that stretched from Central Asia and northern India to the Aegean and Egypt. The Persians also created a new imperial sensibility, by combining already antique Mesopotamian themes of power with Classical Greek grace, all within the fabric of their own Iranian heritage. One very impressive result of this synthesis was Persepolis, the imperial seat in south-west Iran, whose stark beauty of immense scale, vivid carved scenes of courtly ceremony, and ranks of broken pillars marks one of the world's archaeological treasures.

of hills at the eastern edge of the Marv Dasht, a broad plain in the Fars province of modern Iran. Darius began to build in roughly 513 BC, and construction continued under the reigns of his son Xerxes I (485–465 BC) and grandson Artaxerxes II (464–424 BC). Some building was carried out in a more desultory way until the reign of Artaxerxes III (358–338 BC), soon before Alexander the Great swept away the Persian empire.

This new city centred on an enormous stone terrace that covered 450 by 300 m (or about 13 hectares) and rose 14 m above the surrounding plain. A massive double return staircase gave access to the platform at its north-west side. The Gate of All Lands stood opposite the top of the terrace staircase. A square structure with four interior columns that soared 12 m into the air, this imposing gate presented three doorways that directed traffic from the terrace staircase on the west towards the east or south into the two halves of the place. A pair of enormous bulls, over 6 m high, flanked the outer portal, and a pair of human-headed winged bulls the inner portals; this deliberate recollection of Assyrian palace decoration laid implicit claim to the legacy of Near Eastern imperial power.

The south portal faced the principal public building at Persepolis, the *apadana* or audience hall. This structure sat on its own stone podium, 110 m to a side and 2.6 m high. The hall itself formed a 60 m square, with 5 m mudbrick walls. Inside the hall, six rows of six columns supported the 19 m high ceiling, the beams of which were cedar. Deep colonnaded porticoes fronted the hall on three sides. On the west, the portico faced the edge of the main terrace, overlooking the plain. The north and east porticoes were reached by several staircases that climbed the *apadana* podium, each portico possessing a central pair of converging staircases plus single ones at either end. The north and east façades of the *apadana* podium are decorated with figures carved in relief, some of the finest examples of Achaemenid Persian art. The reliefs portray twenty-three pairs of delegates from the different parts of the empire, wearing their characteristic native clothing and bearing tribute gifts for the king, who is shown with the crown prince giving audience. In the background march the royal guard and officers of the court. These scenes are often held to represent the celebration of the New Year's festival.

Darius built a palace tucked against the south-west side of the *apadana*, next to the western edge of the main terrace. Like the *apadana*, the palace sat on its own podium with converging central staircases on its west side. Suites of rooms flanked the

Although Alexander the Great burned Persepolis to the ground, he could not destroy the enduring majesty of this place, looking out on to the Marv Dasht plain beyond.

The rock-cut tombs of Persian kings at Naqsh-i Rustam now stand empty, long since looted of their treasures.

spaciously pillared central hall. The building is remarkable today for the stonework that framed doors, windows and niches in walls otherwise built of brick, and especially for the door jambs decorated with figures of the king as hero struggling with real or mythical animals. Xerxes constructed a palace for himself near the southern end of the main terrace. Also on a separate podium, the building is larger than Darius' palace, but is laid out along similar lines. Flanking Xerxes' palaces on two sides are suites of columned rooms, arranged along a central corridor. This complex is traditionally, albeit contentiously, identified as Xerxes' harem.

Separated from the *apadana* area by a casemate wall, and accessible through the Gate of All Lands, the eastern half of the main terrace contained additional, less distinguished buildings. Foremost among these is the Hall of One Hundred Columns, an

LEFT: The cedar beams that roofed the great Persian pillared halls ran across impost blocks decorated with the heads and torsos of various animals like bulls and lions; the imaginary creature depicted on this block combines an eagle and a lion.

BELOW: The stone carvers at Persepolis adopted the antique Near Eastern motif of combatant animals, here a lion attacking a bull on the steps of the Triplyon, a structure that separated public space from more private quarters.

RIGHT: The Persian king was frequently depicted distinctly larger than his attendants, who protected his comforts with parasol and fly-whisk.

audience hall that Artaxerxes I finished. The so-called Treasury is tucked into the south-east corner of the site, a solid complex of pillared halls from which modern excavations recovered an archive of clay tablets.

Persepolis cannot be reckoned a city in the usual sense, for the place seems inadequately endowed with basic necessities like kitchens, toilets and drains. The buildings on the terrace seem to have functioned more as a ceremonial centre than the royal seat. The Persian kings were a peripatetic lot, even when not on campaign, and often moved residence according to the season. Susa, an ancient city in south-east Iran at the edge of the Mesopotamian plain, was a preferred capital, and Babylon (p. 92), also often hosted the royal household. And even as a ceremonial centre, Persepolis had to share duties with the older Parsagadae, where coronations of the Achaemenid kings continued to be held, thus harking back to the foundation of empire.

A permanent, even large, population, may have occupied less ostentatious quarters on the plain in front of the Persepolis terrace. An archive of administrative tablets records the disbursements of rations to workmen at Persepolis (as well as shipments of foodstuffs between towns around Persepolis). Near the end of Xerxes' reign, the number of workmen registered in the ration lists totals around 1300 individuals. These men plus their families surely lived outside the monumental buildings of state. Remains of buildings have occasionally been reported from the plain below the terrace, but little systematic information is available to show the extent of this settlement. None the less, an inscribed pillar base implies that Xerxes had a palace there, suggesting that even the royal entourage lived on the flats during its periodic visits, and used the monumental buildings on the terrace only for specific ceremonial occasions.

One such was the burial of newly dead Achaemenid kings. At a place called Naqsh-i Rustam, 6 km north of Persepolis, the tombs of four kings, beginning with Darius himself, are cut into a cliff face. The façades of these tombs are ornamented with a carved representation of a colonnaded building with an elaborate niched doorway. Above the building is a depiction of the king worshipping at an altar while being supported by figures of people from different parts of the empire. Although long since looted of their contents, the burial chambers in the rock doubtless held treasures worthy of the dead king.

The end of Persepolis was also the end of the Persian empire. Xerxes had tried to add Greece to the Persian dominion. Although failing (leaving behind the legacy of Thermopylae, Marathon and Salamis as the struggle for freedom in the face of overwhelming odds), Xerxes did succeed in occupying Athens for a period, when he burned the Parthenon (thereby requiring the rebuilding of the temple that survives today). Alexander the Great, the youthful king of Macedonia, returned the favour over a century later, when he invaded Asia and defeated the Persian king, campaigning into Central Asia and north-western India. Alexander occupied Persepolis in 330 BC, looting the place of its stored wealth. And after a night of drunken revelry, Alexander and his captains put the place to the torch, in revenge for the burning of Athens 150 years earlier. ■

PERGAMON

Pergamon was a centre of literature, art and science, whilst its sculptors influenced the development of Hellenistic sculpture throughout Asia Minor. Initially an ally of Rome in Asia, Attalus III bequeathed his kingdom to the Romans in 133 BC, and a few years later Pergamon and its territory effectively became the newly created province of Asia.

The emergence of Pergamon is one of the outstanding success stories of the Hellenistic world. It was of no importance before Lysimachos, one of Alexander the Great's successors, established his treasury there; but when he died, Philetairos took over the wealth and turned Pergamon into his powerbase. The dynasty, which he established ruled western and southern Asia Minor for 130 years. Successive kings also transformed the city into one of the most splendid architectural and cultural centres of the Hellenistic east.

into Asia a generation before, and effectively saved Hellenistic civilization in Asia Minor.

The site of Pergamon is undoubtedly one of the most impressive of the region. Situated inland between two tributaries of the river Caicus in modern Turkey, the citadel of Pergamon sits on the ridge of a mountain which rises over 355 m above sea level, and is virtually sheer

Before Lysimachos, one of Alexander's successor generals, chose Pergamon to be the location of his treasury, the city was of no consequence. When Lysimachos died in battle in 281 BC, Philetairos, the man whom Lysimachos had placed in charge of the treasure, kept control of Pergamon and the treasury and established an independent kingdom. Pergamon's greatest success came in 230 BC when Attalus I, the first of the dynasty to use the title 'king', defeated the plundering Gallic tribes who had crossed

on all sides except to the south. Here, Lysimachos' wealth, the natural resources of the kingdom, and the booty which accrued from their expansionist policies, were utilised to spectacular effect by the Attalids. King Eumenes II in particular, who reigned during the period 197–159 BC, extended the city down the slope away from the citadel and transformed it into one of the most beautiful cities of the Greek world, creating a monumental and worthy capital for his kingdom.

The main civic buildings are set on a series of large artificially constructed terraces. The structures, which include the king's palace, an arsenal, a *temenos* (sacred precinct) dedicated to the ruler cult, the library and a precinct to Athena, are arranged fan-like around the imposing theatre, which itself gives commanding views of the countryside around.

As patrons of the arts and of culture in general, the kings of Pergamon generously sponsored educational institutions such as the philosophical schools of Athens. The Attalid court attracted many of the outstanding and distinguished scholars and intellectuals of the day. Leading scientists, poets, teachers and philosophers were drawn to the city. Moreover, the Attalids themselves were avid collectors of books and manuscripts and, in consequence, the library on the citadel was particularly impressive. It was claimed that the total number of books in the library was 200,000 (although the existing building, as it stands, only has room for approximately 17,000), and so seriously rivalled the great library of Alexandria (p. 40), until the collection was removed by Mark Antony and given to Cleopatra.

The jealousy between Alexandria and Pergamon, it is claimed, helped the latter city to develop parchment as a medium for writing. The story (albeit erroneous), goes that Ptolemy of Egypt restricted the export of papyrus in order to try to restrict Pergamon's growing importance as a place of learning and repository of manuscripts. This restriction forced the Pergamenes to resort to writing on skins and bind them as books rather than rolling the texts as with papyrus.

The interest of the Attalids in the education and training of the youth of the city is also seen in the construction of a gymnasium below the citadel. This imposing building, measuring about 200

LEFT: Curates Street, Ephesos. Street paving became common in the cities of the Roman Empire.
RIGHT: The acropolis of Pergamon with the theatre in the foreground.

by 150m, is the largest gymnasium in the Greek world. It was constructed on three levels, with each section assigned to a specific age group – 'boys', 'youths' and 'young men'. Within the complex there were exercise yards, the remains of a small theatre-shaped room for lecturing, a library, baths, and a temple in all probability dedicated to Heracles and Hermes, deities usually associated with the physical and intellectual activities which went on inside a gymnasium. The organization of activities and the provision of services in the gymnasium often devolved on members of the aristocracy as a public duty, and they assumed the title 'gymnasiarchos'. One such official at Pergamon was Diodorus Pasparos who, it is recorded, provided an *exedra* – an open-fronted room – on the eastern side of the upper gymnasium in 127 BC.

The achievements of Pergamon in the field of education were equalled, if not surpassed, by its sponsorship and patronage of the visual arts and in particular sculpture, which led to the development of a distinctive style, named 'Pergamene'. The frieze on the altar of Zeus in the citadel complex, depicting the battle between the giants and the gods, offers one of the best examples of Pergamene sculptural achievements. The altar itself was constructed during the period 180-169 BC to commemorate the victory of Pergamon over the marauding Gallic tribes.

With the death of Attalus III in 133 BC, Pergamon passed into Roman control according to the conditions of the king's will, and a few years later it was incorporated into the newly formed province of Asia. In the 2nd century AD there was a revival of interest in Pergamon, especially as a centre of medicine and healing. The eminent doctor, Galen, second only to Hippocrates in the history of ancient medicine, came from the city; and the original Hellenistic Asklepieion, a sanctuary dedicated to Asklepios, the god of healing, situated on the edge of the city was transformed into a major healing centre. The sanctuary itself was greatly

ABOVE: A sculpture of Nike (winged victory) from Ephesos.
LEFT: The Trajaneum at Pergamon, a temple dedicated to the Emperor Trajan.

extended and embellished under the Emperor Hadrian and ranked as one of the wonders of the world.

The features of the sanctuary reflect the combination of the miraculous and the superstitious with practical medicine, which contributed to the healing and curative processes. The sanctuary contained consulting rooms, an incubation area, a circular temple to Zeus-Asklepios, a library, a small theatre and supplies of running water. Aelius Aristides, the famous orator and writer of a the 2nd century AD, spent much of his time at the Asklepieion at Pergamon in an attempt to cure himself of a series of illnesses, from which he apparently suffered. For one cure the god commanded him to smear himself with mud, run around the sanctuary three times, and then wash the mud off at the sacred spring. Aristides informs us that it was so cold that all the water was frozen, and of the two friends who accompanied him, one turned back and the other had to be taken to the baths to defrost. Aristides, however, survived – possibly a case of hypochondria!

Habitation at Pergamon continued down into the 8th century AD when it was overrun by Arabs. By this time the zenith of the city's glory and power had long since vanished. ■

The temple to Hadrian at Ephesos.

DURA-EUROPOS

In the spring of 1920, while bivouacking on the ruins of an ancient fortress near the Euphrates River, a British army patrol discovered walls painted with brilliantly coloured, life-sized figures. As it turned out, the paintings reported by the British lieutenant depicted his Roman predecessor Julius Terentius sacrificing to the gods in what is now called the Temple of the Palmyrene Gods at the city of Dura-Europos.

French and American archaeological teams dug at the site between 1922 and 1937, uncovering a frontier town, built by the Greeks and then passed from hand to hand, as the Seleucids and Romans in the west and the Parthians and Sassanians to the east struggled to control this borderland. Its geopolitical setting makes Dura-Europos an important place for understanding international relations of the time (c. 300 BC–AD 250). But the excavators also revealed unparalleled evidence for the cultural and religious melting pot that was Hellenistic Syria. Most spectacular was the discovery of the oldest church yet known, and one of the earliest synagogues outside Palestine.

Dura-Europos lies on the escarpment that forms the southern edge of the Euphrates valley, just inside Syria's border with Iraq. Erosion has dissected this escarpment with many steep gorges, or wadis, and two such wadis bracket the city. This setting thus affords the natural protection of extremely difficult approaches on three sides. A high wall to the west protected the city from this direction, and less substantial walls enhanced the natural advantages of the other three sides. The walls enclosed some 180 hectares, making Dura no mere encampment. Seleucus I, the successor to Alexander the Great in Syria and the founder of the Seleucid dynasty, first built Dura in roughly 300 BC. For the first century or so of its existence, the town was small and, it seems,

A walled town, Dura Europos had the added protection of sheer drops on three sides, and a glorious vista across the Euphrates River valley.

unwalled. Some second century BC texts found in the city suggest that many, if not all, the settlers in this early town were *kleruchoi*, army veterans given a piece of land and a place to live out their retirement. This policy, common in the Classical world, not only rewarded soldiers for their decades of faithful service, but also established a reserve garrison on the frontiers. However, only the Palace of the Strategos (the military governor of the town) and the centrally located *agora* (the open market square) can definitely be assigned to this early phase of the city's construction. The location of a town wall is unknown, but may have been fairly near the cliff edge, and obscured by later building.

Around 150 BC city planners effected a momentous change to the urban fabric, by applying the so-called Hippodamic plan (named after Hippodamus, a fifth-century social theorist from western Turkey) that established a regular formal grid of streets. This created equally sized (70 by 55 m), rectangular city blocks, a format that can roughly be paralleled in many modern cities. At about the same time, the builders laid down the western city wall, thus closing off the town in this direction, and giving the place a boundary on its fourth side. The Palmyra Gate, so called because it opened on to the track that crossed the desert to this famous caravan city (p. 130), gave access to the city through the massive west wall. The main street of the new grid ran from the Palmyra Gate towards the Palace of the Strategos and the river, passing through the open *agora*.

The Parthians, a people from north-east Iran who had busily been creating an empire to the east, took Mesopotamia during the middle decades of the second century BC, and continued to press westward. The coming storm seems to have hastened completion of the west wall, which shows less careful workmanship in its northern end. The urgent effort bore little fruit, and the Parthians seized Dura in 114 BC, but the Parthian occupation did little to disrupt the functioning of the town. Indeed, its new rulers extended the city street grid to cover all the available space within the walls. The Parthians left their imprint in more subtle ways. The open spaces of the *agora* came to be filled with many small shops, rather like the suq (bazaar) of the traditional towns in the same region. Many civic buildings, and especially temples, embellished the city, and even some Greek gods came to be portrayed in Parthian garb.

In due course, the city passed into Roman hands, briefly in the early second century (AD 116–118, when Trajan marched to the Persian Gulf), and then more permanently in AD 168. The Roman occupation effected some noticeable changes to the city. The Roman garrison occupied its north end, and there erected a temple to Jupiter, a palatial residence for the garrison commander and a bath; troops occupied many existing residences that had been remodelled as barracks. The Romans had held Dura for less than a century, when the Sassanian army, the newly arisen Persian

supplanters of the Parthians in the east, sacked the city in AD 256 after a long siege.

Its position on a frontier exposed Dura-Europos to many different traditions, and the city's inhabitants came together from diverse cultures. Texts on papyrus and parchment, as well as the more casual graffiti, reveal a polyglot population. The official records, kept in Greek or Latin, keep track of mainly military affairs (troop rosters, patrol reports, equipment inventories and so forth), while the civilian population also wrote in Aramaic, Palmyrene (a local version of Aramaic script) and Safaitic (an Old Arabic script often associated with nomads). The city contained temples of deities from many different pantheons – the gods of Greece and Rome, such as Zeus (Jupiter) and Artemis, were neighbours to gods of Syria or Phoenicia, such as Atargatis and Hadad, and those of Palmyra and Parthia. In some cases, different gods came to be merged into each other, for example the Greek Zeus Kyrios with the Syrian Baal Shamin, a melding process that helped create a cultural synthesis.

Most of these sanctuaries had been built fairly early in the city's history, and had been maintained as temples for the following two or three centuries. Three shrines were spectacularly different. When the Sassanian army besieged Dura, the city's defenders heaped up an embankment of sand and gravel across the west wall, in a futile effort to strengthen the city defences. However ineffectual these reinforcements proved to be, the embankment did render the invaluable service of covering, and so protecting, not only the wall itself but also the row of houses across the street from the west wall. This protection ensured the preservation not merely of the wall and magnificently intact Palmyra Gate, but even of more perishable objects like wooden doors and elaborately decorated Roman shields. More importantly, three houses adjoining the west wall yielded the most spectacular, and historically significant, finds of the city. These structures began life as ordinary residences, similar to those throughout the town, with their banks of rooms arranged around a central courtyard. However, at various times during the last century of the city's existence, the three houses had been converted into shrines of three different religions: the cult of Mithras, Judaism and Christianity.

The mithraeum, the sanctuary of Mithras, was created in the northern, military section of town soon after the Romans took control of the city. This location reflects the popularity among Roman soldiers of the Mithras cult, with its emphasis on discipline and struggle with the forces of chaos. The shrine underwent several renovations, becoming larger and more formal, and, in its final phase, elaborately decorated in paint and moulded plaster with scenes of the cult.

Although Dura had contained a Jewish population since Seleucid times, the synagogue was built only in the last quarter of the second century AD, when one room of a private house was adapted for use as the Hall of Assembly, with a Torah niche and benches around all four walls. The building was later remodelled (in c. AD 245) as a larger and more formal synagogue that incorporated the adjoining building (previously a separate residence) as a vestibule and caretaker's quarters. The original house was given a colonnaded entry court that led to the larger Hall of Assembly. The long western wall contained the Torah niche, and painted scenes from biblical stories ornamented all four walls. This sacred structure is one of the oldest known synagogues of the Diaspora.

The Christian chapel was created, only a decade or two before the Sassanian siege, by knocking down a partition wall to create a long hall with a low podium at one end. Diagonally across the courtyard, a small room contained a square baptismal font, about a metre deep, with an arched canopy overhead. Painted scenes from both the Old Testament and the Gospels ornamented the walls of this baptistry. This chapel, created from a private house, is the oldest archaeologically identifiable church. ■

KREMNA

The city of Kremna fully justifies its name (in Greek, *kremna* means crags). It is an almost impregnable natural fortress, situated on a limestone plateau, rising sheer from the surrounding valleys. Historical references to the city are virtually non-existent. The Roman geographer Strabo mentions that it was captured by the Galatian king Amyntas. When he died, Augustus, the first emperor of the Roman world, set up a colony of veterans on the site, one of more than twelve which were established to control and pacify this part of the newly created province of Galatia.

Prior to its inclusion in the province, Kremna had been fully influenced by the Hellenized world, and a typical three-sided

Pisidia is the rugged, inhospitable region of south-western Turkey. In antiquity its people were regarded as warlike and uncivilized. Yet archaeology is revealing cities of typical Hellenized/Roman character here, which belie the region's semi-barbaric reputation. The city of Kremna tells a story of splendour and prosperity, which was brought to an end by a spectacular siege, as the Romans attempted to recover the city from a group of bandits.

agora, the remains of which can still be observed, is proof of both the prosperity of the city in this period and the Greek influences to be found in this remote and inaccessible place. However, as part of the province of Galatia and as an established Roman colony, Kremna flourished and became a typical, Romanized urban centre of the empire. Beginning with the efforts of the Emperor Hadrian, the greatest period of the city's prosperity came in the second and third centuries AD. During this time the majority of its public buildings were erected, buildings which reflect the prosperous

The south gateway at Kremna.

urbanized life which is typical of the Roman empire at its height. There are temples, a colonnaded street and a forum with basilica. Public amenities were extremely important, and the city could boast two theatres. One overlooks the southern part of the main civic area. The other, unfinished, was cut from the living rock of the southern cliff. Both gave spectacular views over the valleys to the south and the mountains beyond.

Of even more importance to everyday life was the bath house. At Kremna no expense was spared to ensure such an amenity and it remains today one of the most impressive buildings in the city. The problem was that there was no suitable source of water at a sufficient elevation to supply the bath-house, so an aqueduct was built to bring water from a nearby spring into the city. This aqueduct was a remarkable piece of Roman hydraulic technology. Not only did it negotiate a deep valley by means of a siphon, constructed from thick sections of terracotta piping, but because the source was lower than the baths, at one point the water was raised mechanically to achieve a sufficient elevation to fill the large

The bath house at Kremna was later converted into a library and gallery.

water storage cistern, which supplied the bath-house.

Kremna in the second and third centuries was a small but flourishing Roman city. Then, in AD 278, disaster struck. The late Roman historian, Zosimus, gives a dramatic account of how a group of bandits from the Taurus mountains, led by a certain Lydios, attacked the coastal regions of southern Turkey and, when chased off by the Romans, fled to Kremna. The Romans pursued and laid siege to the city. Scholars have doubted the veracity of Zosimus' story but a recent British survey of the site recovered extensie evidence of a siege. The remains included two siege walls, a large siege mound, a couner-mound built by the defenders, numerous sling bullets and fragments of artillery projectiles, and two well-cut stone balls, which the defenders probably rolled down the slopes in an efort to destroy the lighter Roman siege works. There was even an inscription, dedicated to the Emperor Probus, in whose reign the siege took place. Although after the Romans had retaken the city occupation continued, Kremna never recovered, and it is perhaps ironic that the Roman forces which came to restore the city to full Roman control, were so instrumental in its demise. ■

SAGALOSSOS

Sagalossos comes into the full light of recorded history when Alexander the Great besieged the city in 334 BC. When it fell, 500 defenders, including a small contingent from neighbouring Termessos, were killed. In the same action Alexander lost his friend, Leandros. Despite its capture, the city prospered to the extent that, when the Roman general Manlius Vulso was operating in the area in 189 BC, Sagalossos was forced to pay fifty talents of silver and contribute 20,000 *medimnoi* (30,000 bushels) of wheat and barley.

Hellenistic Sagalossos occupied the upper slopes of the hill and included an impressive *heroon* (a shrine dedicated to a local hero), the upper *agora*, a large trapezoidal area measuring approximately 70 by 36 m, an important temple sanctuary, built on a high stepped podium and a fine Hellenistic fountain building. The splendour and decoration of these and other Hellenistic buildings

At an elevation of c. 1600 m above sea level, Sagalossos is not only the highest but also the largest city in the Pisidian region of Turkey. Despite its present remoteness, in antiquity the city was an important regional centre. In the quality and grandeur of its buildings and its extensive commercial contacts, it ranks with some of the more illustrious cities in western Asia Minor, and fully justifies its claim to be the 'first city of Pisidia'.

are proof of the quality of the artists and architects available within the city, while the styles coming from western Asia Minor, and even as far away as Syria, emphasize the importance of the city and the widespread cultural contacts on which Sagalossos could draw.

As its wealth and importance increased, so the city expanded. Like so many other cities of the empire, Sagalossos witnessed a veritable explosion of public building activity during the reign of the Emperor Hadrian. Buildings were refurbished and new ones erected. Of particular importance to the status of Sagalossos was the award of the title of *Neokoros*. Translating as 'temple warden', it is usually an indication of the presence of a temple dedicated to the provincial imperial cult, and might have been awarded for the renovations to the Augustan temple of Apollo Klarios, rededicated to Apollo Klarios and the emperors, through the benefactions of a local family, Ti. Flavius Collega and his wife Fl. Donille. Such benefactions from the élite were extremely common, and are an indication of the civic pride and patriotism with which the local aristocracy embellished their home towns.

A second imperial temple followed shortly afterwards. This time dedicated to the Emperor Antoninus Pius, it was built on a natural outcrop, which dominated the middle and lower parts of the city and gave commanding views towards Alexander's hill, where the defenders of the city held out against Alexander's forces, and the surrounding countryside.

The prosperity of Sagalossos, which is reflected in both the number and size of its buildings, and the quality of their decoration, was based not only on the fertility of its dependent territory but in particular on its thriving pottery industry. A large part of the eastern side of the city was dedicated to pottery and lamp production, and there is evidence that pottery was produced here from the Hellenistic period to the early

LEFT: The theatre at Sagalassos.

ABOVE: The large baths at Sagalassos. Baths became one of the most important urban buildings of the Roman Empire.

RIGHT: The paving of the upper agora with its large nymphaeum (monumental fountain house).

sixth century AD. Sagalassos became famous for its pottery manufacture, and its goods were exported throughout the eastern Mediterranean and possibly as far south as Egypt.

Although the site of Sagalassos abounded with natural supplies of water, these sources were still inadequate to meet the domestic, recreational and industrial demands of the city. Additional supplies were needed, and these were brought into the city through aqueducts. There were at least six such water channels, and two on the eastern side of the site were particularly impressive. Following a sinuous course from springs over 5 km away, they were cut from the rock. At one point an impressive gallery was built into the vertical cliff face to accommodate the water channel.

The prosperity of Sagalassos continued throughout the fourth century AD. However, military conditions in Asia Minor deteriorated in the fifth century AD. For protection a defensive wall was hastily erected to enclose the upper part of the city. The suddenness of the crisis is indicated by the large quantity of re-used material utilized in its construction and the abandonment of much of the city outside the wall to the invading enemy.

If water was instrumental in the success of Sagalassos it also played an important role in its ultimate demise. Although life continued within these defences, the rest of the city was abandoned. It is likely that the city was finally deserted as a result of earthquakes which are historically attested for 518 and 528. These destroyed the city's artificial water supplies, and in turn this caused the eventual relocation of the population to the present-day village of Aglasun, in the valley below. ■

ABOVE: The rock-cut passage of one of the aqueducts which brought water into the city.

RIGHT: The seating of the theatre remains largely intact.

PALMYRA

East met west at the desert caravan city of Palmyra. Positioned along one of the long-distance trade routes which brought luxury goods from the east into the Roman empire, Palmyra flourished in the second and third centuries AD. Changing trade routes and an abortive attempt at independence in the troubled years of the third century AD destroyed for ever the prosperity of this flourishing city in the desert.

Palmyra (Tadmor), 'the bride of the desert', is situated at an oasis on the northern edge of the Syrian desert. Founded, according to legend, by king Solomon, its importance stems from the fact that it controls one of the shortest trans-desert caravan routes which ran between the ancient city of Emesa (Homs) in Syria and Dura-Europos (see p. 122) on the river Euphrates, and so was well positioned to exploit the long-distance trade between east and west.

By the middle of the first century its increasing prosperity was acknowledged when, in 41 BC, Mark Antony led a cavalry raid across the desert to plunder the settlement. However, when he arrived at Palmyra, he found the place deserted. The population had abandoned it and fled eastwards with all its moveable possessions across the Euphrates to Parthia. This story is significant because it emphasizes Palmyra's central position between west and east. Whilst the city increasingly came under Graeco-Roman influence, the local population, comprising Amorite, Aramaic and growing Arabic stock, maintained its close natural links with the east. This balance between eastern and western influences was maintained and contributed to its success. Inscriptions are often bilingual in Aramaic (which remained the local language of everyday communication) and Greek. The rich merchants, on whom the economic success of Palmyra was founded, took both local and Roman names, and the public buildings were an amalgamation of Roman architecture with local artistic traditions and details.

The peak of Palmyra's success and prosperity came during the second and third centuries AD as the city exploited the trade, which brought luxury goods for the élite of the Roman world from the east by sea via the Persian Gulf and the Euphrates to Dura-Europos. From here the goods were carried across the desert by camel train through the territory of Palmyra to the prosperous commercial cities of Syria and from there westwards. Nor was trade a one-way phenomenon – the city was also a pivotal

LEFT: A funerary sculpture from Palmyra.

RIGHT: A richly decorated monumental archway on the main colonnaded street of Palmyra.

point in the spread of Graeco-Roman commodities to the Parthians.

Numerous inscriptions from Palmyra give remarkable insight into the camel trains, the policing of the routes, and the revenues from which the city drew its wealth. Inscriptions, honouring the successful and rich of Palmyra, indicate how the camel trains were organized, either through individuals, groups of merchants or at times with the city itself contributing, if the camel train was particularly large – a clear indication that it realized that its wealth was based on trade.

One of the most important and illuminating of the Palmyrene inscriptions is the so-called Tariff of Palmyra. Dating to *c.* AD 137 it is a collection of existing and new financial and tax laws.

BELOW: A funerary sculpture of a woman.

RIGHT: Surviving arcade of Classical columns.

Inscribed in both Palmyrene script and Greek, the tariff details the goods which were passing through the territory. From it can be learned what was traded, the relative importance of the different commodities and the taxes levied. It is clear from the text that the wealth of the city was not dependent on the taxation of long-distance trade alone. Taxes were levied on all goods and services in the city and its territory. This included water and even the services of prostitutes, whose monthly tax was equivalent to the cost of one act. It can come as no surprise that the 'treasurers' of the city outranked in order of importance even the popular assembly.

The prosperity of the city is reflected in its temples, public buildings, the finely decorated colonnaded street, the sumptuously ornamented private houses of the merchants and traders, and the imposing tower tombs built for the dead. Within the civic centre the most imposing of the public buildings was the great temple with surrounding *temenos* (sacred precinct) to the Babylonian deity, Bel. The temple was begun in the reign of the Emperor Tiberius (AD 14–37), with both financial help and possibly even technical expertise from Rome, but the *temenos* was not fully completed until the Antonine dynasty (AD 138-192). The amalgamation of western and eastern influences is evident in its design, construction and decoration. Its architecture is fully rooted in the traditions of Hellenism, with Greek inspiration obvious on the north and south walls of the cella, where Ionic half-columns are situated against the walls; the columns of the peristyle are Corinthian. The west wall with its imposing, monumental doorway has evident influences from Ptolemaic Egypt. The layout of the temple and *temenos* is Semitic, whilst the sculptural decoration is eastern in character. Such amalgamation of different styles and influences is typical of much of the public architecture at Palmyra and is confirmation of both the city's pivotal location between east and west and the international flavour of those who visited it.

The Emperor Hadrian's visit to Palmyra in AD 129 began the city's great period of wealth and grandeur. The cost of the lavish celebrations, which were organized to commemorate Hadrian's visit, was met by one of the city's richest merchants, Malé Agrippa. A decade later he also financed the rebuilding of the temple to Baal Shamin. Unfortunately, success lasted only for just over one century. Because of its location on the edge of Roman influence in the east, and its natural links with the Euphrates valley and beyond, the city had always maintained an air of semi-independence. In the troubled times of the middle to late third century AD, under Odeaenathus and in particular queen Zenobia, the city seized full independence from Rome, and for a time maintained it against the incursions of the Sassanians. Eventually, recovered by the Emperor Aurelian, it again revolted in AD 273 and was captured, looted and destroyed. After its recapture, limited occupation continued and the Emperor Diocletian built a camp there. However, Palmyra never recovered, and the growing importance of the long-distance trade routes to the north of Palmyra from the Euphrates via Thapsacus and Aleppo to Antioch ensured that the economic basis on which the prosperity of the city had been founded was lost for ever. ■

SAMARRA

The early Abbasid caliphs (AD 750–945) founded Baghdad in central Iraq, almost as the heir to Babylon, from where they ruled a vast dominion. With the ocean-going trade with India and China considerably augmenting the state revenues of tribute, incredible wealth flowed into the new metropolis. In the ninth century, this wealth paid for the foundation of a new capital city at Samarra, north of Baghdad.

Although it remained the royal seat of the Abbasid caliphate for less than six decades (AD 836–892), nearly continuous building on a lavish scale very quickly created an impressive band of construction that stretched 50 km along the banks of the Tigris. Covering nearly 60 sq km (not quite ten times the size of Nineveh or Babylon), this short-lived royal seat is the largest archaeological city in the Near East, and perhaps in the world.

After the Arab armies had carried Islam out of Arabia, Syria was the initial centre of power, with Damascus as the Umayyad capital. Doctrinal, ethnic and economic tensions soon led to unrest in the east. Overthrowing the last Umayyad caliph in AD 750, Abu'l Abbas donned Muhammad's mantle as the leader of the Muslim community, and shifted the centre of the Muslim world to Iraq. Soon thereafter, al-Mansur (AD 754–775) founded Baghdad on the banks of the Tigris River, at a strategic crossroads of overland routes from the Far East and the riverine connection towards India. The legendary court of Harun al-Rashid (AD 786–809) and the fabulous stories of Sindbad reflect the immense wealth amassed by the shipping magnates in the India trade. By the early ninth century, Arab shipping sailed directly to China, thus cutting out the middlemen and further increasing profits.

But beneath this veneer of wealth, the Abbasids were running into trouble. Civil wars and provincial revolts were becoming a persistent fact of life. The Zinj, East African slaves who worked immense plantations in southern Iraq, rose in a revolt that lasted fourteen years (AD 855–868) before being put down. Turkish and Persian mercenaries from Central Asia increasingly filled the ranks of the caliphate army, leading to further alienation of the people from their rulers. According to a contemporary account, the arrogant Turkish mercenaries came into bitter conflict with the civilian population of Baghdad. After rioting in the city, the caliph al-Mu'tasim (AD 833–842) sought to move his household to a new capital, so as to avoid renewed violence.

He picked Samarra, on the east bank of the Tigris, about 120 km north of Baghdad, and began building a city there in 836. At this time, Samarra held no special importance. Al-Mu'tasim wielded the full potential of his position in creating the new city. According to Ya'qubi, a ninth-century geographer, the caliph 'had architects brought . . . [and] they selected a number of sites for the palaces. He gave each of his followers a palace to build . . . Then he had plots of ground marked out for the military and civil officers and for the people, and likewise the Great Mosque. And he had the markets drawn out round the mosque with wide market rows, all the various kinds of merchandise being separate [like the markets of Baghdad] . . . He wrote for workmen, masons, and artificers, such as smiths, carpenters, and all other craftsmen to be sent, and for teak and other kinds of wood, and for palm-trunks . . . and for marble workers and men experienced in marble paving to be brought.'

The centrepiece of al-Mu'tasim's new city was Dar al-Khilafa, a palace complex that covered 175 hectares, fronting on the Tigris River. It comprised the palace itself, plus vast gardens, polo grounds with attached viewing pavilion and stables, and quarters for the palace guards and servants. The palace comprised two distinct sections: the public space (the Dar al-'Amma) where the

The great Congregational Mosque at Samarra, with its massive walls and large central courtyard.

ABOVE: Twenty-four windows gave light through the southern wall of the Congregational Mosque, to the deepest interior colonnaded hall.
RIGHT: Elaborate designs ornamented houses and palaces at Samarra.

caliph held audiences on Mondays and Thursdays, and the private space (the Jausaq al-Khaqani) of residential suites, harem and support facilities. A flight of stairs 60 m wide led from a square at the edge of the river up to a large room with an 11 m high vaulted ceiling that served as a reception room, with smaller flanking guard rooms. Beyond this monumental palace entrance lay a suite of ante-chambers that gave on to a square courtyard with a fountain. At this point, the visitor could turn northwards to the private chambers of the caliph or southwards to the harem suites, or could continue straight towards the audience hall, a domed throne room and other chambers of state. The palace was richly decorated with carved stucco (and marble in the throne room), and the harem walls bore figured murals. The teak beams and ceilings, elements of which have survived, were ornamented with painted carved designs, or with flat decoration in paint and gilt. The names of craftsmen appear as surreptitious graffiti in Greek, Syriac and Arabic on ceiling beams.

The city reached its full size under Mutawakkil (AD 847–861), an enthusiastic builder responsible for the Great Congregational Mosque, as many as twenty palaces, and an entire new city called al-Mutawakkiliyya to the north. Mutawakkil's Congregational Mosque was enormous, its outer walls forming a 240 by 156 m rectangle, with exterior buttresses and sixteen doorways. Inside, twenty-four rows of pillars supported a now vanished roof, with a

large central open space. Glass mosaics, preserved only as dispersed inlay elements, ornamented the interior wall. The minaret stood on a separate square platform outside the mosque, but connected to it by a ramp. A minaret, itself 52 m high, presented a ramp spiralling around the outside of the round tower. Many architectural historians suggest that this unusual form was based on Assyrian ziggurats. The Congregational Mosque lay on the north-western side of the existing city, which now developed to its greatest size. Contemporary observers describe seven parallel avenues, including one along the riverbank with dock facilities to handle important river traffic, and another extending from the south gate of the Dar al-Khilafa past the residences of eminent Turks. A third avenue ran from a residential quarter for palace servants along the west side of Dar al-Khilafa itself, then made its way south, passing in succession the main market area around the older mosque of al-Mu'tasim, the main prison, police headquarters, the slave market, the royal stables, and the tax registry.

Mutawakkil constructed many other noteworthy edifices. His new palace complex at Balkuwara lay to the south, in the midst of an army cantonment adjacent to the Tigris. The compound wall stretched along 1.2 km, and the main palace building alone covered about 12 hectares. He laid out three racecourses, complete with spectators' stands, near the Congregational

Mosque, and for pleasant diversions of a different sort a walled hunting park with its own palace south of Balkuwara. The caliph's most intensive building took place in al-Mutawakkiliyya, north of the old city, where he laid out a completely new city (reputedly saying 'Now I know that I am indeed a king, for I have built myself a city and live in it'). Naturally the place came with its own palace (al-Ja'fari, whose compound covered roughly 1.3 sq km) and congregational mosque (the Abu Dhulaf mosque, a somewhat smaller version of the Great Congregational Mosque to the south). This new city was abandoned when Mutawakkil died at an assassin's hand.

These royal palaces, state offices and grand mosques tend to overshadow more ordinary living quarters. Some of these were military, cantonments for Turkish and Central Asian Persian garrisons, or troops led by princes. These cantonments formed distinct towns, sometimes even walled off, each complete with its own street grid, a palace for the commanding officer or prince, and quarters for the troops. Elsewhere the more numerous residences of civilians stretched along the city streets. These buildings, like those in the cantonments and within the palace complexes, tended to reflect standard designs. An anteroom gave entrance from the street to a central rectangular courtyard, facing which were reception rooms giving on to the open space. In larger houses, which might contain up to fifty rooms, one or more inner courtyards lay beyond the reception areas. Surround-

ing the courtyards were rooms for sleeping and daily activities, storerooms and other facilities. The largest houses were independent units, standing alone, while somewhat smaller dwellings were often paired in a sort of duplex arrangement. The smallest residences formed tenement-like structures, with five or ten units sharing party walls in a row. The private houses, like the palaces, might be decorated with various designs in stucco, including a vine-and-leaf motif borrowed from the Classical world, and geometric arrangements of plant elements (leaves, buds, palmettes), trefoils, spirals and other shapes.

Construction of the new capital at Samarra was a heavy drain on the state coffers during the ninth century. According to contemporary accounts, Mutawakkil alone spent 250–300 million dirhams on his building projects. Sums of this magnitude represented a sizeable proportion of state revenues (equivalent, for example, to the total yield over three centuries at one of the major silver mines), and helped to deepen the deficit of lavish court life. Despite the revenues gained from the sea trade, the Abbasid caliphate was going broke. Samarra's location proved too isolated, and perhaps too expensive, and Mu'tadid (AD 892–908) returned the capital to the more centrally located Baghdad at the beginning of his reign. Then in 945, after decades of the Abbasids teetering precariously on the brink of disaster, a rebel Iranian dynasty invaded and conquered Baghdad. Although the Abbasid line continued over the next three centuries, these were princelings in control of small territories, or puppets serving at the whim of other masters. Samarra itself experienced massive depopulation as soon as the royal centre shifted back to Baghdad, and functioned mainly as a Shiite pilgrimage centre from the tenth century onwards. ■

BELOW: The spiral minaret of the Congregational Mosque at Samarra still stands tall a thousand years after its construction.
RIGHT: The well-built brick walls of monuments like the Congregational Mosque, with its semi-circular buttresses, survived centuries of neglect.

FATEHPUR SIKRI - THE CITY OF VICTORY

Fatehpur Sikri is located high on a rocky outlier, 37 km west of Agra, India, in the south-west corner of the Indo-Gangetic Plain. The site was first occupied by Shaikh Salim, a Sufi (Muslim) saint who lived an ascetic and very pious life on this barren ridge above his childhood home of Sikri, choosing the spot for a hermitage. The Emperor Akbar (reigned AD 1556–1605) used to hunt in this area and knew it well.

Akbar's greatest wish was to have a son but, despite having a large number of wives, he had failed to produce one. Hearing of the aged Shaikh, he visited him for counsel in 1568. The Shaikh assured him that he would have three sons, and Akbar then ordered a great mosque to be built at the site.

Sure enough, Akbar's first son was born the following year, and was named Muhammad Salim after the Shaikh. Akbar returned to stay with the old man in 1571, and ordered splendid buildings to be erected for his own use, and made his noblemen construct houses for themselves. Most of the basic construction involved the empire's best architects, who had been working on the Agra fort (using stone quarried from the Fatehpur Sikri ridge), and was

A jewel of Indo-Muslim architecture, the late sixteenth-century AD city of Fatehpur Sikri was built and used by the Emperor Akbar (Arabic for 'Great') during part of his reign, but it lost its role and its importance after he left, and was never to regain its original glory.

finished within a year. The materials used were a mixture of red sandstone and the darker red stone of the ridge itself which, according to a seventeenth-century traveller, could be 'cleft like logges and sawne like plankes'. The emperor took a deep interest in the whole project, even quarrying some stone himself and doing other menial tasks.

In 1572 he marched out to conquer Gujarat, which was ruled by a different Muslim dynasty – and, on returning victorious in 1573, he named the site *Fathpur*, meaning the City of Victory. He established his court there and, for the following twelve years, this was the hub of the great Moghul empire.

The city, designed from the start to be the cultural, commercial and administrative centre of the empire, was 9.75 km in circumference, with embattlemented walls 6 km long, enclosing it from the north to the south-west. On the western side it was protected by an artificial lake. Akbar usually entered it by the Agra gate, and the imperial band was stationed there to announce his comings and goings.

All the palace buildings – the fully planned complex which has survived best – were oriented with the mosque, most of them being entered from the east. The complex is a classic of Indo-Muslim architecture, laid out on Persian principles but built and decorated in the Indian manner (for example, some columns have capitals in the form of stylized elephant heads): the result is a unique jewel. As in most of the Moghul complexes, there is a special raised platform, or 'throne pavilion', where the emperor sat to dispense justice – an executioner with instruments of torture stood by throughout, but was there only to instil terror, not to be called upon. Akbar also showed himself to the people from this platform every day, about three hours after sunrise – some

View from the water pavilion showing the Wind Tower (left) and the 'Jewel House' (right).

would eat nothing unless they had seen his face.

Among the best-known and well-preserved buildings is the harem complex, with its roof of azure blue glazed tiles, its principal entrance guarded by eunuchs. The Wind Tower (Panch Mahal) is a bizarre but beautiful columnar structure, comprising four storeys which decrease in size, set up asymmetrically above a ground floor containing eighty-four columns. There are fifty-six on the floor above, twenty on the next, twelve above that, and a single domed kiosk on four pillars at the top, making a total of 176 pillars. This light and airy building, a summer palace for the ladies and for parties, was an excellent place to escape from the stifling heat.

The Ankh Michauli, or 'Blind Man's Buff House', is said to be where Akbar played hide-and-seek with the women of his harem. Beside it, the 'Treasury Kiosk' (wrongly known as the 'Astrologer's Seat'), about 3 m square, with very extravagant stone brackets, was probably where Akbar would sit on cushions and watch the distribution of copper coins, heaped up in the courtyard, to subordinate officers and deserving people.

The nearby 'Jewel House' (Diwan-i-Khass) is dominated by a massive, richly carved pillar which supports a superb capital and, above it, a circular balcony joined to the corners of the building by four little bridges. Its purpose is uncertain – it is often said to be Akbar's private audience chamber, or the place where he held religious discussions with those below, as he sat or paced on the balcony and bridges above. However, the building may simply be a storehouse for his imperial hoard of gems and jewels.

Finally, the great mosque (Jami Masjid, or 'congregational mosque') is the main building of Fatehpur Sikri, measuring 133 by 165 m, and its courtyard 109 by 133 m. Shaikh Salim, who died here in 1572 aged ninety-two, and to whom the mosque was ascribed by Akbar, is buried in the courtyard in a tomb of stunning beauty, one of the finest pieces of marblework in India, completed in 1580–81. The monumental gate leading to the mosque – the Buland Darwaza – towers above a flight of thirty steps. Its door, up to several metres above human reach, is covered with the shoes of horses and draft cattle, probably hammered in for luck by peasants seeking the Shaikh's intercession for the cure of sick animals. In the same way, threads and pieces of cloth can still be seen attached to stone screens in his tomb, tied there especially by barren women.

In 1585 Akbar had to leave Fatehpur Sikri to defend his north-west frontier, pacify Afghan tribes and conquer Sind. He remained in the north, based at Lahore, until 1598, and Fatehpur Sikri was neglected; although the Shaikh's family kept the royal buildings in good order, the empty houses of the nobles decayed, and by 1591 many roofs of stone houses had gone, and most buildings of unburnt brick had collapsed. When Akbar returned

LEFT: The marble mausoleum of Shaik Salim in the courtyard of the great mosque.
ABOVE: Nineteenth-century view of the interior of the 'Jewel House' showing the central pillar with its huge capital, and the bridges above.

in 1598, he set up his court at Agra – some believe this was because the water supply had failed at Fatehpur. The following year he marched south to supervise wars in the Deccan, and in 1601 passed a few days at Fatehpur Sikri on his return, but he remained at Agra until he died on 17 October 1605.

In 1619 his son Salim – now the Emperor Jahangir – stayed for three months at Fatehpur Sikri because there was plague at Agra. He showed Akbar's palace to his son, and visited the Shaikh's shrine. At this time the nobles' buildings were renovated and furnished, and the town prospered again under the Shaikh's descendants who held high positions during Jahangir's reign.

The real decay and destruction of the city began in the late seventeenth century. It had a final moment in the sun in 1719 when Emperor Muhammad Shah was crowned there, but the empire was disintegrating, and the only visitors henceforth were pilgrims to the shrine. The East India Company seized Agra in 1803, and set up an administrative subdivision at Fatehpur Sikri which lasted until 1850, with a new township being built largely with stones from the ruins. In 1876 the British government of India launched a project to conserve the remaining monuments, and repairs finally began in 1881. Thanks to these efforts, the City of Victory can still be visited, and despite its often stark appearance one can still marvel at Akbar's architectural jewels. ∎

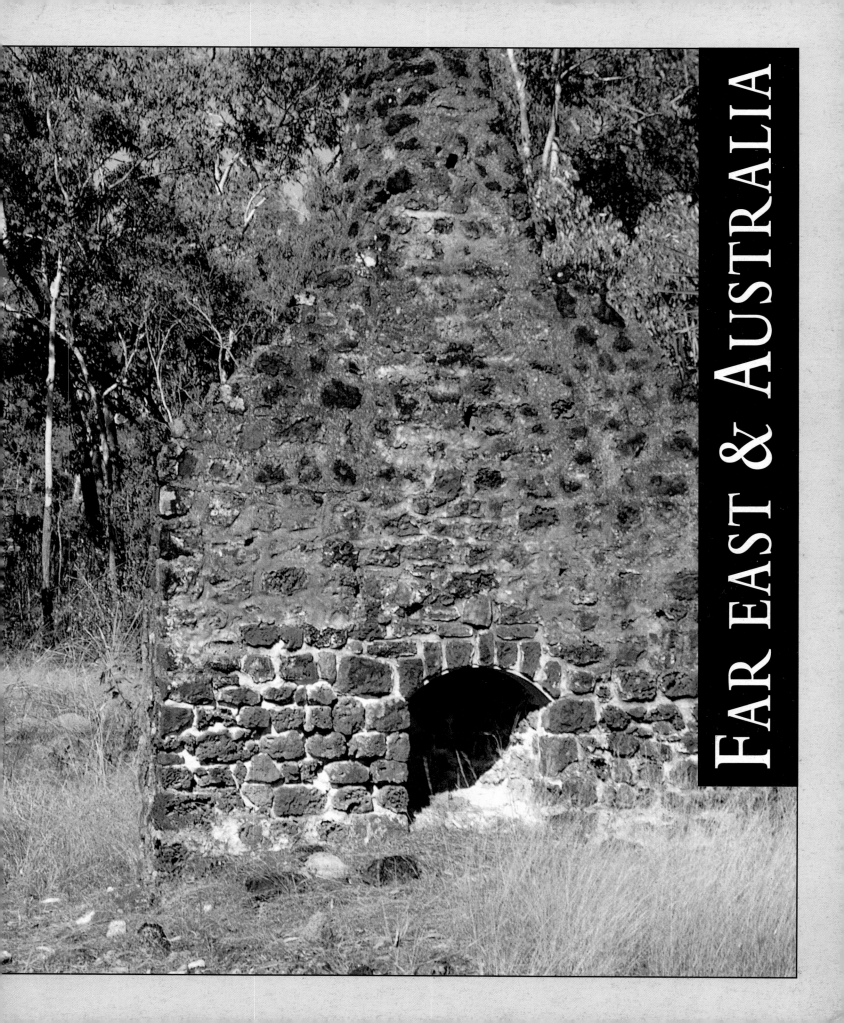

ANYANG AND THE LATE SHANG STATE

The Shang was the first state and the earliest civilization of East Asia. The Shang kings ruled a large area of north China centred on the middle Yellow River valley from about 1700 to 1050 BC. Shang culture is known particularly for its elaborate bronze vessels and its inscribed oracle bones. The bronzes were made in a variety of shapes using advanced piece mould-casting techniques. The oracle bones were used in divinatory ceremonies by the Shang rulers who looked to the gods for help with foreseeing the future. Almost all of our knowledge of the Shang period has come from the late Shang city of Anyang which was occupied during the last three centuries of the Shang era.

In the spring of 1928, fighting between bandits and government forces prevented the people of the small village of Xiaotun in northern China from tilling their fields. When the fighting stopped, in desperation they began to dig up and sell the inscribed oracle bones that had long been found around their village. In August an archaeologist from the Academia Sinica was sent to investigate this source of oracle bones, and in the autumn of the same year excavations were begun at what was to prove one of the great sites of Asian archaeology: the Shang city of Anyang.

Oracle bones from the Anyang area had been known to Chinese scholars from the end of the nineteenth century. The bones, mostly turtle shells and the shoulder-blades of cattle, had been dug up by the local peasants on several occasions and sold as 'dragon bones' to be ground into Chinese medicines. Dong Zuobin had studied these bones and their ancient inscribed characters for some years. When Dong was sent to investigate Xiaotun in 1928, he assumed that the source of oracle bones there had already been exhausted. It soon became clear, however, that there were plenty more bones to be uncovered, and a large-scale excavation was begun by the Institute of History and Philology of the Academia Sinica.

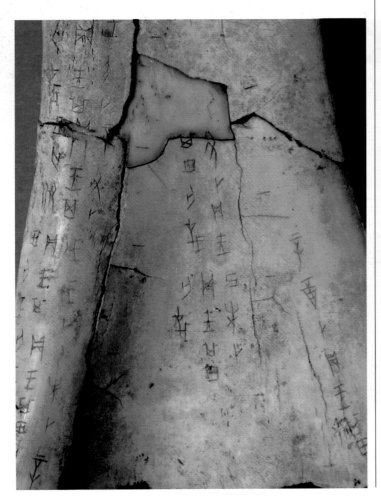

LEFT: Inscribed oracle bone from Anyang. Bones such as this provided the initial clue to the discovery of the site.
ABOVE: Intricately engraved creature in semi-precious stone, found at Anyang during excavations.

Bronze wine vessels of the Shang dynasty. Bronze casting reached great artistic heights during the Shang period.

The 1920s were a momentous decade in Chinese archaeology, witnessing several major discoveries such as the cave of Peking Man at Zhoukoudian, the Neolithic site of Yangshao, and the Bronze Age city of Anyang, and professional archaeological excavation in China can be said to have begun with these famous discoveries. The Anyang excavations, directed by Li Chi, who is often called the father of modern Chinese archaeology, lasted from 1928 until the Japanese invasion in 1937, and played a particularly seminal role in training Chinese archaeologists. After the Second World War, many of the finds from Anyang were sent to Taiwan where they now remain.

The site of Anyang stretches for nearly 6 km along both sides of the Huan River, north-west of the modern town of Anyang in Henan Province. Shang Anyang contains a variety of separate sites which together formed the ancient city. Most important are the royal cemetery at Xibeigang and a palace complex at Xiaotun. A variety of other workshops, graves and residential areas for both commoners and the élite show that Anyang already possessed the diverse specialist functions associated with a true city.

The Xiaotun site, which covers an area of about 10,000 sq m,

seems to have been the central focus of Anyang. Several groups of large constructions with stamped-earth foundations were uncovered, comprising both residential and ceremonial buildings. Burials, some with horse-drawn chariots and human sacrifices, were associated with these buildings, as were ordinary pit dwellings and oracle bones. At Xibeigang, eleven large shaft tombs, nearly 1200 small pit burials and various buildings and workshops were uncovered. The shaft tombs were mostly cruciform in shape with long ramps leading down into the chamber. Most of the royal tombs had been robbed before excavation, but one at Xiaotun dug in 1976 had escaped plundering. This tomb was incredibly rich in Shang art, producing more than 440 bronzes, nearly 600 jades and over 560 bone artifacts. Inscriptions on several of the bronzes identify the tomb as that of Fu Hao, a consort of the fifth Shang king, Wu Ding.

Tens of thousands of fragments of oracle bones have been discovered at Anyang. Sacrifices, military campaigns, hunting expeditions, the weather, agriculture, tribute payments and sickness were just some of the topics subject to divination, which was performed by applying a hot brand to a previously drilled pit in the surface of the bone. The cracks which appeared on the opposite side of the bone were then interpreted and the result was sometimes written on to the bone's surface. These inscriptions have proved an invaluable source of information about Shang government.

A huge variety of other artefacts was discovered at the Anyang site ranging from bronze, bone and stone sculptures to more mundane animal bones and domestic pottery. The animal bones included several exotic species such as whale, elephant, tapir and peacock. Nearly a quarter of a million potsherds came from the pre-war excavations at the site. Several thousand human skeletons were also found, although these became dispersed after the war, with only a few hundred being sent to Taiwan with the other artifacts. Many skulls came from sacrificial pits, most of which contained around ten skulls each. Initial studies on these skulls emphasized the variety of 'racial' characteristics, with some scholars identifying Caucasoid, Eskimo and even Melanesian individuals. The assumption was these were non-Chinese slaves or prisoners of war who were sacrificed by the Shang rulers. More recent anthropological analyses have concluded that the Anyang population was physically quite homogeneous, but this does not exclude the possibility that many

ABOVE: Limestone buffalo from the tomb of Fu Hao.
BELOW: Delicately engraved birds and turtle, used as ornaments.
RIGHT: Bronze vessel with feet, and bird motif on its lid. Such bronzes were typical grave goods in Shang-period tombs of China.

of the sacrificial victims came from ethnic or cultural minorities in north China.

Anyang was clearly one of the great cities of Bronze Age Asia, but what was its exact role in the late Shang state? Many scholars have argued that Anyang was a Shang capital, but this interpretation has been doubted by others. It is possible that the concept of a fixed capital may not yet have existed; certainly it is known from the oracle bone inscriptions that the Shang kings spent a great deal of time touring their domains. The geographical extent of Shang power is another problem. Although Shang bronzes and other artefacts are found in a wide area across northern and central China, it seems likely that the territory under direct political control of the Shang was a much smaller region centred on the Yellow River. Anyang was built over 3000 years ago to bolster the power and prestige of the Shang kings: it is ironic that because of our poor archaeological knowledge of Shang sites other than Anyang, it continues to serve that worthwhile purpose most effectively! ∎

149

FUJIWARA

ujiwara is located in the Asuka region of the southern Nara Basin, which had been home to several imperial palaces from at least the sixth century. These palaces became larger over time, but were primarily administrative and ritual centres, lacking the variety of activities found in a true city. To avoid impurities associated with death, a new palace was built in a different location on the accession of each new ruler. By the 670s, however, this traditional system of imperial palaces had become incompatible with the demands of an increasingly bureaucratic state, and the Emperor Tenmu decided to build a permanent capital at Fujiwara. Construction work was temporarily abandoned when Tenmu died in 687, but was later continued by his widow, Empress Jito. The completed Fujiwara was used from 694 until 710 when the capital was moved some 15 km north to Nara.

Fujiwara is mentioned in a number of early written texts, but archaeology has been crucial in determining the exact location of the site and in reconstructing details of its urban history. The eighteenth-century rise of a nativist scholarship which stressed the indigenous aspects of Japanese culture led to increased debate over the location of Fujiwara, but it was not until the first archaeological excavations were conducted from 1934 to 1943 that the site of the capital was confirmed. Excavations resumed in the 1960s and have been carried out continuously since 1969 by a branch of the

By the late seventh century AD, the Yamato state had consolidated its control of much of western and central Japan, and work was begun on a capital in the Nara Basin. The new capital was to be a magnificent symbol of Japan's status as a leading centre of East Asian civilization. The city was called Fujiwara-kyo – the 'Capital of the Wisteria Plain'.

lavishly funded Nara National Cultural Properties Research Institute. By 1996 some 10.5 hectares of the Fujiwara Palace had been dug, an area comprising only about 10 per cent of the whole palace compound. A similar area (about 10 hectares) of the capital site has also been excavated so far.

Although its occupation was relatively short-lived, Fujiwara can be considered Japan's first urban centre. Just as the Yamato state was itself based heavily on administrative models borrowed from China, the architectural plan of Fujiwara attempted to replicate (though on a much smaller scale) the great continental cities such as the Tang capital of Changan. Like Changan, the Fujiwara city plan was based on a grid known as the *jobo* system. Major streets, known as *oji*, divided Fujiwara into twelve *jo* from north to south and eight *bo* from east to west. According to the reconstruction by Toshio Kishi, Fujiwara covered an area of 3.2 km north–south and 2.1 km east–west. Recent excavations have suggested the possibility that the city was actually considerably larger than this, but confirmation awaits further research. The overall population has been estimated at between twenty and thirty thousand people. An entry for 704 in a document known as the *Shoku Nihongi* relates that residents of Fujiwara were given rolls of cloth. Some 1505 households received this cloth, and it is possible that this was the total number of households in the capital at that time. We know that eighth-century households were quite large, since those which were listed in a 733 tax register from the Nara capital had an average of 16.4 members each.

The palace, which was home to the emperor and the main bureaucratic offices, occupied about 1 sq km in the north-central section of the capital, and was surrounded by a 5 m wide outer ditch, a wall and a narrower inner ditch. The main entrance to the palace was through the Suzaku Gate which led to the major state buildings, the Imperial Audience Hall (*Daigokuden*), where the emperor conducted both political and religious business, the Halls of State (*Chodoin*) and the emperor's private

Scale model of the Fujiwara Capital viewed from the north. The palace complex is in the centre of the city.

Excavations in progress at the Fujiwara Capital site.

As Japan's first urban centre, Fujiwara faced the considerable problems of how to feed its large population and how to dispose of the rubbish and other waste its inhabitants produced. The emperor and the aristocracy who resided in Fujiwara were supported by tax payments from the provinces. Over 7000 inscribed wooden slips, or *mokkan*, excavated from the capital site detail some of the goods brought to Fujiwara in this way. Two official markets are known to have existed in the city, although their locations have not been confirmed archaeologically. Rice, cloth and coins were used for economic transactions, with Japan's first official coinage issued from Fujiwara in 708. The fact that Fujiwara has produced the earliest archaeological latrines from Japan suggests that urban waste disposal was requiring new, more permanent facilities than had previously been in use. The latrines excavated from Fujiwara, however, are all quite basic facilities where wastes would simply have flowed out into ditches running along the side of the street. Finds of parasite eggs in the soil of these latrines suggest that the people of Fujiwara were eating raw vegetables as well as fresh-water fish such as carp and trout that had not been properly cooked.

In the third month of 710, the Empress Genmei moved the capital of Japan to Nara at the northern end of the Nara Basin. Fujiwara was stripped of all building materials that could be reused for construction of the new capital, and by the ninth century much of Fujiwara had been returned to agricultural usage. The reasons for the move have been much debated, but probably included a desire to break away from the Asuka region where capitals had been located for at least a century. The larger Nara capital was seen as lending authority to the new Ritsuryo administrative system. Another factor suggested by historian Hisashi Kano relates to the symbolic geography of Fujiwara. From his palace in the north of the city, the emperor looked south to survey his dominions, but the hills at the southern end of the Asuka region meant that the south of the capital could in effect overlook the palace, disrupting the symbolic landscape. Shifting the capital further to the north was an effective solution to this problem. ■

residence, the *Dairi*. The Imperial Audience Hall was 45 m wide, 21 m deep and 25 high and was the largest building in Japan at that time. Aside from their sheer size, the architectural impact of the palace buildings was heightened by their location within huge open plazas.

Aristocratic residences were situated close to the palace. One such mansion covering an area of 12,000 sq m has been excavated about 300 m south-west of the Suzaku Gate. Lower ranking officials and commoners lived in more modest dwellings further out from the palace. Several large Buddhist temples were another feature of the capital, Buddhism having become a state religion after being first introduced into Japan in the sixth century.

Construction of the Fujiwara capital was a major undertaking. Archaeological investigations have revealed special canals thought to have been dug to transport timber and other building materials into the city, since they were filled in before actual occupation began. Two main methods of structural support were employed in ancient Japan. In one, used at Fujiwara for the Imperial Audience Hall and the Halls of State, wooden pillars were placed directly on to large foundation stones. In the other, the wooden pillar and a smaller foundation stone were buried in a small pit. The Fujiwara Palace was the first non-religious building in Japan to be roofed with ceramic tiles. These tiles comprise a large proportion of the archaeological finds from Fujiwara, and detailed studies of their chronology and production have been conducted. It has been estimated that over two million tiles were needed for the Fujiwara Palace complex.

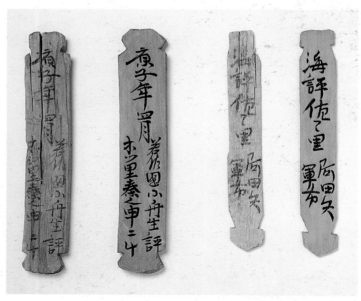

Inscribed wooden tablets excavated from Fujiwara. Such tablets were used as baggage labels in ancient Japan.

ANGKOR: THE CITY BUILT BY ANGELS

The rise of civilization in South East Asia still remains poorly understood, but political, religious and trading contacts with China and India appear to have played a decisive role. By the sixth century AD, Chinese records give the name 'Zhenla' to the area of the middle Mekong River and Lake Tonle Sap in modern Cambodia. The nature of this Zhenla is much debated but it seems to have been a term for a series of regional chiefdoms that possessed large, defended settlements and temple architecture showing strong Indian influence. By the beginning of the ninth century, Zhenla was unified into a powerful Khmer empire by King Jayavarman II. King Yasovarmon I moved its capital to Angkor in the last decade of the ninth century, from where the Khmer empire dominated mainland South East Asia until the early fifteenth century, when Angkor was

The complex of temples and other buildings that formed the city now called Angkor was one of the great wonders of ancient Asia. A mere two centuries after the fall of Angkor, historians of neighbouring Siam expressed doubts that it had been constructed by human hands, noting that 'they say angels from heaven came to help in building this magnificent city'.

sacked by Siamese troops.

The word Angkor derives from a Sanskrit term meaning 'holy city', but Angkor was not a city in the same sense as many of the other settlements described in this book. It was a huge, sprawling complex of temples, monuments, reservoirs and canals that grew in several stages over the centuries. A significant quantity of pottery and other occupational debris is known from surface collections inside Angkor, but in the absence of large-scale excavations it is not clear to what extent thordinary Khmers lived in the city complex.

The spatial structure of Angkor was determined by Indian religious concepts. The city was oriented around a central pyramid temple built on Phnom Bakheng, the only natural hill in the area. This temple was linked with Mt Meru, the central mountain of traditional Indian cosmology. Over time, the basis of the iconography at Angkor changed from the Hindu cult of Siva to Mahayana Buddhism, but a constant factor was the desire of Khmer kings to build monuments to their immortality. Perhaps most successful in this was Suryavarman II, who in the twelfth century built the most famous temple complex of the city – Angkor Wat.

Angkor's success was due in large part to its location on the north-west shore of Tonle Sap, the largest lake in Indochina. In the wet season, water from the Mekong River flows back north into Tonle Sap more than trebling the surface area of the lake from 30,000 sq km in the dry season to 100,000 sq km in the wet. The lake provided a ready source not only of fish but also of water for irrigation. An elaborate system

LEFT: King Suryavarman II's temple mausoleum at Angkor Wat is one of the greatest architectural accomplishments of ancient Asia. RIGHT: The southern gateway of Angkor Thom.

of reservoirs, canals and moats was dominated by two huge man-made reservoirs, or *baray*. The Eastern Baray is 7.12 by 1.7 km in area and could hold as much as 60 million cubic metres of water. The Western Baray was slightly larger in size. There is some debate over the extent to which these reservoirs were used in agricultural irrigation, and it may be that sufficient water was obtained from the nutrient-rich floods of Tonle Sap. Further research will help to clarify the function of the reservoirs, but the rise of Angkorian civilization would not have been possible without a large agricultural surplus, and it is relevant that a Chinese visitor to Angkor in the 1290s recorded that three or four rice crops were cultivated there each year.

The eventual decline of Angkorian civilization was probably due to a complex set of circumstances. The military expansion of the neighbouring Siamese and Cham states was, of course, one significant factor. A substantial fall in agricultural output seems to have also been important, but here it is difficult to determine cause and effect. Changing religious and political affiliations may have altered the traditional structure by which agricultural surpluses were exploited by the kings of Angkor. What were perhaps originally quite minor disruptions in the intricate system of Angkorian irrigation could have had major knock-on effects across a wide area. The French historian Fernand Braudel suggested that the demise of Angkor may have been due to an increase in the incidence of malaria. The muddy, stagnant water of most rice paddy-fields serves to hinder the breeding of mosquito larvae. If, because of war or other factors, the paddy system had not been properly maintained, however, then the water may have become clear and calm − the favoured breeding ground for the most dangerous species of mosquito.

After Angkor was sacked by the Siamese in 1431, most of the city was abandoned, but Angkor Wat was taken over by Buddhist monks and became an important pilgrimage centre.

European study of Angkor began almost 150 years ago. It was rediscovered by a Catholic missionary in 1850, and numerous surveys of the complex were conducted from as early as the 1860s. By the end of the nineteenth century, the French had gained control of Vietnam, Laos and Cambodia and had established the Ecole Française d'Extrême Orient to research the archaeology and philology of the Indochina region. In the early 1970s the Angkor region was captured

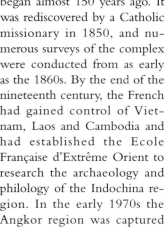

ABOVE: Eastern end of the north library at Banteay Srei.

LEFT: Angkor Wat.

A carved stone relief in the west gallery at Angkor Wat depicts a battle scene. Angkor was sacked by Siamese troops in 1431.

by the Khmer Rouge. There followed a twenty-year period of neglect and wilful destruction of the monuments. Sculptures were removed to sell on the illegal antiquities market; buildings were damaged by vibration from tanks and aircraft and sometimes even used for target practice; encroaching vegetation, wind and rain all took their toll, with a freak storm in August 1989 uprooting 1200 trees which damaged a number of temples. Once the Cambodian Peace Settlement was signed in 1991, Angkor was quickly placed on the UNESCO World Heritage List. Since then there has been a concerted effort by several international organizations to repair and maintain the monuments, to conduct basic research across the Angkor complex, and to train local Cambodian scholars in the skills necessary to preserve Angkor for the twenty-first century. Though significant advances have already been made, much work remains to be done at this world heritage site. ∎

HIRAIZUMI: JAPAN'S GATEWAY TO THE NORTH

Hiraizumi was the capital of the Northern Fujiwara clan who ruled the Tohoku region of north-eastern Honshu as a semi-independent kingdom in the twelfth century AD. The Northern Fujiwara were a family of aristocratic origin who, by the end of the eleventh century, had wrested control of the To-

Japan's first urban centres were the great capitals of western Honshu: Fujiwara (p. 150), Nara and Kyoto. These cities were above all political symbols of the power of the Yamato state but as the authority of that state began to wane from the ninth century, other urban forms developed in the provinces. Hiraizumi was one of the most important of these provincial cities, mirroring Kyoto in the splendour of its religious architecture and yet owing its wealth and vitality to trade and interaction with the world of north-east Asia that lay outside Japanese control.

hoku from the Japanese state in a series of wars and revolts. Some time between 1094 and 1104, Kiyohira, the first Fujiwara chieftain, chose Hiraizumi in modern Iwate Prefecture as his new capital for strategic reasons, and for its existing status as a religious centre based on the holy mountain Kanzan. Hiraizumi grew rapidly through the twelfth century, but as a city it did not survive the fall of the Northern Fujiwara in 1189. While the main temples remained, by the late seventeenth century the appearance of Hiraizumi was vividly captured by the famous haiku poet Matsuo Basho: 'Summer grass: all that remains of warriors' dreams.'

Archaeology is essential to a full understanding of Hiraizumi, because most of the existing records are biased against the Northern Fujiwara, portraying them as barbarian outlaws. A number of small-scale excavations, mainly within temple precincts, had been conducted at Hiraizumi since the 1950s, but it was not until the late 1980s that wide-area salvage archaeology began to give us a detailed picture of the ancient city. From 1988 to 1993, some 40,000 sq m were dug between the Chusonji and Motsuji temples and the Kitakami River. This area was previously believed to contain the residences of the first two Fujiwara chieftains, but the

large residential fortress that was unearthed was dated on ceramic grounds to the third quarter of the twelfth century and was therefore most probably the residence of the third chieftain, Hidehira. This complex was surrounded by a huge ditch, 7–8 m wide and 3 m deep, a type of defensive feature which was common in the Tohoku region in late antiquity but rare in western Japan.

Excavations in the central area of Hiraizumi have produced a variety of artifacts consistent with its status as a major provincial city. Ceramics include both domestic and imported wares. Some 100,000 unglazed earthenware bowls, weighing over fifteen tons in total, appear to have been used once in rituals or banquets and then thrown away, a custom clearly introduced from Kyoto. Only a very few of these bowls, which are known as *kawarake*, have been found at other, contemporary sites in the Tohoku region. The fine ceramics excavated at Hiraizumi testify to the active trading role of the city. Domestic earthenware came from the Tokoname and Atsumi kilns near modern Nagoya. White and green Song dynasty porcelain was excavated in some quantity, Hiraizumi having produced more imported Chinese porcelain than any other contemporary site except Kyoto and the Kyushu port of Hakata.

Wooden artifacts excavated from Hiraizumi include clogs, combs, rulers, various containers and chess pieces. Thousands of *chugi* – wooden spatulas used instead of toilet paper – were also discovered in pits that were either latrines or cesspools. *Chugi*

LEFT: Unglazed earthenware bowls used for banquets.
ABOVE: Iron pot excavated from Hiraizumi excavations.

The Kitakami River can be seen at the bottom of the picture.

were introduced into Japan from China, perhaps in the seventh century AD, and were still used in some rural areas until after the Second World War. Pictorial evidence such as the twelfth-century Gaki Soshi scroll confirms their use at the time of Hiraizumi.

Archaeology has thus begun to provide a quite different picture of ancient Hiraizumi from the traditional image based on the famous Buddhist art and architecture of the city. Some scholars have seen this Buddhist culture as a mere imitation of Kyoto, but more persuasive is a recent view which emphasizes the complex symbolic oppositions to the Kyoto-based Heian state that are inherent in Hiraizumi art. The Konjikido Hall within the Chusonji temple, for example, is unique in Japanese Buddhism in being both a hall and a tomb for the mummified remains of the four Fujiwara leaders. The main twelfth-century temples are the Chusonji with its gold-roofed Konjikido Hall, the Motsuji, and the Muryokoin. Although there is some evidence that these temples were built to conform to an urban plan, the overall layout of Hiraizumi remains unclear. The size of the city is a further problem: although Hiraizumi is often described as the largest provincial city in twelfth-century Japan, we have no real idea of what sort of population it may have held.

The wealth and power of the Northern Fujiwara were based on extensive trade with both the north (Hokkaido, Sakhalin and the Maritime Provinces) and the south (Japan). This trade, which included gold, horses and furs, followed the breakdown of the tribute-based economy of the ancient Japanese state and can be seen as part of a wider commercial revolution that swept East Asia in the early medieval era. Already in the tenth century, Japanese documents record sea-lion skins, bear furs, sand gold and konbu seaweed as tax payments from northern Tohoku. Most of these items would have been obtained via trade with Hokkaido rather than produced locally. By the twelfth century, this trade had be-

come the mainstay of the power of the Northern Fujiwara. The basic pattern of trade between Japan and north-east Asia perfected by the Northern Fujiwara continued into the medieval period long after the fall of Hiraizumi and had major effects on all the societies that participated in it. In Hokkaido, for instance, it led to profound changes in the culture of the indigenous Ainu people as the introduction into Hokkaido of cast iron pots of a type found at Hiraizumi led to the abandonment of Ainu pottery production and a shift in cooking techniques from ceramic ovens to iron pots suspended over an open fire. Far from being the isolated Stone Age relics of popular imagination, the Ainu were a people whose recent culture was formed through contacts with the outside, contacts which reached a critical intensity with the rise of Hiraizumi. ∎

PORT ESSINGTON

The Victoria military settlement at Port Essington on the Cobourg Peninsula on the north coast of Australia was the third unsuccessful British attempt to settle the region. The venture began in 1838 with the dispatch of an ill-equipped detachment of Royal Marines. The unfortunate members of the garrison struggled to survive in an alien environment in extreme isolation in order to establish British sovereignty in northern Australia.

Unlike most other Australian colonial settlements, there was no convict labour for most of the eleven years the settlement lasted, so the garrison was very much reliant on its own limited resources. The evidence from the surviving structures and archaeological excavations, together with the documentary sources, illustrate the practical problems faced by the settlers and the solutions they improvised.

Earlier attempts in the 1820s to settle the top end of what is now the Northern Territory of Australia were made with the intention of developing trading contacts with the Indonesian Archipelago. The Admiralty, however, proposed the Port Essington settlement more as a flag-waving exercise to forestall attempts at colonization by the French or Americans. The aim was to establish British 'permanent possession of the entire coast of Australia', as James Stephen of the Colonial Office put it. Commercial factors were less important than the political and strategic objectives and were only raised when the Treasury was approached (unsuccessfully) for financial backing. Undeterred, the Admiralty pressed ahead regardless, and dispatched two ships and a detachment of Royal Marines under the command of Sir James J. Gordon Bremer.

The architectural history of Port Essington can be divided into three phases. At first, things went reasonably well. Seven prefabricated timber buildings had been brought from Sydney, including dwellings for the commandant and officers, barrack rooms, kitchen, hospital, storehouse and church. Clearing the land proved laborious and difficult, and the buildings were erected on piles because levelling the stony ground was so arduous. (This technique was later widely used in tropical Australia because it improved ventilation and helped to control termites.) The single men's huts, of bark or reeds with a thatched roof, only lasted two or three years before termites destroyed the framework. The huts were then burnt and rebuilt on the same site. A defensive earthwork and a pier were constructed. but the local ironstone proved difficult to work so only one side of the pier was properly dressed stone.

In November 1839 a tropical cyclone devastated the settlement. Most of the buildings were destroyed, and HMS *Pelorus*, which was in harbour at the time, ran aground. The crew of the *Pelorus*, who remained throughout 1840, were a welcome addition to the labour force, and prompted a change in construction methods. One of the crewmen was a brickmaker by trade, and his skills meant that bricks could be produced, albeit of poor quality. Buildings were brought to ground level and given brick and stone foundations. Two that had survived the storm were enclosed at the lower level, a retrograde step as they were later rendered uninhabitable by termites. By the beginning of 1842, married quarters, a magazine, charcoal and lime kilns, a bread oven and a smithy had all been completed.

The third phase of building at Port Essington coincided with the visit in late 1844 of a team of twenty convicts, all quarrymen and masons, who had been building a beacon on the Barrier Reef. They stayed for four months and, as well as a beacon at the mouth of Port Essington, also built two additional family cottages and the hospital kitchen, and rebuilt the smithy. All these buildings, in contrast with the more amateurish and improvised earlier structures, were clearly built by professionals. The plan for the kitchen, for example, seems to have been adapted from a standard nineteenth-century British design, with a raised internal floor and stone doorsteps. The walls were well laid and even, and the corners,

Le Breton's illustration of the pier and harbour at the Victoria settlement, Port Essington, in 1839.

The remains of some buildings at Port Essington still survive, including this hospital kitchen.

entrances, windows and chimney were finished with good quality dressed masonry.

Apart from the Marines themselves there were also a small number of wives and children and some civilian officials at Port Essington, but the settlement was always very small, never exceeding eighty people. According to surviving documents, life was difficult, tedious and uncomfortable. Producing crops was a matter of trial and error and the slow accumulation of experience, as the seasons and climate were poorly understood. Livestock was imported, although the losses in transit were enormous. One shipment of forty-five cattle landed only fourteen survivors, two of which died almost immediately. Sheep did particularly poorly in the climate and stock had to be hand-fed to prevent them eating poisonous plants – yet another drain on the labour force.

The health of the settlers was generally poor. The death rate was very high; nearly a quarter of all those posted to Port Essington died. Malaria was the main killer. The doctor later recalled the worst epidemic during the wet season of 1848-9. 'I cannot think of Port Essington without a shudder, what a fearful state we were in in 1849 when all but yourself and two others were attacked by fever . . . Do you recollect during my lucid intervals your visits to my bedside for instructions how to treat the sick? The care of the sick and dying lasted six weeks.'

Unlike at most other Australian settlements, relations with the local Aboriginal people were cordial. The Aborigines were of course accustomed to the annual visits of Macassan fishermen from Celebes (now Sulawesi) for *trepang* (sea-cucumber), considered a delicacy in China. McArthur, who succeeded Bremer as commandant, seems to have pursued a policy of tolerance and non-violence. The small size of the garrison and the absence of free settlers meant that the British posed no threat to the economic basis of Aboriginal life, nor was there any serious attempt to Christianize the Aborigines.

The Aborigines adopted European goods, including metal for fishing spears, clothing, which they traded, and tobacco. Glass was also welcomed as a substitute for stone and many glass artifacts were found during excavations. According to the naval artist Harden Melville, the young men preferred the doctor to extract their incisors instead of knocking them out with a stone at their initiation ceremonies as was the local custom. The Aborigines supplied the garrison with shellfish, turtle, honey and the hearts of the cabbage tree palm, which supplemented the game – kangaroo, birds and fish – taken by the settlers.

Among the surviving structures at Port Essington is a row of five semi-circular stone chimneys. These belonged to the married quarters. These are identical to the distinctive Cornish round chimney once thought to be found only in Cornwall. An illustration of a similar chimney at Glenelg in South Australia dates from 1836-8. Marines from Glenelg were among those posted to Port Essington in 1838 and it seems likely that at least one Cornishman was among them. Apart from the chimneys, the cottages, in the same way as the single men's huts, were built of bark or reeds and thatched with grass. Square holes with shutters similar to the ports of a vessel provided light and air. Excavation of one cottage showed that it had a clay floor, in contrast to the shell floors of most other buildings. The interior of the cottage was swept clean and little was found. Glass artifacts against one wall, however, showed that Aborigines camped outside while it was occupied.

Isolated, ignorant of the environment, ill-prepared, and with minimal support from a distant bureaucratic centre, the settlement at Port Essington was too small to be viable. It was eventually abandoned in 1849. The area was never reoccupied and the ruins testify to the difficulties the British encountered in establishing settlements in tropical Australia. ■

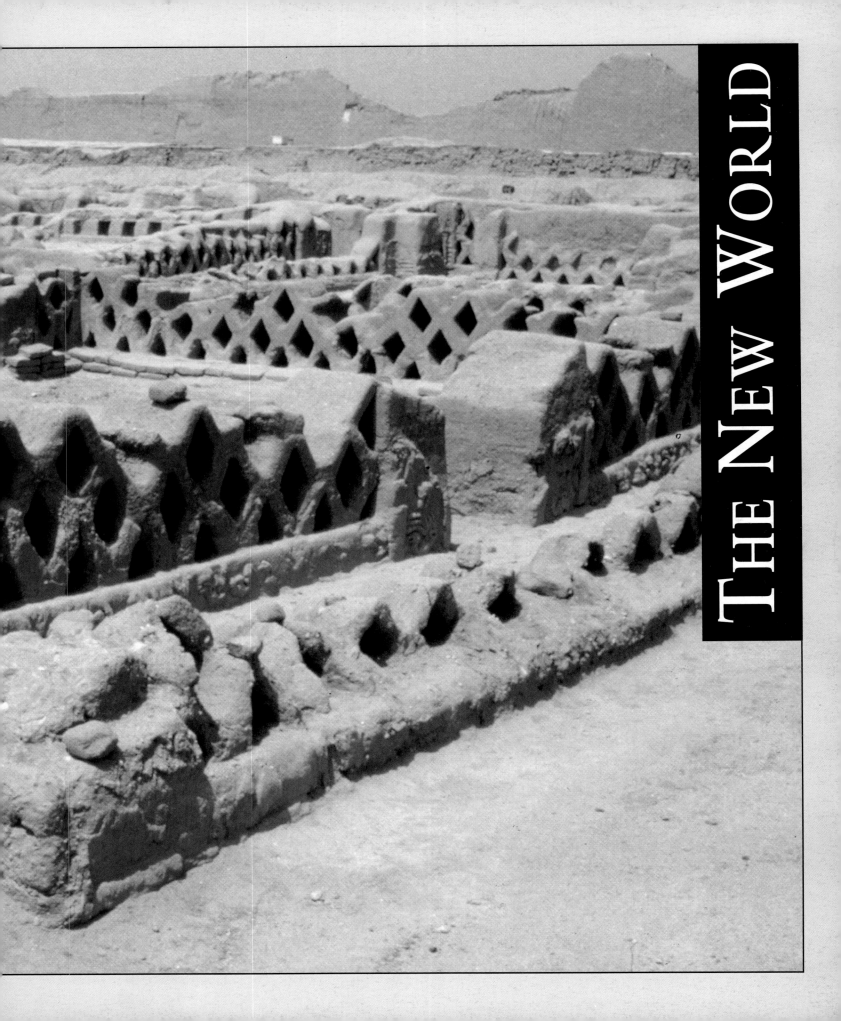

CAHOKIA: ANCIENT CITY OF THE AMERICAN HEARTLAND

This area of the North American continent had been occupied for thousands of years prior to the construction of Cahokia by hunters and gatherers. Pottery was introduced to this region around 600 BC. During the first millennium, local inhabitants began to construct permanently occupied villages based on the hunting and gathering of local wild resources, as well as the cultivation of sunflower and squash. Soon after, there is evidence for the introduction of corn as an important component of their diet, and this occurred along with a growth in population and an increasingly complex social organization. From about AD 1000, Cahokia began to rise to the height of its power. Archaeologists still dispute the ultimate origins of the place. Clearly the cultural base of Cahokia society was indigenous. However, it is also possible, perhaps likely, that Cahokia, given its similarities to contemporary cultures in Mexico, such as its overall plaza-dominated plan, may have been inspired either directly or indirectly by contact with them.

The site of Cahokia is in fact just one of a complex of mounds that once dotted the entire area. However, because of European settlement that started in earnest at the beginning of the nineteenth century, and the reworking of land for agriculture, most of these mounds are now lost. Cahokia is located in the flood-lands of the confluence of the Missouri, Mississippi and Illinois rivers,

When thinking of ancient cities of the Americas, most people's minds immediately drift to the lush forests of Mexico. And yet, right in the heartland of North America, 1000 years ago there arose a magnificent ancient civilization, as complex in its own way as the better-known archaeological cultures of Mexico, but as overlooked as the Maya and Aztec civilizations are celebrated. Just east of the modern town of St Louis, across the Missouri River in the state of Illinois, stands the archaeological site of Cahokia.

and thus controlled not only the rich alluvial plains of this area, known also as the American Bottom, but also access to these major river systems.

The Cahokia site covers about 800 hectares, of which the inner 80 were enclosed by a log wall. It comprises about a hundred earthen mounds, in shape either conical, flat-topped or ridge-topped. Some of them were used as the burial places of important people, and others as platforms for wooden buildings that have long since decayed, the residences of Cahokia's lesser élite. The largest of these mounds is called Monks Mound (so-named because, when first visited by the antiquarian Henry Brackenridge in 1811, Cahokia was occupied by a group of Trappist monks). It is over 30 m high and approximately 300 by 240 m in area. It was constructed in stages over several centuries, between AD 900 and 1150 (according to recent radiocarbon dating), so that today it appears as a series of terraces of different heights. The mound required over 7 million cu m of earth, all of it taken from nearby borrow-pits, the remains of which are still clearly visible. Monks Mound is the largest pre-Columbian structure in North America, and in fact is surpassed in size only by the Great Pyramid in Cholula and the Pyramid of the Sun at Teotihuacán,

An artist's reconstruction of the Central Plaza at Cahokia.

Lesser mounds, some used for burials, others for buildings, surround Monks Mound.

both of which are in Mexico. On top of the mound archaeologists found the remains of a large building measuring 30 by 12 m, as well as other structural remains. This was presumably the residence of the leader of the community.

In front of Monks Mound is a plaza, some 300 by 400 m, surrounded by seventeen smaller mounds, once surmounted by wooden buildings, the residences of Cahokia's lesser élite. The plaza as well as the mounds, in total over 80 hectares, were enclosed by a palisade. And beyond this central enclosure were other plazas, other mounds and other settlements.

Mound 72 at Cahokia is a superlative example of burial practices at the site. This mound, of the ridge-topped variety, was at one time at least 3 m high, and approximately 42 by 20 m in area. It consisted of a set of smaller mounds that had subsequently been covered together, some time towards the end of the tenth century. Over 250 individual skeletons were recovered from it. One individual – presumably a man of great importance in Cahokia society – had been buried on a platform of shell beads. Next to him were other skeletal remains accompanied by grave goods, most notably a cache of several hundred beautifully carved projectile points. The stone type and shape of these points suggest contact

with areas as far afield as Oklahoma, Tennessee and Wisconsin. Also in the grave were a copper-covered staff, sheet copper and mica.

Cahokia, with its central plaza dominated by Monks Mound, was the heart of a sprawling metropolis of farmers, craftsmen and traders, with contacts that spread through much of the Midwest of the North American continent. It supported a population conservatively estimated at 10,000 people but which may perhaps have been as many as 30,000. The Cahokia metropolis was made possible only by community building activity and this, as well as the evidence for long-distance trade, indicates the complex and hierarchical social organization of an ancient city.

How strange, then, that Cahokia is rarely given its due as one of the great archaeological treasures of the continent. Perhaps the reason lies in nineteenth-century politics, for at that time many Americans were reluctant to see Cahokia and the hundreds of other spectacular mound sites of the continent as the work of ancient Indians. Indeed, they preferred to attribute these sites to fanciful builders, such as lost Welshmen or errant Phoenicians. Archaeologists today think that this idea was rooted in the racism of the nineteenth century, for if indeed Indians could build such monuments, then how could they be treated as savages and their land taken from them? Thanks in part to archaeology, however, such fantasies can no longer be seriously entertained, and the real story behind these magnificent mound sites is now known. ∎

CITIES OF THE NORTH AMERICAN DESERTS

The northern area of the American Southwest, part of the San Juan River system, was inhabited during the last 2000 years of the prehistoric period by a series of peoples that were once called the Anasazi. Archaeologists, however, now prefer to call them Ancestral Pueblo, for the descendants of these prehistoric Indian populations still live in pueblo villages like Zuni, Taos and Hopi. About 2500 years ago these farmers began growing corn, beans and squash, plants that were first cultivated in Central America several thousand years earlier. Later on, they started to grow plants like cotton and tobacco but, with the exception of the dog and the turkey, they never relied on domesticated animals. These people left behind them archaeological ruins of all kinds, from small semi-subterranean pit-houses to large, multi-roomed apartment-like complexes, some of them four or even five storeys high. The pinnacle of ancestral Pueblo architecture is nowhere better seen than in the archaeological sites of Chaco Canyon, and in particular Pueblo Bonito, an ancient town in the desert.

The American Southwest is a barren land. Its windswept deserts scorch in the summer and freeze in the winter. There seems too much of everything: too much sun, too much wind, too much drought. And even when it does rain, it seems to rain all at once, and much of the moisture's goodness is lost. Yet here, 1000 years ago, there developed a remarkable prehistoric culture based on a remarkable knowledge of how to farm the desert to produce crops of maize, beans and squash. These people left behind some of the most magnificent archaeological remains of the continent.

Chaco Canyon is located in northern New Mexico, surrounded by the Navajo Nation Reservation. The canyon lies on an approximately east–west orientation following the course of Chaco Wash, but the waters of the wash itself only run intermittently throughout the year. The section of canyon that contains the majority of archaeological sites is about 20 km long, and thirteen large site complexes, as well as many other smaller ones, can be seen here. Chaco was inhabited by Ancestral Pueblo peoples from as early as 300 BC, but the climax of their occupation occurred between AD 1000 and 1150. Estimates of the Chacoan population at this time range from 2000 to 6000 people.

The environment of Chaco Canyon is a forbidding one. In order to ensure an adequate food supply, the ancient inhabitants of Chaco early on devised a complicated system of water control so that the natural run-off could be used to best effect. Along the north side of the canyon, for example, are the remains of an extensive system of diversion dams, canals and ditches to take as much water as possible to the well laid-out field systems adjacent to the large towns.

That peoples could live in such an apparently inhospitable place, not only growing enough food to survive but also producing such magnificent architecture is remarkable enough. But Chaco Canyon is also the centre of an extensive network of smaller sites, called Chacoan outliers, extending several hundred kilometres to the north, south and west, many of which are connected by well-made roads. These roads are up to 96 km long and 13 m wide. While most are now mere linear depressions in the ground, often only visible from the air, some sections still retain masonry kerbs. The elaborateness of this road

The 'apartment-style' buildings at Chaco Canyon bespeak a complex social organization.

Apartment rooms were used for dwelling, storage, and many other purposes.

system indicates a very intensively organized and maintained communication system.

The network of Chacoan sites scattered throughout the San Juan Basin and joined by this road system is sometimes called the Chaco Phenomenon by archaeologists, and the causes underlying its development have been the source of much debate. Most interpretations revolve around economic factors for the rise of Chaco (the canyon was the centre of, among other things, turquoise production for the northern Southwest). Outlier sites harvested or produced specialized resources that were then shipped to the central canyon area for redistribution back out into the network. One example of the network's complexity can be found at Chimney Rock. This Chacoan outlier site is located in the forests of southern Colorado, over 160 km to the north of Chaco Canyon. It has been suggested by scholars working at the site that resources like timber, meat and hides were floated by workers down the San Juan River and its tributaries until they reached the Chacoan road system of northern New Mexico, then to be transported overland to Chaco itself. Other archaeologists have argued that the outlier sites were something more akin to religious colonies, and the roads symbolic and practical connections between the colonies themselves. Most recently, it has been suggested that the roads served to move soldiers quickly between outlier sites, the whole network itself being the basis of something approaching a feudal system by which the élite of Chaco could exploit and control the surrounding countryside. Perhaps there is an element of truth in all of these theories.

The presence at Chaco Canyon sites of Mesoamerican items such as copper bells and macaw skeletons was once thought to indicate a Mexican trade connection, and perhaps was the very stimulus for Chaco's rise. Recent analysts are more cautious, suggesting that trade between the two areas may have been modest, the result not of a monolithic trading entity run by professional Aztec traders, but rather of small-scale exchanges by which Mesoamerican material reached the Southwest incrementally.

Chaco Canyon contains thirteen towns, of which the largest is Pueblo Bonito, although it would be inaccurate to assume that

The great Kiva at Pueblo Bonito; a religious and communal centre for ancestral Pueblo life in the canyon.

this town was drastically more important than the others in the canyon. This site has, however, drawn the attention of archaeologists, since it was first seen by Europeans in the middle of the nineteenth century. (Of course, these sites had never been lost to the Indian inhabitants of the area.) It was the focus of an early investigation by Neil Judd for the National Geographic Society in 1921, and today most visitors equate Chaco with Bonito.

Pueblo Bonito comprises a D-shaped series of connected rooms, surrounding a central open area or plaza. The central wall that divides the pueblo is close to a north-south orientation. The D shape of the pueblo opens it to the south, and this, together with its vertically stepped architecture, gives the site maximum solar exposure. (Many other sites had astronomical significance too; for example, the supernova of July 1054 is recorded at Peñasco Blanco.)

Pueblo Bonito stood four or perhaps even five storeys high. Over 300 individual ground-floor rooms, and perhaps as many as 650 in total, have been identified. These rooms were used for both habitation, storage and other specialized activities; some were later sealed and used for burials. There were at least thirty-two *kivas*, and two great *kivas*: these are semi-subterranean chambers, often circular in shape that were used – as they are today by

modern Pueblo peoples – for religious ceremonies and as important centres of community life.

Buildings were constructed of well-shaped stones held together by adobe (mud cement and plaster). Typically, walls were of rubble core masonry – parallel wall sides were constructed and then filled in with adobe and rough stone. The interiors of the walls were plastered and whitewashed and often decorated with painted designs. Wall exteriors were often plastered too. Room features included wall niches, wood platforms, windows and firepits. Archaeologists uncovered beautiful pottery, and human burials with arrows, bird effigies and turquoise pendants, all items indicative of a high social status.

Based on the analysis of tree-rings taken from construction beams, it is estimated that work began on Pueblo Bonito in the early 900s. In the eleventh century additions to the basic plan were made, and between AD 1075 and 1115 major building work, including extensions in the form of wings, was undertaken. Minor construction and repairs continued constantly until the early twelfth century when building activity stopped. The importance of Pueblo Bonito to its inhabitants is shown by the fact that, during the eleventh century, they shored up the so-called Threatening Rock, a huge slab of cliff that threatened to topple over and crush a large part of the site. When this finally happened – in 1941 – sixty-five rooms and a beautiful section of the north wall were destroyed. ■

Kiva.L

The great cliff dwellings of Mesa Verde in southern Colorado continue to impress visitors with their grandeur.

TEOTIHUACÁN

The Central Mexican city of Teotihuacán was one of the greatest metropolises of Mesoamerica during the Classic Period (AD 250–900). The city's widespread influence is evidenced in monuments and artefacts from the eastern Gulf Coast to the western Zapotec-controlled region of Oaxaca. In the south, the Maya of Guatemala constructed temples and manufactured vessels which mimicked those produced at the vast site. Though Teotihuacán's ancient economic and artistic reach is well documented, relatively little is understood about the city's political structure or, for that matter, about the people who constructed its distinctive massive pyramids.

Excavations conducted during the 1960s revealed that Teotihuacán had early origins dating to the first century AD, and that the metropolis reached its peak during the sixth and seventh centuries. The city was laid out on a grid plan with its central core covering 13 to 14.5 sq km. Large, single-storey apartment compounds scattered throughout the site housed extended families numbering from sixty to a hundred people. The first large construction campaigns date to somewhere between AD 100 and 200. During this time, the Teotihuacanos laid out a street, 40 m wide, running north-south for 5 km. The Aztecs, believing ancient gods to be buried along this avenue, called the road Miccaotli, the 'Street of the Dead'. The Pyramid of the Sun, located east of the street, was constructed shortly afterwards and is distinguished by five unequal tiers fronted by a single stairway that bifurcates at the bottom. This huge monument, over 220 m wide at the base, soars to a height of some 65 m. The stone veneer surface covers an interior core of three million cubic tons of adobe and rubble.

The placement and appearance of the structure have suggested a number of possible functions. It was most certainly a backdrop for ritual and public events, and its astronomical alignment, with the summer solstice zenith in mind (when the sun is directly over the pyramid and casts no shadow on either its north or south

OPPOSITE: One of the most revered constructions at the site of Teotihuacan was the Pyramid of the Sun. A shrine or temple may have once topped this huge structure.

LEFT: In a painted mural from the Tepantitla apartment compound, small humans are shown dancing amidst the butterfly-filled, after-life paradise known as Tlalocan.

BELOW: A ritual mask, or possibly part of an incense burner.

side), must have been cause for civic celebration. Alternatively, a shrine fronting the pyramid's base marks the location of a long underground cave which terminates in a quatrefoil chamber almost directly under the pyramid platform. Ancient offerings of vases and figurines, along with multiple artificial walls which blocked off the tunnel, point to a periodic ritual use. Although the tunnel was permanently sealed in the fifth century by the Teotihuacanos, later offerings indicate that the Aztecs broke into it centuries later.

Scholars have put forward a number of hypotheses regarding the significance of the cave. Some believe that it functioned as a pilgrimage site for centuries prior to the construction of the pyramid. According to others, the pyramid was erected over the cave in order to mark the Teotihuacán 'axis mundi', the centre of the world. As such, the cave under the Pyramid of the Sun would have been perceived as the *locus* of Teotihuacán origins. It is known that later peoples, like the Aztecs, believed that caves were sites of birth, emergence and creation. The pyramid's cave could therefore have functioned as a place where one communicated with the ancestors, where the past could be made present.

The Pyramid of the Moon, located at the north end of the Street of the Dead, was constructed shortly after the Pyramid of the Sun. It was framed by a hill known as Cerro Gordo, and its builders emphasized the visual similarities between architecture and landscape. The structure is somewhat smaller than the Pyramid of the Sun, standing only 45 m high and about 145 m wide at the base but, like the Pyramid of the Sun, the Pyramid of the Moon is believed to have been erected in a single phase of construction. It has been suggested that the Pyramid of the Moon and its hill were both dedicated to the Teotihuacán Great Goddess. This creator deity appears in many of the city's murals as a personified mountain and is associated with caves, water,

LEFT: Pyramid of the Moon, maybe dedicated to the 'Great Goddess', a deity of fertility and agriculture. BELOW: Apartments and ritual platforms line a Teotihuacán street. OPPOSITE: An incense burner lid showing a face peering through an ornate headdress.

vegetation, and the concept of fertility.

Shortly after AD 200, the Teotihuacanos divided the city into quadrants by laying two new avenues along the east–west axis of the site. The *ciudadela* (citadel) was constructed at the south-east juncture of the main intersection of the Street of the Dead and the East Avenue. The walls of this enormous square complex span a distance of 400 m on each side and encase a vast open plaza. In-

side the plaza there are the remains of the famous little Pyramid of Quetzalcoatl, and two adjacent complexes believed to have functioned as the administrative centre for the city. The Pyramid of Quetzalcoatl was named after the feathered serpents which flank its central staircase and decorate the balustrades. These serpents seemingly slither across a blue background decorated with scattered sea shells indicating an aquatic environment. The squared-off mosaic head-dress which appears intermittently along the serpent's undulating body has been identified as an emblem of a militaristic order.

The rise of militarism at the site is also underlined by recent excavations at the Temple of Quetzalcoatl. To date, archaeologists have unearthed 113 complete skeletons of bound individuals wearing war regalia. Some researchers believe that the warriors were the victims of a despotic rule which arose shortly after AD 150 and were the unlucky members of a defeated earlier regime. Their interred bodies functioned as dedicatory offerings for the building and as a permanent warning to citizens and visiting merchants conducting business inside the *ciudadela*'s walls.

By the sixth century, Teotihuacán's population had grown to perhaps as many as 200,000 people. The citizens built new and more complex structures in order to house the swelling urban masses and military orders. The richly embellished Palace of Quetzalpapalotl probably housed one of the growing orders of warriors. Inside, Quetzal-decorated piers support an entablature carrying stepped elements and a symbol known as a 'Mexican Year Sign'. These interlocking trapezoids were associated with the calendar by the Aztec and with ritual warfare by the Maya.

The increased signs of militarism appearing in the pictorial arts of the city seem to coincide with its decline during the eighth century. Around AD 750 ceremonial structures and other public buildings, particularly those around the Street of the Dead, were systematically burned, never to be used again. All evidence seems to point to some sort of internal uprising. Beyond the popular unrest, the external matrix of Teotihuacán's power was also under assault, possibly due to the rise of cities far from Central Mexico. As these other states became increasingly powerful and commercially competitive, Teotihuacán appears to have lost control over the long-distance exchange network that had led to its prosperity. With problems at home and abroad, the city was abandoned by AD 800, its former greatness intimated only in sixteenth-century Aztec anecdotes and in the ruins scattered across the vast city. ■

TIKAL

Tikal, located in the Department of the Petén in Guatemala, was one of the largest and most influential of all the cities. Its origins date to before the Classic Period (AD 250–900), around 600 BC. Tikal's location, midway between two rivers, allowed the rulers of the site to control both overland and riverine trade routes. Even though the city's population swelled to over 50,000, the Maya were able to feed their growing numbers by optimizing the use of arable land. The artificially raised fields and hillside terraces which are scattered across the region point to the ancient intensive agriculture which was probably under the control of the ruling élite. Like most Maya cities, Tikal was organized on the basis of ranked lineages, with

For over 600 years (AD 250–900), the ancient Maya spread their civilization over the vast area now comprising Guatemala, Belize, northern El Salvador, Honduras, and Mexico's south-eastern provinces of Tabasco, Yucatan and Quintana Roo. Early settlers to the region clustered their city-states near or along the banks of rivers. As populations grew, the larger states solidified their dominance over the smaller cities by means of ritualized warfare and control of economic resources.

the highest ranking families constantly jockeying for political control. At the head of the dominant lineage was a ruler whose power was based not only on military might but also on the concept of divine right.

Modern knowledge of Tikal's history began about thirty years ago when the American archaeologist, William Coe, headed the University of Pennsylvania Tikal Project (1956–69). In the process of mapping the site and recording its monuments, Coe discovered that the city consisted of groups of masonry buildings which were connected by paved causeways, called *sac bes* ('white roads'). Clusters of sacred and residential constructions were generally grouped around individual plazas on top of man-made and natural hills. At its political

Left: Like many of the constructions on the top of Tikal's Great Acropolis, Temple II functioned as both a tribute to the ruling élite as well as a mortuary structure.

Above: The corbelled vaulting system inside these structures from the Central Acropolis is particular to Maya architecture and decreased the mass of the upper part of the buildings.

Right: The 'stela and altar complex' is one of the hallmarks of Maya civilization. The altar placed before the stela may have served as a platform for the ruler.

ABOVE: Like most Maya altars, Altar 4 was carved on its side. The deity emerges from a shell, indicating the watery underworld known as Xibalba.

LEFT: Hieroglyphic decipherment breakthroughs have enabled the texts from Tikal's stelae to be read, allowing Mayanists to reconstruct the history and royal lineages of the site.

RIGHT: Pyramids and palaces are clustered around central plazas on the top of Tikal's acropolises.

zenith, the huge city supported some 3000 structures.

At the top of one of the largest of the city's hills is the Great Acropolis. This huge mound with its plaza supported pyramids and religious structures, and functioned as a burial site for many of Tikal's great kings. One of the mortuary constructions is Temple I which looms 45 m above the plaza and is at the apex of a pyramidal base of nine tiers. The small corbel-vaulted temple is accessed via a narrow staircase which fronts the pyramid. Three interior chambers are separated with doorways spanned by carved wooden lintels. The text from Lintel 3 identifies the pictured ruler as Ah Cacaw ('Lord Chocolate Bean'), who ruled Tikal in the seventh and eighth centuries. While the structure was started by Ah Cacaw, it was finished by his son, Ruler B, who took the reins of power in AD 734.

Apart from housing the body of Ah Cacaw in a tomb located

below the structure, this monument probably served symbolically as a man-made 'world mountain'. The temple-caves over such constructions were used to perform auto-sacrificial rites and were the means through which the Maya rulers communicated with their ancestors. It is likely that after the passing of Ah Caca, his son, Ruler B, visited the monument to seek audience with his dead father.

Before each of the pyramids of the Great Acropolis, there are numerous free-standing monolithic sculptures known as stelae, generally accompanied by altars which may have served as pedestals for the rulers. This pairing of monuments, known as the 'stela and altar complex', is characteristic of many Maya sites and is one of the hallmarks of Maya civilization.

Stelae were generally decorated with the likenesses of great kings regaled in all their splendour. On Tikal Stela 16, for example, the ruler Ah Cacaw stands frontally with his head in profile. His costume includes representations of jade beads and long plumes of the Quetzal Bird. A Maya artisan carved this monument during the ruler's eighth-century reign in commemoration of a successful period ending during the city's halcyon days. ∎

COPÁN

As in the case of Tikal (p. 172), the site of Copán was first inhabited during the Pre-Classic Period and was in close proximity to fresh water. By AD 200 the Maya started the first architectural constructions: the Great Plaza, the Great Ballcourt and the Acropolis. By AD 426 Copán's ruling dynasty was founded by a king named Yax Kuk Mo' (Blue-Quetzal-Macaw). He and his sixteen descendants would rule the site for the next 400 years.

Most of the city's huge pyramids, stelae and altars proclaim the successful war campaigns and histories of Copanec rulers. Individual kings generally couched their deeds in the contexts of those of earlier dynasts. For example, Altar Q, carved under the direction of the city's last king, Yax Pac, portrays all sixteen rulers

Copán, one of the largest of the ancient Maya sites, is on the southern periphery of Mesoamerica. Established in the first millennium BC, Copán steadily grew in both size and population. Under the guidance of powerful dynasts, the city's political control spread to adjacent sites. Distant alliances were made with larger Maya polities hundreds of miles away. In at least one instance, economic relations seem to have been cemented with royal marriage between a Copanec king and a woman from the great city of Palenque to the northwest.

of the site around its perimeter. On the front of the monument, Yax Kuk Mo' hands the sceptre of royal authority to his descendant, Yax Pac. Atop this monument, the text reinforces Yax Pac's claim to power by making reference to the accession of the earliest dynast.

Although Yax Kuk Mo' was responsible for building the first version of the Great Ballcourt, it was remodelled in the eighth century by his descendant, 18-Rabbit. Measuring 25 by 7 m, this I-shaped playing field is one of the largest made by the Maya. The sacred nature of the game is shown by the presence of six macaw-headed markers along its sides. These, and the ballcourt itself, refer to two episodes from the ancient narrative of the hero twins, Hunahpu and Xbalanque, later recorded in a seventeenth-century

LEFT: An image of God III from the stairway of the East Court. The jaguar ears flanking the face indicate this deity's underworld association.
ABOVE: The head of the 'Old Man of Copán', once part of a huge statue.

Top: Altar Q depicts sixteen of Copán's most important dynasts. Here Yax Kuk Mo' hands a sceptre of royal authority to his descendant, Yax Pac.

Left: The Principal Bird Deity, and a skeletal head adorn the back rack of a ruler from Stela H at Copán.

Above: On the front of Stela H, 18-Rabbit is shown as 'First Father'.

volume known as the *Popol Vuh*. As the story goes, the twins were the first players of the game. In one episode, their raucous playing so disturbed the Lords of the Underworld, that they were called down to atone for their disrespect. After playing the game for the Underworld deities and being subjected to a series of tests, the twins eventually defeated the evil gods. In another episode, the bird Vucub Caquix 'Nine Parrot' had falsely presumed dominion over the sun and the moon and was generally terrorizing all living creatures. The twins were able to re-establish order in the world by shooting down this arrogant supernatural bird. The Ballcourt at Copán, then, reflects the worldly obligations of the kings towards their city. Like Hunahpu and Xbalanque, the kings

BELOW: Jade pendants depicting seated rulers are part of burial goods from Copán.
RIGHT: Temple 18, one of the last structures built at the site of Copán. The small crypt under the platform may have once held the body of Yax Pac, whose image is sculpted on the four piers of the building.

were responsible for maintaining civic order, dispatching all would-be usurpers of power. It was believed that the players who lost this game went to the Underworld, where they would play the game for the amusement of the Lords of the Underworld and would deliver messages for their king.

Archaeological evidence points to the abandonment of the

great Maya cities in the ninth century. Although the reasons for the collapse are unknown, many theories have been put forward including ecological disaster, war and famine. Portents of the impending calamity are found in the last structures of Copán. Buildings such as Temple 18 pale in comparison to the earlier enormous constructions spread across the city. On four of the piers from this small temple, Yax Pac is portrayed as a war-lord, holding spear and shield and dressed in cotton armour. Since the city was under external and internal assault at this time, this portrayal of the king and the size of the monument can be understood as a visual indicator of the waning power of the ruler and the decline of the great city and civilization. ■

TIWANAKU

Tiwanaku was the capital city of one of the first of the expansive empires in the Andes, and its influence on contemporary and later civilizations is difficult to exaggerate. Emerging from a long tradition of lakeshore towns that relied on herding, farming and fishing, Tiwanaku became the dominant city in the Titicaca Basin sometime around AD 400. The distinctive architecture, monuments and iconography of the Tiwanaku soon spread throughout what is now southern Peru, northern Chile and much of the Bolivian highlands, as the Tiwanaku built colonies in lowland areas important for agriculture and trade, and used long-distance trade to obtain a wide range of resources unavailable in their highland homeland.

The city lies on the southern end of the Titicaca Basin, an area of interior drainage between the eastern and western mountain ranges of the Andes. The major feature of the basin is Lake Titicaca, the highest navigable lake in the world. The city of Tiwanaku is located approximately 15 km from the present-day lakeshore, where the climate is milder and the soils are better than is the case in much of the surrounding *altiplano*, or high plain. At 3850 m above sea level, Tiwanaku may be the highest ancient capital city in the world.

In this remarkable setting, this unique and carefully planned city was constructed using elaborate stonework. Laid out along a

In 1549 the Spanish chronicler Cieza de León visited the highland city of Tiwanaku, in what is now Bolivia, and provided the first known description of its ruined monuments. Cieza was impressed by the stone architecture and monuments of Tiwanaku, and, influenced perhaps by the stories the local people told of the city and its origins, he speculated that the ruins represented the oldest site in the Andes. Although we now know that Tiwanaku itself emerged from a long tradition of local cultural development, we also have a much greater understanding of the importance of this great highland centre, which colonized and traded in vast areas of the south-central Andes between about AD 500 and 1000.

grid that follows the cardinal points, the city covers about 16 hectares. Large monumental structures in the centre are surrounded by as yet unstudied areas where most of the inhabitants probably lived. The city itself was the centre of an empire, while smaller towns with features similar to those found at Tiwanaku were located across the high plains of the surrounding region.

The stonework in the city is one of its most notable aspects. The elaborate masonry of the monumental buildings features huge cut stone blocks held in place not only by careful positioning but also with I-shaped copper bars set into grooves in the stone blocks. Some of the large blocks have carved images on their façades. Huge monumental carved stone doorways and giant stone monoliths featuring carvings of figures holding *keros* (ceremonial goblets), staffs, and even trophy heads are found throughout the central area of the city.

The core of Tiwanaku is made up of several large monumental structures, the largest of which is the Akapana pyramid, a terraced mound built by erecting five tiers of stone walls and filling the area behind them with earth. Researchers have believed for many years that the Akapana was a natural hill modified by the Tiwanaku, but the most recent investigations suggest that most of the hill is man-made. The stone-faced pyramid is about 200 m long and 17 m high. On the top of the pyramid, a central sunken

ABOVE: The Gateway of the Sun, illustrated by E. G. Squier.
RIGHT: The temple at Tiwanaku, with stele at its centre.
OPPOSITE: Detail from the Gateway of the Sun, Tiwanaku, carved from a single block of stone.

court 50 m long sits between two sets of stairs that form eastern and western entrances to the Akapana. The remains of rectangular stone rooms indicate that some of Tiwanaku's élite may have lived on top of this most prominent of the city's monuments. Human burials, and offerings of animal remains, metal, carved and polished stone, and ceramic objects are found in and around the structures.

The Kalasaya is a huge rectilinear platform located just north of the Akapana. It is about 130 m long, and raised above ground level by a stone wall formed of large upright sandstone blocks alternating with coursed stone masonry. Built along an east–west axis, with a rectangular court on its eastern side, the Kalasaya is impressive for its regularity and structure. A tall stone statue, known as the Ponce monolith, sits in the middle of the sunken court.

Stairs set into the east wall of the Kalasaya lead down towards the semi-subterranean temple, one of the hallmark architectural features at Tiwanaku. The walls of this structure match those of the Kalasaya, being constructed of large vertical sandstone blocks alternating with sections of horizontally placed coursed stone blocks. The entry to the temple was down a set of stairs on its south side. A huge stone stela, known as the Bennet monolith, is placed at the centre of the structure, with smaller stone monolithic carvings around it.

The Pumapunku is a second major mound found at Tiwanaku. It is some distance from the other structures in the core of the city, to the south-east of the Akapana. Like the Akapana, the Pumapunku is a stepped mound with massive stone blocks forming its outer walls. It is a T-shaped structure with a central patio or courtyard. Other large structures, and large stone carvings such as the famous Gateway of the Sun, are also located in this area. Years of excavations, as well as reconstructions, have led to the displacement of some of the monolithic monuments in the centre of Tiwanaku, but the basic structure of the city remains.

The areas surrounding the centre of the city include residential quarters where the peasants, artisans and herders may have lived. Although there is not yet a great deal of evidence from the capital itself, studies of other Tiwanaku cities nearby indicate that there were distinct precincts of Tiwanaku sites where residents

Detail of stele in the centre of the semi-subterranean temple.

Beaten metal mask with polished face surrounded by symbolic patterns. The face is strikingly modelled.

yielded fine wool for clothing and other textiles. Llamas were used as beasts of burden, and huge llama caravans moved goods from Tiwanaku colonies and trade centres in the lowlands up to the capital.

Tiwanaku was one of the longest lived of the prehispanic empires in South America, and the city had an enduring influence on Andean civilization. The distinctive art style seen in Tiwanaku's pottery and stone carvings spread throughout the south-central Andes during the city's reign. Long after its fall, Tiwanaku's highland economy, iconography, and ideology went on influencing the development of both coastal and highland civilizations in a huge range of settings. Ongoing study of this ancient city continues to reveal its secrets, even a thousand years after it fell. ■

lived and worked at different specialized activities, such as pottery making, stoneworking, and metalworking.

Tiwanaku was the capital of a large empire, the heart of which was the Titicaca Basin. The economy of the city and the empire was based on a combination of farming and herding, as well as some fishing. Although only certain crops can grow in the *altiplano* region, agricultural productivity was greatly enhanced by a highly developed system of reclamation of rich lakeside lands. These areas, subject to flooding, were ideal for a system of intensive raised field agriculture, which more than doubled the productivity of agriculture around Lake Titicaca. The rich soils and relatively stable temperatures in raised fields also allowed the production of crops not easily grown in the highlands.

Llamas and alpacas, the domesticated species of Camelids or South American camels, were also important to the economy of Tiwanaku. In addition to providing meat, they were important for their wool and were used as transport. Alpacas, in particular,

The Fraile Monolith, holding a Kero, or ceremonial drinking cup.

EL TAJÍN

Europeans and Euro-Americans first took note of El Tajín in the late eighteenth century. During his travels, Diego Ruiz, a colonial official associated with the tobacco trade, stumbled upon the Pyramid of the Niches, one of the site's largest constructions. Inquiring locally, he was told that the building was known by a Totonac name, 'El Tajín', meaning the place 'of the lightning bolt' and also the name of the Totonac rain god. Ruiz's drawings and the attendant report, which were published in a Mexico City newspaper, provoked further interest as to the nature of the ancient city. For the next hundred years, scholars, including the great explorer Alexander Von Humboldt, commented upon the building's unique appearance. However, it was not until the start of the twentieth century that the first scientific inquiries

The ancient city of El Tajín is located on the Gulf Coast of Mexico. Although this site's origins date to the Classic Period (AD 250–900), its florescence occurred during the Epiclassic Period (AD 900–1100). The city's success can be attributed to its control over the rich agricultural products of the area. During its heyday, El Tajín became the region's major distributor of maize, cotton, cacao and rubber. The city's economic influence was accompanied by a wide dispersal of its distinctive art style which can be seen in artifacts from sites in north-central Veracruz, along the Gulf Coast and the eastern portions of the central highlands.

were made at the site, and not until 1935 that the extent of the site was realized. The Mexican archaeologist Augustín García Vega was the first to note that the Pyramid of the Niches was not an isolated construction, but part of an immense city composed of dozens of buildings covering hundreds of hectares. So vast was it that the archaeologist José García Payón devoted almost forty years of his life, from 1938 until his death in 1977, to uncovering the ruins.

The six-tiered Pyramid of the Niches was one of the first complexes to be excavated. In ancient times its flagstone-covered rubble core supported a temple. Though the temple was destroyed long ago, its 20 m high base stands as a lasting testament to the skills of the indigenous architects. Modern reconstructions of the pyramid's colours reveal that the ancient appearance of the build-

ing must have been truly stunning. The bright red surface of the structure was interrupted by 365 niches, all painted black, representing individual world caves, possibly a reference to the home of the deity. Their number may have had calendrical significance. A central stairway fronting the building had flanking dark blue balustrades which were decorated with fret designs. Some scholars believe that the frets represent lightning, one of the attributes of the god, Tajín. It has also been shown that the carved tablets associated with this building portray the rain god, an indication that the information given to Ruiz 200 years ago was correct.

Another unique aspect of El Tajín is the eleven ballcourts scattered across the heart of the city. Their prevalence at the site indicates that the importance of El Tajín went beyond its control of the local economy. Clearly, this great city was a regional centre for the ritual play of the ancient game. The ballcourts at Tajín are generally placed in relation to geographic features or major temples, and all the playing fields have the characteristic I-shape associated with most Mesoamerican courts.

Multiple functions for the ballgame at El Tajín have been suggested. For instance, it may have served as an athletic event or a type of gladiatorial contest where the loser was sacrificed; or the function may have been more related to religious concepts. The game could have been the means through which human blood was obtained and offered up to the gods or, as in the case of the ancient Maya, the ballgame may have represented a re-enactment of a sacred mythological story.

It has been argued that the ballgame at El Tajín was primarily a mode of communication between man and the gods, a view based on imagery found in monuments such as the South Ballcourt (AD 600), located between two temples just south of the Pyramid of the Niches. The six vertical panels which flank the walls of the court are carved with scenes of ritual significance, relating to either ballgame preparation or to the Underworld aftermath of the game. For instance, the south-west panel, designated Panel #2, depicts an event prior to the game. Here, the player relaxes on a bed while musicians serenade him. His semi-divine status is suggested by the seated posture he assumes — a pose generally associated with the Pulque God at El Tajín. The overall sacred nature of the event is reinforced by the presence of a floating skeletal figure, representing Venus, and the death god who rises from a jar situated in a vat of *pulque* (the fermented juice of the maguey plant, imbibed on ritually important occasions to induce a slightly trance-like state).

Scenes of the ballgame's aftermath are located on the central panels of each wall. The site of the action in Panel #5 has been identified as the 'Temple of the Underworld', a designation supported by symbols associated with human bones, and the moon. Here the ballplayer points to Chac Mool, a Pulque-associated deity. Presiding over the scene are the Rain God, Tajín, and the Wind God.

In all Mesoamerican groups, rituals involving sacrifice tended to be political as well as sacred in nature. So while the games at El Tajín were clearly sacred, they had an underlying political component which served to reaffirm élite power and prerogative. This is indicated by the Building of the Columns, dated to the eleventh century AD. Though now destroyed, this building was once supported by sculpted columns depicting images proclaiming the exploits of the Epiclassic ruler, '13 Rabbit'. While the overarching theme of the columns is one of conquest, as indicated by a disembowelled victim sprawled out before the seated ruler, this takes place in the context of ballgame-associated paraphernalia. Owing to the presence of game equipment, it has been suggested that such events took place within a ballcourt, and that the public dispatch of the unlucky captives may have directly followed the game. Hence, during the last years of the great city, the sacred ballgame was increasingly linked with secular notions of conquest.

The city's collapse dates to the late Epiclassic Period and, by AD 1100, El Tajín was largely abandoned. Because of the evidence of burnt temples and smashed sculpture, it was believed until recently that El Tajín's end was sudden and violent, and had involved invasion and conflict. However, it is now supposed that at least one of the episodes of destruction was an internally directed event and may indicate the presence of the Mesoamerican practice of ritually 'killing a building' for the sake of installing a new lineage at the site. This new evidence points to increasing factionalism within the site itself, rather than to a crisis brought about by external pressures. If the hypothesis of internal disintegration proves to be correct, then the columns of '13 Rabbit' may be symptomatic of this ruler's last-gasp attempt at promoting a positive image of his own failing power and the waning status of the city. ■

BELOW: The militaristic sculpture from the Building of the Columns. RIGHT: The Temple of the Niches derives its name from the 365 niches which decorate its four sides. The structure may have had calendrical associations and have been dedicated to the Totonac rain god, Tajín.

CHAN CHAN

Beginning around AD 850, the rulers of what was to become the powerful Chimor empire built a city that was virtually unique in its planning and use. Architectural canons rooted in a long tradition of coastal Andean construction were used in new ways to create a city that served as a production and trade centre for hundreds of years. Traditional platform mounds, the most impressive feature of earlier settlements, were used at Chan Chan, but they do not seem to have been central to it. Large walled compounds were the core of the city, and the city was the core of the coastal empire of Chimor.

The city walls at Chan Chan encompassed more than 20 sq km of adobe, rammed earth and cane structures that housed thousands. The centre of the city, an area of about 6 sq km, comprised eleven huge rectangular compounds enclosed by thick adobe and rammed-earth walls that reached 3 m in height. The compounds, often called *ciudadelas* (little cities or citadels), may have served as the palaces of the royal rulers of Chimor.

Most of the compounds are divided into three distinct sectors: a northern section, which included the main entrance to the compound, as well as a series of courtyards, storage and administrative areas; a central sector, which may have included the king's resi-

At the mouth of the Moche River, on the desert coast of Peru, lie the ruins of the thousand-year-old adobe city of Chan Chan. One of the largest and most impressive ancient cities in the New World, Chan Chan was the capital of the prehispanic kingdom of Chimor, which ruled a stretch of coastal desert more than 1000 km long between about AD 1000 and 1450. In the mid fifteenth century, the Chimor were conquered by the Inka, and the city lost its status as capital of a kingdom. Today, what remains of Chan Chan lies just to the north of the modern city of Trujillo, Peru, threatened by ever expanding settlement, but still standing as a monument to an ancient coastal kingdom.

dence during his lifetime, and which also housed a large T-shaped burial platform that served as his final resting place; and a southern sector that featured a large shallow walk-in well, as well as structures and *ramadas* (shelters or shade areas) made of cane.

The inside of the *ciudadelas* is mazelike, with long narrow passageways with high adobe walls on either side, leading to a series of increasingly restricted courtyards, storage rooms and sets of U-shaped rooms referred to as *audiencias*, or reception rooms. Archaeologists suggest that the architecture of the *ciudadelas* reflects the hierarchical nature of the social, political and economic life of the city, with access to the inner sanctums of the *ciudadelas* restricted to the most privileged élite rulers of Chimor. Here, a select few viewed the stored treasures of an empire.

Throughout the city, adobe buildings, well built but on a much smaller scale than the *ciudadelas*, were inhabited by administrators and other élite residents. Most of the remaining inhabitants of the city, including craftspeople, lived in houses and compounds of irregularly shaped rooms made of cane. Some lived in areas adjacent to the *ciudadelas*, but most inhabited the southern and western sections of the city. Although the residents of the cane houses at Chan Chan may not have had all of the privileges of its rulers, they did enjoy a special status within the kingdom: they were allowed to wear earspools, unlike the common folk. Chan Chan was a city inhabited by royalty, and by those who did the work most valued by the kings.

The residents of Chan Chan were supported by a large population of farmers and fishermen who lived outside the city. During their rule, the Chimor oversaw the construction of an extensive network of irrigation canals to provide water to increasingly large tracts of desert lands. Intensive agricultural production of maize and other products fed

Oblique aerial photograph of part of the core of the city of Chan Chan.

Detail of architecture inside an area that may have been used for storage inside one of the ciudadelas and Chan Chan, showing restored section of adobe friezes.

the city of Chan Chan, whose residents also enjoyed the fruits of the sea, which were harvested by an army of fishermen living along the shore, and salted and preserved inside the city. The rulers of Chan Chan also relied on tribute and taxes of labour and goods from conquered or otherwise annexed territories to the north and the south of their heartland in the Moche Valley.

Archaeological studies of the cane houses found throughout the city indicate that thousands of craftspeople and specialized traders living in areas surrounding the *ciudadelas* provided the élite with imported and manufactured goods that included finely woven textiles, wooden and stone carvings, metalwork and pottery. Raw materials, such as stone, metal, wood and wool, and even partially manufactured goods, were brought to Chan Chan from the edges of the Chimor kingdom and beyond, mostly by caravan. The llama served as the main pack animal, and huge caravans of llamas were dispatched from the capital to the sources of exotic goods required by the craftspeople for the manufacture of the goods demanded by their rulers. At least two separate areas within Chan Chan have been identified as caravanserais, centres of trade where the llama packers lived and traded. The traders enjoyed the privilege of living inside the city – an indication of their importance to the Chimor.

Ethnohistorians believe that the kingdom of Chimor was a hierarchically organized society, ruled by a series of kings under a system of dual leadership, with two families of kings serving complementary roles. Inheritance may have been preferentially from brother to brother, until the last brother died and leadership passed to a new generation. When a king died, he was buried on a huge platform in the central section of his *ciudadela*, surrounded by elaborate burial goods such as metal, textiles, pottery and wooden carvings. Members of his household, who may have included relatives, retainers and servants, were buried in small tombs surrounding his burial platform. After his death, the *ciudadela* in which he had ruled continued to function, cared for by his descendants, even as the seat of power of the city was transferred to another king, who ruled from a different *ciudadela*.

After generations of development, the Chimor came under Inka rule in the mid fifteenth century. Some of the city's treasures and shrines were taken to Cuzco, the capital city of the Inka. Eventually, the city was abandoned. The finely crafted treasures which had been kept in the *ciudadelas* and buried with the rulers of Chan Chan, attracted treasure hunters and looters beginning with the Spanish colonization of Peru. Colonists, as well as the Spanish crown, were hungry for gold, and they looted much of the site, leaving little for archaeologists to study in and around the burial platforms. The bones of the ancient kings of Chimor, along with many of their treasures, have disappeared during the past 500 years. Nevertheless, what remains of the site provides testimony to the extent and organization of the ancient kingdom of Chimor and its impressive capital city of Chan Chan. ∎

TENOCHTITLÁN

Until recently, modern attempts to visualize the Aztec city have been hampered by the fact that, shortly after their arrival, the Spaniards razed most of Tenochtitlán in order to build what is today Mexico City. Fortunately, colonial authors concerned with the conversion of the natives, or their exploitation, chronicled aspects of Aztec religion and history. According to their accounts, the Aztecs migrated south from their north-western home in Aztlán during the twelfth century. After their arrival in the Valley of Mexico, they settled on an island in the eastern part of the lake. The Aztecs related that the location of the capital was eventually chosen according to the instructions of their war chief, Huitzilopochtli. As the story goes, after the heart of a defeated enemy, named Copil, was thrown into the lake, Huitzilopochtli directed his followers to search for the place where it had landed. The location was marked by a cactus growing out of a rock and supported an eagle with outstretched wings. It was here, in 1345, that the Aztecs established their city, calling it Tenochtitlán, the 'Place of the Fruit of the Cactus'. Over time the Aztecs physically joined Tenochtitlán with an older neighbouring island city, called Tlatelolco.

The history of imperial expansion begins in 1375 when the Aztecs elected the first of ten absolute rulers called Huei tlatoque, or 'great speakers'. The early Aztec kings legitimized their power by marrying into older established Toltec lineages and forming

When the Spaniards led by Hernán Cortés entered the Valley of Mexico and first viewed the Aztec capital of Tenochtitlán they were astonished by its size and beauty. Huge causeways connected the great island-city to the shores of Lake Texcoco and to lesser municipalities. Plots of land, created by dredging up soil from the shallow lake bed, supported the city itself. City blocks were accessed by numerous canals and, here and there, on 'floating gardens' called *chinampas*, grew food crops and flowers. One of Cortés' soldiers compared the city to Venice, though since it had a population of 200,000 and an empire spreading southwards into Central America, none of the European metropolises could match the size or power of this New World capital.

political alliances with other cities. In the fifteenth century, the Aztecs allied themselves with two other great cities and systematically conquered other cities within the Valley of Mexico and beyond. As the empire expanded, the huge causeways were built to facilitate transport of agricultural products into the capital. The pochteca, an organized merchant class, brought in exotic goods from distant lands and kept a protective eye on the newly conquered territories.

Policies of political expansion and religion were fused and echoed in the construction of Tenochtitlán. At the heart of the city, the walled sacred precinct was the convergence point for the four main causeways. Like other Native Americans, the Aztecs recognized five directions: east, north, west, south and centre. The central direction was the most important because it was the earthly *locus* where all directions met, and because it was where heavenly and underworld realms could be accessed. It is therefore no accident that the Aztecs placed their most sacred buildings within the walls of the precinct.

The most important of all the structures, the Templo Mayor ('Great Temple'), housed the cult statues of the two greatest deities in the Aztec pantheon: Tlaloc ('Long Cave'), an ancient Toltec fertility god, and Huitzilopochtli ('Hummingbird Left'), the Aztec deified war leader and sun god. Colonial images reveal that the pyramidal base supported two temples – one for each of the deities – and was reached via a double staircase running down

ABOVE: Symbolic sculpted eagles found within the sacred precinct of Tenochtitlán.
RIGHT: Serpents found during the Templo Mayor excavations.

Carved skulls decorate the base of the Tzompantli, or skull rack, in Tenochtitlán's sacred precinct.

Long Cave = Var?

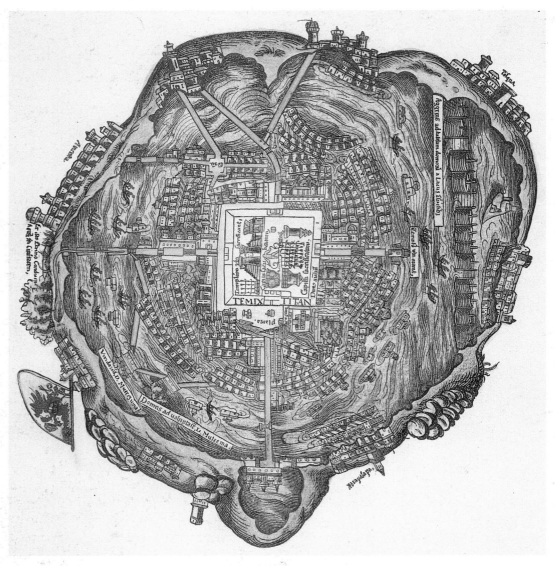

LEFT: The 'Map of Cortés' showing the walled sacred precinct.
RIGHT: Figures found leaning against the stairs, Templo Mayor.

was revealed on 22 February, 1978 when workers discovered a huge horizontal carved stone associated with the temple's fourth phase of construction (1469–81). The piece depicts a naked, dismembered woman bound with cords of knotted serpents. This 'captive' wears bells over her cheeks, and in this way Matos was able to identify her as Coyolxauhqui ('She Who Wears Bells'), the evil sister of Huitzilopochtli. In their myth, the Aztecs stopped during their migration at a hill known as Coatepec, 'Snake Mountain'. It was here that Coyolxauhqui attempted to kill her mother, Coatlicue ('Snake Skirt'), because she, Coatlicue, had become pregnant with Huitzilopochtli and was husbandless. At the moment of attack, Huitzilopochtli sprang from Coatlicue's womb, fully armed, killing Coyolxauhqui and throwing her dismembered body down the mountain. The Coyolxauhqui Stone found at the base of the Templo Mayor suggested to

its westward facing front. Although Cortés almost completely destroyed the temple during the sixteenth century, its earlier phases were excavated in 1978 by the Mexican archaeologist Eduardo Matos Moctezuma. His work revealed that the Great Temple had been rebuilt at least seven times and that the last phase, the version seen by Cortés and his men, might have stood as high as 60 m.

Beyond reaffirming the physical appearance of the temple, archaeologists were able to contextualize the structure in light of its religious and political functions. An analysis of the pyramid's northern temple has concluded that this side of the Templo Mayor symbolized the mythic, seed-filled mountain-home of Tlaloc, Tonacatepetl. This was supported by the discovery of sculptured frogs along the structure's platform, and jade figurines and vessels representing Tlaloc himself. Additionally, it has been suggested that offerings of water fowl and fish from far off oceans could be understood not only as gifts to this important deity but as a reference to the city's dominance over distant polities.

Matos associated the pyramid's southern temple with the god Huitzilopochtli and war. As in the case of the Tlaloc-related side of the pyramid, the Huitzilopochtli side was also the reference point for a geographic place. The most telling clue to its identity

Matos that the pyramid represented Coatepec, the place of Huitzilopochtli's first and most important military victory. Further support for his identification is found in the carved serpent heads which project from the pyramid's balustrades. These function as toponyms, symbols that indicate a place name. In this case, they are to be read as 'Snake Mountain'.

It is clear, then, that the Templo Mayor represented more than one mythical mountain. Matos believes that, as a whole, the pyramid recalled the mythic past in support of the city's and empire's present. The imagery associated with Tlaloc and Huitzilopochtli reflected the economic basis of the Aztec empire – agriculture and war. While the Tlaloc side of the Templo Mayor represented agricultural fertility and water, it also referred to the more ancient states of the Valley of Mexico. The deity's presence in his temple implied the Aztecs' ability to secure his benevolence both in the valley and in the distant food production areas along the coasts. Huitzilopochtli's imagery evoked notions of manifest destiny and is a testament to the military might required to bind parts of the empire with its centre. The Templo Mayor both celebrated and justified the expanding Aztec economy and the political control of Tenochtitlán over its vast empire. ■

MACHU PICCHU

Bingham was searching for another lost city – Vilcabamba – when he stumbled upon the ruins of Machu Picchu. The city was so overgrown with vegetation that he could barely make out the fine Inka stonework or the lay-out of the site. After clearing and mapping the ruins with his team, Bingham revealed the city to the world, publishing a huge spread, with spectacular photos of Machu Picchu and other sites, in the April 1913 issue of the *National Geographic*. He had come to believe that Machu Picchu was in fact Vilcabamba, from which the Inka Manco Capac had resisted the Spanish.

Historical and archaeological research has not borne out Bing-ham's theories about Machu Picchu. Instead, they have shown that what Bingham had actually found was a city that was proba-bly built by the Inka emperor Pachacuti, perhaps to serve as a royal retreat. The location of the site, and its architecture, provide

Carved from living rock at the edge of the Sacred Valley of the Inka, surrounded by mountain peaks, lies the city of Machu Picchu, perhaps the most famous lost city in the Americas. A four-day walk from the Inka capital of Cuzco, Machu Picchu perches high above surrounding river valleys on the eastern slopes of the Andes. Abandoned by the time the Spanish arrived in Peru, and quickly overgrown by the jungle, the city lay hidden from all but a few local farmers until the early twentieth century when the American explorer Hiram Bingham brought Machu Picchu to the attention of the world. Today, the beauty and mystery of the site attract thousands of visitors each year.

clues as to the true nature and function of Machu Picchu.

For the Inka, mountain peaks, stones, brooks, and other natural and modified features of the landscape were *apus*, shrines, or dwellings of spirits and gods. Mountain peaks are sacred in the Andes, and major ones are often the subject of pilgrimages and rituals, even today. In the mid fifteenth century AD Machu Picchu was carefully placed among sacred mountain peaks, in a unique and spectacular setting, with views of moun-tains in all directions. The city is also a prime observation spot for the movements of the sun, and archaeologists and astronomers have identified a number of natural and constructed points in the

BELOW: The Intihuatana at Machu Picchu, with the Huayna Picchu in the background on the left side.
RIGHT: The terraces of an agricultural sector at Machu Picchu.

ABOVE: Characteristic terraces show how the Aztecs adapted their building to suit the terrain.

LEFT: Ruined ritual or domestic buildings in the central zone of the site.

city that were used for making astronomical and solar observations.

The architecture of the city provides further clues to its real function. Sacred precincts, specialized constructions and fine architectural details abound at Machu Picchu, not storage silos or administrative buildings as might be expected for a centre of state administration. The city lacks the features of a seat of government or of a town of mainly economic or military importance. Although the agricultural products of the areas surrounding Machu Picchu – coca and other crops – may have been important to the empire, the city itself did not function primarily as an agricultural or administrative centre. Rather it was probably a retreat, something akin to a royal estate, where the emperor went to engage in religious and other activities away from his capital city.

Machu Picchu does not seem to have been occupied full time by the emperor or his permanent retainers. Rather, a group of residents cared for the city and kept it ready for visits from the

Inka and his relatives and retainers. Groups of weavers, artisans, and perhaps priests or other religious practitioners may also have lived at Machu Picchu. The major activities in the important structures at the site do not appear to have been mundane day-to-day affairs.

Machu Picchu, like most cities, has various sectors where different activities took place. There are small and large buildings, some with finely cut stone masonry and others with less elaborate construction. Carved rock outcrops abound at the site, as do points where the movements of the sun could be observed, an all-important activity for the maintenance of both religious and agricultural calendars.

Machu Picchu is set out along the contours of the hill slopes, in regular patterns that reflect the elaborate planning and careful construction of the city. The buildings are laid out along the spine and saddle of a relatively low point between two mountain peaks, with plaza areas in the centre and agricultural sectors running along the edges of the city. Stone stairways descend the steep slopes, through the agricultural and built-up sections of the city. Long pathways with stone doorways lead from area to area.

Tourists entering the site today walk through the southern section of agricultural terraces, and they soon come across a group of sixteen small pools that were fed by a series of waterfalls that cascaded down into these ritual baths of the Inka. Nearby is a sec-

BELOW: Remains of a structure at Machu Picchu, showing the characteristic steep pitch of Inka roofs.
RIGHT: The inhospitality of the landscape provides a stunning backdrop.

tion of large buildings often interpreted as royal residences. Also in this area is the monument known as the Temple of the Sun, where some of the finest stonework in the city is found. This structure is a circular stone tower that surrounds a sacred rock outcrop that was used to observe and mark the movements of the sun. The walls of the tower have small niches in them for offerings, and a window in the Temple of the Sun is aligned with the rock so that light forms a striking line on the solstice each June.

Some of the most interesting and impressive constructions at Machu Picchu are found in a western sector of the site. The structure known as the Temple of the Three Windows, which was greatly admired by Bingham, features a huge rock used to form the base of one entire wall. The lower portions of three trapezoidal windows were carved into the rock. The windows were then finished with fine cut stone masonry that completed the walls.

Also in this area is a structure known as the Principal Temple, which has a foundation made of huge rocks, and is finished with extraordinary stone masonry with multifaceted cut stone blocks. Attached to this is a room, often referred to as the 'sacristy', reflecting a modern belief that the Inka priests used it to prepare for the rituals they were about to perform in the main temple.

One of the fascinating features of the city is a carved stone known as the Intihuatana, sometimes called the 'hitching post of the sun' by English-speaking guides and guidebooks. This vertically projecting carved stone is similar to stones that were once found at many Inka cities. It may have been used for marking the movements of the sun and keeping track of the changing seasons.

The Spanish identified this type of stone with religious practices which they hoped to stamp out as they worked to convert the natives, and they destroyed many of these stones in their effort to eradicate native religion. The one at Machu Picchu is one of the very few to have survived intact, because the Spanish did not know of its existence.

Even after years of study and tourism, Machu Picchu maintains its beauty and its aura of mystery. The mountains towering above the jungle, and the constructions that follow the contours of the hill slopes and reflect the shapes of the surrounding peaks, create a unique and spectacular site. Although it was abandoned more than 500 years ago, Machu Picchu serves as a monument not so much to the imperial power of the Inka, but to their architectural genius, and to other, perhaps less worldly concerns. ∎

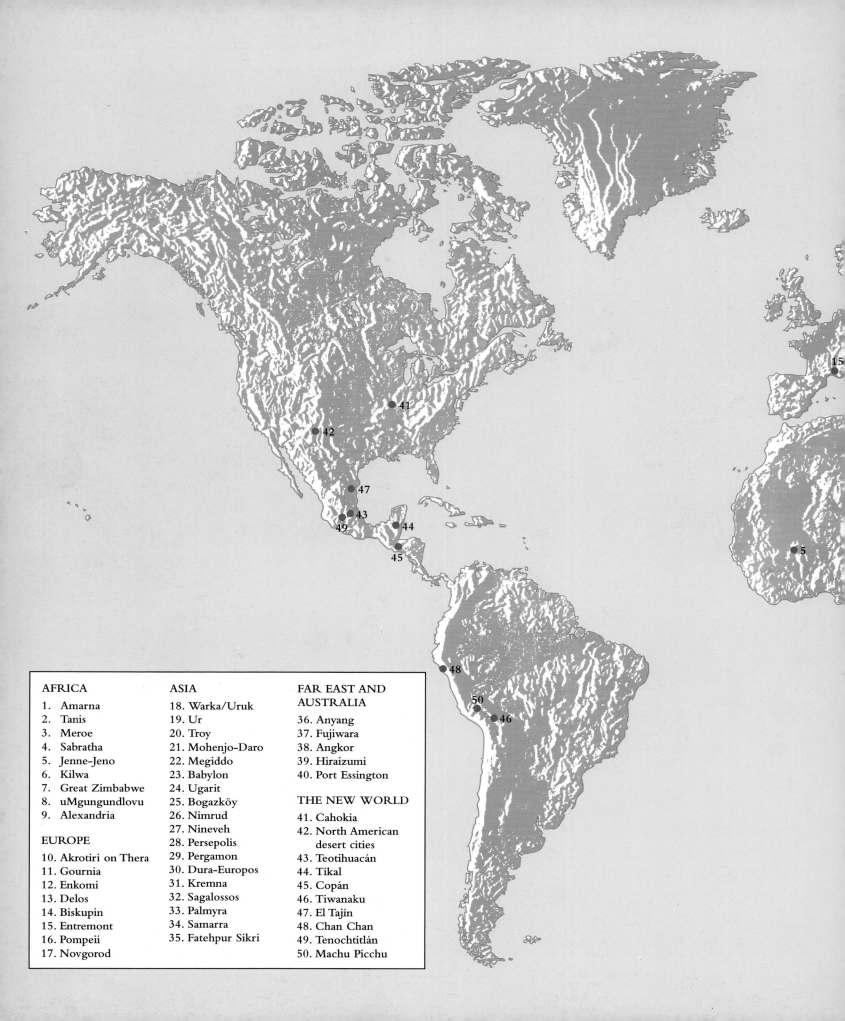

AFRICA

1. Amarna
2. Tanis
3. Meroe
4. Sabratha
5. Jenne-Jeno
6. Kilwa
7. Great Zimbabwe
8. uMgungundlovu
9. Alexandria

EUROPE

10. Akrotiri on Thera
11. Gournia
12. Enkomi
13. Delos
14. Biskupin
15. Entremont
16. Pompeii
17. Novgorod

ASIA

18. Warka/Uruk
19. Ur
20. Troy
21. Mohenjo-Daro
22. Megiddo
23. Babylon
24. Ugarit
25. Bogazköy
26. Nimrud
27. Nineveh
28. Persepolis
29. Pergamon
30. Dura-Europos
31. Kremna
32. Sagalossos
33. Palmyra
34. Samarra
35. Fatehpur Sikri

FAR EAST AND
AUSTRALIA

36. Anyang
37. Fujiwara
38. Angkor
39. Hiraizumi
40. Port Essington

THE NEW WORLD

41. Cahokia
42. North American
    desert cities
43. Teotihuacán
44. Tikal
45. Copán
46. Tiwanaku
47. El Tajín
48. Chan Chan
49. Tenochtitlán
50. Machu Picchu

Sava

Entremont

Marseilles

Tiber

Rome

ADRIATIC SEA

Naples ○ ● *Pompeii*

TYRRHENIAN
SEA

Cagliari

IONIAN

Palermo

Tunis

Susah

MEDITERRANEAN SEA

Sabratha

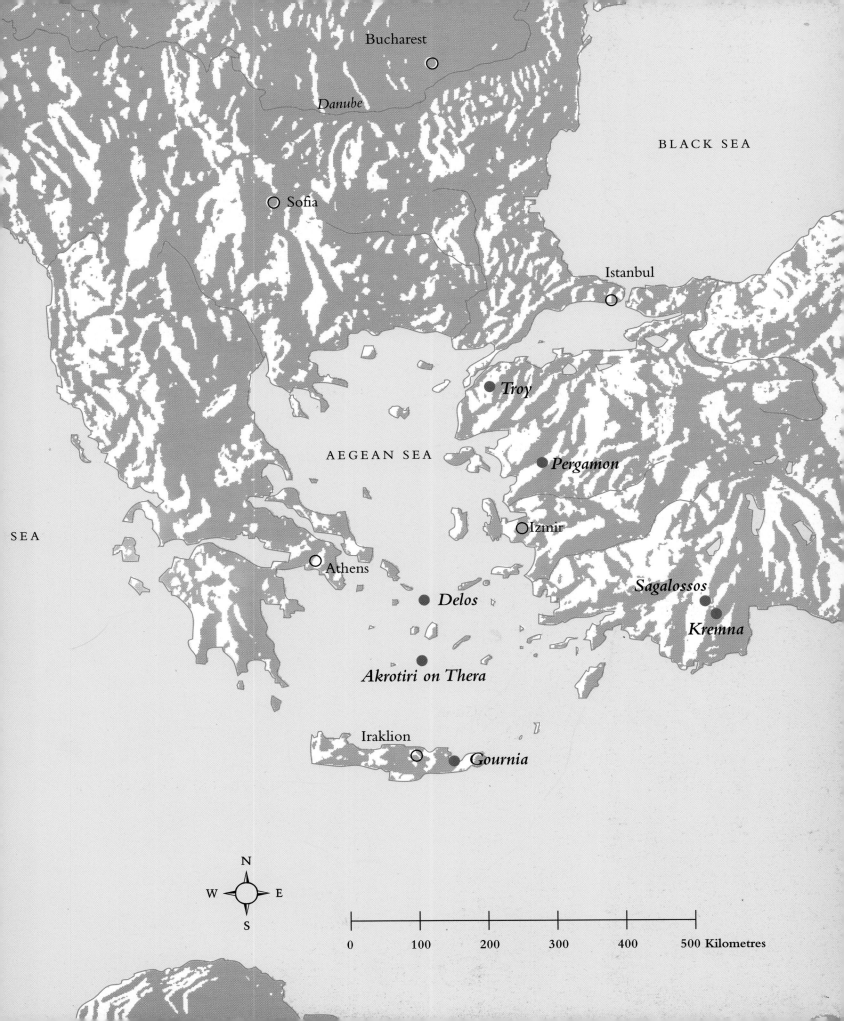

BLACK SEA

Bucharest

Danube

Sofia

Istanbul

AEGEAN SEA

Troy

Pergamon

Izmir

SEA

Athens

Sagalossos

Delos

Kremna

Akrotiri on Thera

Iraklion

Gournia

N
W   E
S

0   100   200   300   400   500 Kilometres

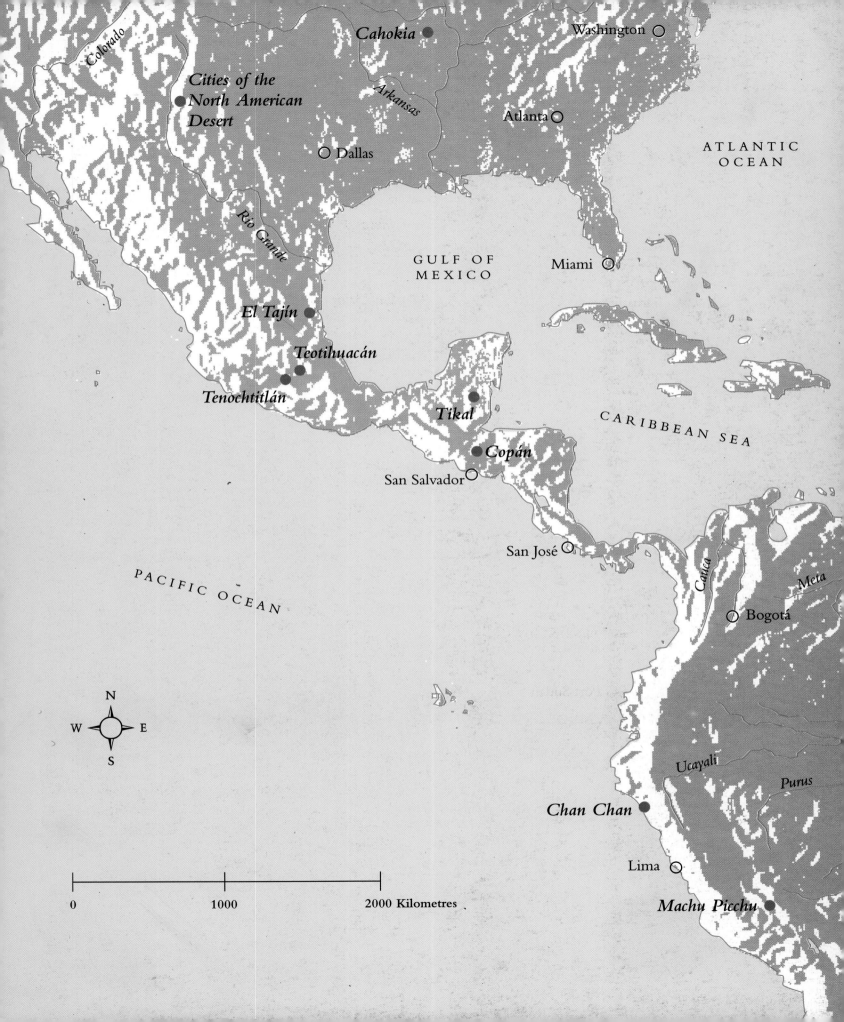

Colorado

Cahokia ●

Washington ○

Cities of the North American Desert ●

Arkansas

Atlanta ○

ATLANTIC OCEAN

○ Dallas

Río Grande

GULF OF MEXICO

Miami ○

El Tajín ●

Teotihuacán ●

Tenochtitlán ●

Tikal ●

CARIBBEAN SEA

Copán ●

San Salvador ○

San José ○

Cauca

Meta

○ Bogotá

PACIFIC OCEAN

N
W E
S

Ucayali

Purus

Chan Chan ●

Lima ○

0   1000   2000 Kilometres

Machu Picchu ●

BIBLIOGRAPHY

AFRICA

1. AMARNA
Kemp, B. J. and S. Garfi 1993. *A survey of the ancient city of El-Amarna*. Egypt Exploration Society: London.

Pendlebury, J. D. S. 1935. *Tell el-Amarna*. London.

2. TANIS
Coutts, H. (ed.) 1988. *Gold of the Pharaohs*. Edinburgh Museums.

Montet, P. 1947–60. *La necropole de Tanis*. Paris.

3. MEROE
Shinnie P. L. 1967. *Meroe*. Thames & Hudson: London.

Welsby, D. 1996. *Kingdom of Kush: the Napatan and Meroitic Empires*. British Museum Press: London.

4. SABRATHA
Kenrick, P. M. *et al.* 1986. *Excavations at Sabratha 1948-1951*. The Society for the Promotion of Roman Studies: London.

5. JENNE-JENO
McIntosh, S. K. and R. J. 1982. 'Finding West Africa's oldest city', in *National Geographic* (September) 162 (3): pp. 396-418.

McIntosh, S. K. and R. J. 1993. 'Cities without citadels: under standing urban origins along the middle Niger', in Shaw, T., P. Sinclair, B. Andah and A.Okpoko (eds.) *The Archaeology of Africa. Food, metals and towns*, pp. 622–41. Routledge: London and New York.

Flood, J. 1995. *Archaeology of the Dreamtime*, 3rd ed., Angus & Robertson: Sydney.

6. KILWA
Chittick, N. 1974. *Kilwa. An Islamic trading city on the East African coast* (2 vols.). The British Institute in Eastern Africa, Memoir Number Five: Nairobi.

7. GREAT ZIMBABWE
Garlake, P. S. 1973. *Great Zimbabwe*. Thames & Hudson: London.

Huffman, T. N. 1987. *Symbols in stone. Unravelling the mystery of Great Zimbabwe*. Witwatersrand University Press: Johannesburg.

Huffman, T. N. 1996. *Snakes and crocodiles. Power and symbolism in ancient Zimbabwe*. Witwatersrand University Press: Johannesburg.

8. uMGUNGUNDLOVU
Parkington, J. and M. Cronin 1979. 'The size and layout of Mgungundlovu 1829–1838', *South African Archaeological Society Goodwin Series 3*: pp. 133-48.

Plug, I. and F. Roodt 1990. 'The faunal remains from recent exca-vations at uMgungundlovu', *South African Archaeological Bulletin* 45: pp. 47–52.

9. ALEXANDRIA
Forster, E. M. 1961. *Alexandria: a History and a Guide*. London.

Fraser, P. M. 1972. *Ptolemaic Alexandria*. Oxford.

La Riche, William, 1996. *Alexandria: the Sunken City*. Weidenfeld & Nicolson.

EUROPE

10. AKROTIRI ON THERA
Doumas, C. G. 1983. *Thera. Pompeii of the Ancient Aegean*. Thames & Hudson: London.

11. GOURNIA
Hall, E. H. 1912. *Excavations in Eastern Crete: Sphoungaras*. University of Pennsylvania Press: Philadelphia.

Hawes, H. A. B., B. E. Williams, R. B. Seager and E. H. Hall 1908. *Gournia, Vasilik, and Other Prehistoric Sites on the Isthmus of Hierapetra, Crete*. Philadelphia.

12. ENKOMI
Courtois, J.-C., J. Lagarce and E. Lagarce 1986. *Enkomi et le Bronze Recent a Chypre*. Imprimerie Zavallis: Nicosia.

14. BISKUPIN
Bogucki, P. 1990. 'A glimpse of Iron Age Poland', *Archaeology* 43 (5): pp. 74–5.

Harding, A. F. 1984. 'Biskupin and its context', *Popular Archaeology* 5: pp. 27–30.

Rajewski, Z. 1970. *Biskupin*. Arkady: Warsaw.

Wells, P. S. 1984. *Farms, Villages, and Cities: Commerce and Urban Origins in Late Prehistoric Europe*. Cornell University Press: Ithaca.

15. ENTREMONT
Benoit, F. 1975. 'The Celtic oppidum of Entremont, Provence', in R. Bruce-Mitford (ed.), *Recent Archaeological Excavations in Europe*, pp. 227-59. Routledge and Kegan Paul: London.

Green, M. J. 1995. *The Celtic World*. Routledge: London.

Musee Granet 1987. *Archéologie d'Entremont au Musee Granet*. Musee Granet: Aix-en-Provence.

16. POMPEII AND HERCULANEUM
Brion, M. 1973. *Pompeii and Herculaneum, the glory and the grief*. Cardinal: London.

Grant, M. 1971. *Cities of Vesuvius. Pompeii and Herculaneum*. Weidenfeld & Nicolson: London.

17. NOVGOROD
Dunaev, M. and F. Razumovsky 1984. *Novgorod. A Guide*. Raduga Publishers: Moscow.

Kolchin, B. A. 1989. *Wooden Artefacts from Medieval Novgorod*. B. A. R.: Oxford.

Medyntseva, A. A. 1984. 'Novgorodskie nakhodki i dokristianskaia pis'mennost' na Rusi' (Novgorod finds and pre-Christian Russian writing), Sovetskaia Arkheologiia, 1984 (4): pp. 49–61.

Yanin, V. I. 1990. 'The Archaeology of Novgorod', Scientific American 262 (2): pp. 84–91.

ASIA

18. WARKA/URUK
Nissen, H. 1988. *The Early History of the Ancient Near East, 9000–2000 BC*. University of Chicago Press: Chicago.

19. UR
Moorey, P. R. S. 1982. *Ur 'of the Chaldees', a revised and updated edition of Sir Leonard Woolley's Excavations at Ur*. Cornell University Press: Ithaca.

20. TROY
Blegen, C. W. 1963. *Troy and the Trojans*. Thames & Hudson: London.

McDonald, W. A. 1990. *Progress into the Past. The Rediscovery of Mycenaean Civilization* (2nd ed.). Indiana University Press:

21. MOHENJO-DARO
Allchin, B. and F. R. Allchin 1982. *The Rise of Civilization in India and Pakistan*. Cambridge University Press: Cambridge.

Wheeler, M. 1968. *The Indus Civilization* (3rd ed.). Cambridge University Press: Cambridge.

22. MEGIDDO
Kempinski, A. 1989. *Megiddo, A City-State and Royal Center in North Israel*. C. H. Beck: Munich.

23. BABYLON
Oates, J. 1986. *Babylon* (rev. ed.). Thames & Hudson: London.

24. UGARIT
Curtis, A. 1985. *Ugarit (Ras Shamra)*. Lutterworth Press: Cambridge.

Drower, M. 1975. 'Ugarit', in *Cambridge Ancient History* II.2A (3rd ed.). Cambridge University Press: Cambridge.

25. BOGAZKÖY
Bittel, K. 1970. *Hattusha, Capital of the Hittites*. Oxford University Press: Oxford and New York.

Macqueen, J. G. 1986. *The Hittites and their Contemporaries in Asia Minor*. Thames & Hudson: London.

26. NIMRUD
Mallowan, M. E. L. 1966. *Nimrud and its Remains*. Collins: London.

27. NINEVEH
Russell, J. 1991. *Sennacherib's Palace without Rival at Nineveh*. University of Chicago Press: Chicago.

Stronach, D. and S. Lumsden 1992. 'UC Berkeley's excavations at Nineveh', *Biblical Archaeology* 55: pp. 227–33.

28. PERSEPOLIS
Cook, J. M. 1983. *The Persian Empire*. Schocken Books: New York.

Wilber, D. 1989. *Persepolis, the Archaeology of Parsa, Seat of the Persian Kings* (rev. ed.). Darwin Press: Princeton.

29. PERGAMON

Hanson, E. V. 1971. *The Attalids of Pergamon.* Cornell University Press: Ithaca.

30. DURA-EUROPOS

Hopkins, C. 1979. *The Discovery of Dura-Europos.* Yale University Press: New Haven.

Rostovtzeff, M. I. 1938. *Dura Europos and its Art.* Clarendon Press: Oxford.

31. KREMNA

Mitchell, S., S. Cormack, R. Furdon, E. J. Owens and J. Ozturk 1995. *Cremna in Pisidia: an ancient city in peace and war.* Duckworth: London (with the Classical Press of Wales).

32. SAGALASSOS

Waelkens, M. *et al.* 1993- *Sagalassos* (vols. I, II, III). University of Leuven Press.

33. PALMYRA

Browning, I. 1979. *Palmyra.* Chatto & Windus: London.

34. SAMARRA

Creswell, K. A. C. 1979. *Early Muslim Architecture* (2nd ed.). Hacker Art Books: New York.

35. FATEHPUR SIKRI

Rizvi, S. A. A. 1972. *Fatehpur Sikri.* Archaeological Survey of India: New Delhi.

FAR EAST AND AUSTRALIA

36. ANYANG AND THE LATE SHANG STATE

Chang, K. C. 1980. *Shang Civilization.* Yale University Press: New Haven.

Keightley, D. N. 1978. *Sources of Shang History: The Oracle-Bone Inscriptions of Bronze Age China.* University of California Press: Berkeley.

Li Chi 1977. *Anyang.* University of Washington Press: Seattle.

37. FUJIWARA

Fujiwara Palace and Capital (1991). Written and published by the Nara National Cultural Properties Research Institute, Nara, Japan.

Brown, D. M. (ed.) 1993. *The Cambridge History of Japan, Vol. 1: Ancient Japan.* Cambridge University Press: Cambridge.

38. ANGKOR

Coedes, G. 1963 (reissued 1986). *Angkor: An Introduction.* Oxford University Press: Oxford.

Higham, C. 1989. *The Archaeology of Mainland Southeast Asia.* Cambridge University Press: Cambridge.

39. HIRAIZUMI

Hudson, M. 1996. 'Mummies of the Northern Fujiwara', in *Tombs, Graves and Mummies* (P. G. Bahn, ed.), pp. 198–9. Weidenfeld & Nicolson: London / Barnes & Noble: New York.

Yiengpruksawan, M. 1993. 'The house of gold: Fujiwara Kiyohira's Konjikido', *Monumenta Nipponica* 48: pp. 33–52.

40. PORT ESSINGTON

Allen, J. 1973. 'The archaeology of nineteenth-century British imperialism: an Australian case study', *World Archaeology* 5: pp. 44-60.

Spillett, P. 1972. *Forsaken Settlement.* Landsdowne: Melbourne.

THE NEW WORLD

41. CAHOKIA

Fowler, M. 1989. *The Cahokia Atlas.* Illinois Historic Preservation Agency: Springfield, Illinois.

42. CITIES OF THE NORTH AMERICAN DESERTS

Lister, R. and F. Lister 1981. *Chaco Canyon.* University of New Mexico Press: Albuquerque.

Frazier, K. 1986. *People of Chaco.* Norton and Co.: New York.

Matlock, G. and S. Warren 1988. *Enemy Ancestors.* Northland Press.

43. TEOTIHUACÁN

Heyden, D. 1981. 'Caves, Gods, and Myths: World-View and Planning in Teotihuacán', in E. P. Benson (ed.) *Mesoamerican Sites and World Views*, pp.1–40. Dumbarton Oaks: Washington D.C.

Millon, R. 1974. *Urbanization at Teotihuacán*, Mexico (2 vols.). University of Texas Press: Austin.

Sugiyama, S. 1989. 'Iconographic Interpretation of the Temple of Quetzalcoatl', *Mexicon* 11 (4): pp. 68–74.

Taube, K. A. 1992. 'The Temple of Quetzalcoatl and the Cult of Sacred War at Teotihuacan', *Res.* 21: pp. 53–87.

44 & 45. TIKÁL AND COPÁN

Ferguson, W. M. and J. Q. Royce 1984. *Maya Ruins in Central America in Color: Tikal, Copán, and Quirigua*. The University of New Mexico Press: Albuquerque.

Freidel, D., L. Schele and J. Parker 1992. *Maya Cosmos: Three Thousand Years on the Shaman's Path*. William Morrow and Company, Inc.: New York.

Recinos, A. 1950. *Popol Vuh: The Sacred Book of the Ancient Quiche Maya*. (transl. D. Goetz and S. G. Morley). University of Oklahoma Press: Norman.

Schele, L. and M. Miller 1986. *The Blood of Kings: Dynasty and Ritual in Maya Art*. Kimbell Art Museum: Fort Worth.

46. TIWANAKU

Kolata, A. L. 1993. *The Tiwanaku: Portrait of an Andean Civilization*. Blackwell: Oxford.

Morris, C. and A. Von Hagen 1993. *The Inka Empire and Its Andean Origins* (chapter 7). Abbeville Press: New York, London and Paris.

Moseley, M. E. 1992. *The Incas and Their Ancestors, the Archaeology of Peru* (especially chapter 8). Thames & Hudson: London and New York.

47. TAJÍN

Bruggemann, J. K. 1991. *Proyecto Tajín*. Instituto Nacional de Antropologia e Historia: Mexico, D. F.

Garcia Payon, J. 1961. *El Tajín*. Instituto Nacional de Antropologia e Historia: Mexico.

Wilkerson, S. J. K. 1987. *El Tajín: A Guide for Visitors*. Museum of Anthropology of Xalapa and the City Council of Papantla, Veracruz: Veracruz, Mexico.

Wilkerson, S. J. K. 1990. 'El Tajín: Great Center of the Northeast', in *Mexico: Splendors of Thirty Centuries*, pp. 155-81. The Metropolitan Museum of Art: New York.

48. CHAN CHAN

Morris, C. and A. Von Hagen 1993. *The Inka Empire and Its Andean Origins* (chapter 8). Abbeville Press: New York, London and Paris.

Moseley, M. E. 1992. *The Incas and Their Ancestors, the Archaeology of Peru* (especially chapter 9). Thames & Hudson: London and New York.

Moseley, M. E. and K. C. Day 1982. *Chan Chan: Andean Desert City*. University of New Mexico Press: Albuquerque.

49. TENOCHTITLÁN

Berdan, F. 1982. The Aztecs of Central Mexico: An Imperial Society. Holt, Rinehart and Winston: New York.

Broda, J. 1987. 'The Provenience of the Offerings: Tribute and Cosmovision', in E. Boone, (ed.), The Aztec Templo Mayor pp. 211–56. Dumbarton Oaks: Washington DC.

Matos Moctezuma, E. 1988. The Great Temple of the Aztecs: Treasures of Tenochtitlán. Thames & Hudson: London.

Sahagun, Fray B. de. 1950–72. Florentine Codex – General History of the Things of New Spain (12 vols.) (translated by C. E.Dibble and A. J. O. Anderson). School of American Research and the University of Utah, Monographs of the School of American Research and Museum of New Mexico: Santa Fe, New Mexico.

50. MACHU PICCHU

Bingham, H. 1948. *Lost City of the Incas*. Duell, Sloan and Pearce: New York.

Hemming, J. 1970. *The Conquest of the Incas*. Harcourt, Brace, Jovanovich: New York.

Morris, C. and A. Von Hagen 1993. *The Inka Empire and Its Andean Origins* (chapter 9). Abbeville Press: New York, London and Paris.

INDEX

ACKNOWLEDGEMENTS

Title page: Ancient Art & Architecture Collection; p. 6l Trip, r AKG London; p. 7l Corbis, r Andrea Stone; pp. 12, 13 E.T. Archive; p. 14 Werner Forman Archive; p. 14–15 ET; pp. 15, 16–7 WF; pp. 18, 19t Steven Snape; pp. 19b, 20, 21 ET; pp. 22, 23, 24l, 24–5, 26, 27 WF; pp. 28, 29t & b, 30, 31 Trip; pp. 32, 33tl & br Rod McKintosh; pp. 34, 35bl & tr, 36, 37 WF; pp. 38, 39 Museum Africa; pp. 40, 41tl & cr Peter Clayton; p. 42–3 AAAC; p44 Weidenfeld & Nicolson Archives; pp. 45, 46–7, 47l, 48–9 AAAC; p. 48tl Robert O'Dea; p. 50 W&N; p. 51t & b AAAC; p. 52 Cyprus Museum; pp. 53l & r, 54–5, 55t, 56–7, 58, 59 AAAC; p. 60 State Archaeological Museum, Warsaw; p. 61 W. Piotrowski; pp. 62bl & br, 63 Centre Camille Jullian; pp. 64, 65b Robert O'Dea; p. 65t WF; p. 66tl & bl ET; pp. 66–7, 68–9 WF; pp. 68, 70 W&N; p. 71 Robert O'Dea; pp. 72, 73t & b Novosti; p. 74–5 AAAC; p. 76 Robert Harding Picture Library; p. 77 AAAC; p78bl RHPL, tr ET; p79 AKG; pp80, 81 British Museum; pp82, 83b AKG; pp 83t, 84–5 Peter Clayton; pp. 84bl WF, 86 AAAC; p. 87bl WF, tr ET; pp. 88, 89, 91tr AKG; p90–1 AAAC; pp92, 94–5 Michael Jenner; pp93, 95tr & br, 96–7 AKG; pp98, 99t & b AAAC; pp. 100, 101 ET; p. 102, 104–5, 106 British Museum; p. 103 WF; pp. 105r, 107 ET; p. 108bl AAAC, tr AKG; p. 109 ET; p. 110 AAAC; pp. 111,112b WF; p. 112t Peter Clayton; p. 113 AKG; p. 114–5 ET; p. 116 Peter Clayton; pp. 117, 118–9, 119tr, 120t Michael Jenner; pp. 120b, 121 Peter Clayton; p. 122 AAAC; p. 123 Michael Jenner; pp. 124, 125, 126, 127t & b, 128, 128–9 Edward Owens; pp. 130, 131, 132l, 132–3, 134–5 Michael Jenner; pp. 136, 137l & r, 138, 139 W&N; p. 140 Paul G. Bahn; pp. 141, 142–3, 143tr W&N; pp. 146l & r, 147, 148t & b, 149 W & N; pp. 150, 151tr, bl Nara National Cultural Properties Centre; pp. 152, 153, 154t & b, 155; pp. 156bl & br, 157 Hiraizumi Board of Education; p. 158 ET; p. 159 Jim Allen; p. 160–1 ET; pp. 162, 163 Cahokia Historical Society; pp. 164, 165, 166 AAAC; pp. 167, 168, 169b WF; p. 169t Paul G. Bahn; p. 170t Peter Clayton; pp. 170b, 171 WF; p. 172 Constance Cortez; pp. 173t & b, 174tl & bl Andrea Stone; p. 174–5 WF; pp. 177t, bl & br, 178bl, 178–9 Andrea Stone; p. 180bl from Sqiers, E. G.: *Peru: Travel and Exploration in the Land of the Incas* (1877); pp. 180br, 181, 182br Karen Wise; p. 182tl WF; pp. 184, 185, 186bl, 186–7 Rex Koontz; p. 188 AAAC; p. 189 ET; p. 190bl & br Paul G. Bahn; p. 191 WF; p. 192 AKG; p. 193 Paul G. Bahn; pp. 194, 195, 196–7, 197tr, 198, 199 Karen Wise.

Abbreviations: AAAC = Ancient Art & Architecture Collection; AKG = AKG London; ET = E. T. Archive; RHPL = Robert Harding Picture Library; WF = Werner Forman Archive; W&N = Weidenfeld & Nicolson Archives.